BERLITZ®

P9-DEQ-615

German
PHRASE BOOK
& DICTIONARY

Easy to use features

- Handy thematic colour coding
- Quick Reference Section—opposite page
- Tipping Guide—inside back cover
- Quick reply panels throughout

How best to use this phrase book

- We suggest that you start with the **Guide to pronunciation** (pp. 6–8), then go on to **Some basic expressions** (pp. 9–15). This gives you not only a minimum vocabulary, but also helps you get used to pronouncing the language. The phonetic transcription throughout the book enables you to pronounce every word correctly.

- Consult the **Contents** pages (3–5) for the section you need. In each chapter you'll find travel facts, hints and useful information. Simple phrases are followed by a list of words applicable to the situation.

- Separate, detailed contents lists are included at the beginning of the extensive **Eating out** and **Shopping guide** sections (Menus, p. 39, Shops and services, p. 97).

- If you want to find out how to say something in German, your fastest look-up is via the **Dictionary** section (pp. 164–189). This not only gives you the word, but is also cross-referenced to its use in a phrase on a specific page.

- If you wish to learn more about constructing sentences, check the **Basic grammar** (pp. 159–163).

- Note the **colour margins** are indexed in German and English to help both listener and speaker. And, in addition, there is also an **index in German** for the use of your listener.

- Throughout the book, this symbol ☞ suggests phrases your listener can use to answer you. If you still can't understand, hand this phrase book to the German-speaker to encourage pointing to an appropriate answer. The English translation for you is just alongside the German.

Second revised edition—15th printing 1993
Printed in Switzerland

Contents

Acknowledgments
We are particularly grateful to Eva Bayer for her help in the preparation of this book, and to Dr. T.J.A. Bennett who devised the phonetic transcription.

Guide to pronunciation

You'll find the pronunciation of the German letters and sounds explained below, as well as the symbols we use for them in the transcriptions.

The imitated pronunciation should be read as if it were English except for any special rules set out below. It is based on Standard British pronunciation, though we have tried to take into account General American pronunciation as well. Of course, the sounds of any two languages are never exactly the same; but if you follow carefully the indications supplied here, you'll have no difficulty in reading our transcriptions in such a way as to make yourself understood.

In the transcriptions, letters shown in bold print should be read with more stress (louder) than the others.

Consonants

Letter	Approximate pronunciation	Symbol	Example	
f, h, k, l, m, n, p, t, x	normally pronounced as in English			
b	1) at the end of a word or between a vowel and a consonant like **p** in up	p	**ab**	ahp
	2) elsewhere as in English	b	**bis**	biss
c	1) before **e, i, ö** and **ä**, like **ts** in hits	ts	**Celsius**	tsehlziuss
	2) elsewhere like **c** in cat	k	**Café**	kahfay
ch	1) after back vowels (e.g. **ah, o, oo**) like **ch** in Scottish loch, otherwise more like **h** in huge	kh	**doch**	dokh

ch	2) sometimes, especially before **s**, like **k** in **kit**	k	**Wachs**	vahks
d	1) at the end of a word or between a vowel and a consonant like **t** in eat	t	**Rad**	raat
	2) elsewhere, like **d** in **do**	d	**durstig**	**doo**rstikh
g	1) always hard as in **go** but at the end of a word often more like **ck** in tack	g k	**gehen** **weg**	**gay**ern vehk
	2) when preceded by **i** at the end of a word like **ch** in Scottish loch	kh	**billig**	**bill**ikh
j	like **y** in yes	y	**ja**	yaa
qu	like **k** followed by **v** as in **vat**	kv	**Quark**	kvahrk
r	generally rolled in the back of the mouth	r	**warum**	vah**rum**
s	1) before or between vowels like **z** in **zoo**	z	**sie**	zee
	2) before **p** and **t** at the beginning of a syllable like **sh** in **shut**	sh	**spät**	shpait
	3) elsewhere, like **s** in sit	s/ss	**es ist**	ehss ist
ß	always like **s** in sit	s/ss	**heiß**	highss
sch	like **sh** in **shut**	sh	**schnell**	shnehl
tsch	like **ch** in chip	ch	**deutsch**	doych
tz	like **ts** in hits	ts	**Platz**	plahts
v	1) like **f** in for	f	**vier**	feer
	2) in most words of foreign origin, like **v** in vice	v	**Vase**	**vaa**zer
w	like **v** in vice	v	**wie**	vee
z	like **ts** in hits	ts	**zeigen**	**tsigh**gern

Vowels

In German, vowels are generally long when followed by **h** or by one consonant and short when followed by two or more consonants.

a	1) short like **u** in c**u**t	ah	**lassen**	**lah**ssern
	2) long like **a** in c**a**r	aa	**Abend**	**aa**bernt
ä	1) short like **e** in l**e**t	eh	**Lärm**	**leh**rm
	2) long like **ai** in h**ai**r	ai	**spät**	**sh**pait
e	1) short like **e** in l**e**t	eh	**sprechen**	**shpreh**khern
	2) long like **a** in l**a**te, but pronounced without moving tongue or lips	ay	**geben**	**gay**bern
	3) in unstressed syllables generally like **er** in oth**er**	er*	**bitte**	**bitt**er
i	1) short like **i** in h**i**t	i	**billig**	**bil**likh
	2) long like **ee** in m**ee**t	ee	**ihm**	eem
ie	like **ee** in b**ee**	ee	**hier**	heer
o	1) short like **o** in g**o**t	o	**voll**	fol
	2) long like **o** in n**o**te, but pronounced without moving tongue or lips	oa	**ohne**	**oa**ner
ö	like **ur** in f**ur** (long or short)	ur*	**können**	**kur**nern
u	1) short like **oo** in f**oo**t	u	**Nuß**	nuss
	2) long like **oo** in m**oo**n	oo	**gut**	goot
ü	like French **u** in **une**; round your lips and try to say **ea** as in m**ea**n (long or short)	ew	**über**	**ew**ber
y	like German **ü**	ew	**typisch**	**tew**pish

Diphthongs

ai, ay, ei, ey	like **igh** in h**igh**	igh	**mein**	mighn
au	like **ow** in n**ow**	ow	**auf**	owf
äu, eu	like **oy** in b**oy**	oy	**neu**	noy

---

* The r should not be pronounced when reading this transcription.

Some basic expressions

Yes.	**Ja.**	yaa
No.	**Nein.**	nighn
Please.	**Bitte.**	bitter
Thank you.	**Danke.**	dahnker
You're welcome.	**Bitte.**	bitter
Thank you very much.	**Vielen Dank.**	feelern dahnk
That's all right/ Don't mention it.	**Gern geschehen.**	gehrn gershayern

Greetings *Begrüßung*

Good morning.	**Guten Morgen.**	gootern morgern
Good afternoon.	**Guten Tag.**	gootern taag
Good evening.	**Guten Abend.**	gootern aabernt
Good night.	**Gute Nacht.**	gooter nahkht
Good-bye.	**Auf Wiedersehen.**	owf veederrzayern
See you later.	**Bis bald.**	biss bahlt
This is Mr./Mrs./ Miss ...	**Das ist Herr/Frau/ Fräulein ...**	dahss ist hehr/frow/ froylighn
How do you do? (Pleased to meet you.)	**Sehr erfreut.**	zayr ehrfroyt
How are you?	**Wie geht es Ihnen?**	vee gayt ehss eenern
Very well, thanks. And you?	**Sehr gut, danke. Und Ihnen?**	zayr goot dahnker. unt eenern
How's life?	**Wie geht's?**	vee gayts
Fine.	**Gut.**	goot

SOME BASIC EXPRESSIONS

Die ersten Worte

I beg your pardon?	**Wie bitte?**	vee **bitter**
Excuse me. (May I get past?)	**Gestatten Sie?**	gershtahtern zee
Sorry!	**Entschuldigung/ Verzeihung!**	ehnt**shul**diggung/ fehrt**sigh**ung

Questions *Fragen*

Where?	**Wo?**	voa
How?	**Wie?**	vee
When?	**Wann?**	vahn
What?	**Was?**	vahss
Why?	**Warum?**	vah**rum**
Who?	**Wer?**	vayr
Which?	**Welcher/Welche/ Welches?**	**vehl**kherr/**vehl**kher/ **vehl**kherss
Where is ...?	**Wo ist ...?**	voa ist
Where are ...?	**Wo sind ...?**	voa zint
Where can I find/ get ...?	**Wo finde/bekomme ich ...?**	voa **finder**/ber**kommer** ikh
How far?	**Wie weit?**	vee vight
How long?	**Wie lange?**	vee **lahnger**
How much?	**Wieviel?**	vee**feel**
How many?	**Wie viele?**	vee **feeler**
How much does this cost?	**Wieviel kostet das?**	vee**feel kostert** dahss
When does ... open/ close?	**Wann öffnet/ schließt ...?**	vahn **urf**nert/shleest
What do you call this/that in German?	**Wie heißt dies/ das auf deutsch?**	vee highst deess/dahss owf doych
What does that mean?	**Was bedeutet das?**	vahss ber**doy**tert dahss
What does this word mean?	**Was bedeutet dieses Wort?**	vahss ber**doy**tert **deezerss** vort

Do you speak ...? *Sprechen Sie ...?*

Do you speak English?	**Sprechen Sie Englisch?**	shprehkhern zee ehnglish
Is there anyone here who speaks English?	**Spricht hier jemand Englisch?**	shprikht heer yaymahnt ehnglish
I don't speak (much) German.	**Ich spreche kaum Deutsch.**	ikh shprehkher kowm doych
Could you speak more slowly?	**Könnten Sie bitte langsamer sprechen?**	kurntern zee bitter lahngzaamerr shprehkhern
Could you repeat that?	**Könnten Sie das bitte wiederholen?**	kurntern zee dahss bitter veederrhoalern
Could you spell it?	**Könnten Sie es bitte buchstabieren?**	kurntern zee ehss bitter bookhshtahbeerern
Please write it down.	**Schreiben Sie es bitte auf.**	shrighbern zee ehss bitter owf
Can you translate this for me/us?	**Könnten Sie mir/uns das übersetzen?**	kurntern zee meer/uns dahss ewberrzehtsern
Please point to the phrase/sentence in the book.	**Bitte zeigen Sie mir den Ausdruck/ den Satz im Buch.**	bitter tsighgern zee meer dayn owsdruck/ dayn zahts im bookh
Just a moment. I'll see if I can find it in this book.	**Einen Augenblick bitte, ich schaue mal im Buch nach, ob ich es finde.**	ighnern owgernblik bitter ikh shower maal im bookh naakh op ikh ehss finder
I understand.	**Ich verstehe.**	ikh fehrshtayer
I don't understand.	**Ich verstehe nicht.**	ikh fehrshtayer nikht
Do you understand?	**Verstehen Sie?**	fehrshtayern zee

Can/May ...? *Kann ...?*

Can I have ...?	**Kann ich ... haben?**	kahn ikh ... haabern
Can we have ...?	**Können wir ... haben?**	kurnern veer ... haabern
Can you show me ...?	**Können Sie mir ... zeigen?**	kurnern zee meer ... tsighgern
I can't.	**Leider nicht.**	lighderr nikht

Can you tell me ...?	**Können Sie mir sagen ...?**	kurnern zee meer **zaag**ern
Can you help me?	**Können Sie mir helfen?**	kurnern zee meer **hehl**fern
Can I help you?	**Kann ich Ihnen helfen?**	kahn ikh **ee**nern **hehl**fern
Can you direct me to ...?	**Können Sie mir den Weg nach/ zu ... zeigen?**	kurnern zee meer dayn vayg naakh/ tsoo ... **tsigh**ern

What do you want? *Was wünschen Sie?*

I'd like ...	**Ich hätte gern/ Ich möchte ...**	ikh **heh**ter gehrn/ ikh **murkh**ter
We'd like ...	**Wir hätten gern/ Wir möchten ...**	veer **heh**tern gehrn/ veer **murkh**tern
Give me ...	**Geben Sie mir ...**	**gay**bern zee meer
Give it to me.	**Geben Sie es mir.**	**gay**bern zee ehss meer
Bring me ...	**Bringen Sie mir ...**	**bring**ern zee meer
Bring it to me.	**Bringen Sie es mir.**	**bring**ern zee ehss meer
Show me ...	**Zeigen Sie mir ...**	**tsigh**ern zee meer
Show it to me.	**Zeigen Sie es mir.**	**tsigh**ern zee ehss meer
I'm looking for ...	**Ich suche ...**	ikh **zook**her
I'm hungry.	**Ich habe Hunger.**	ikh **haab**er **hung**err
I'm thirsty.	**Ich habe Durst.**	ikh **haab**er doorst
I'm tired.	**Ich bin müde.**	ikh bin **mew**der
I'm lost.	**Ich habe mich verirrt.**	ikh **haab**er mikh fehr**eert**
It's important.	**Es ist wichtig.**	ehss ist **vikh**tikh
It's urgent.	**Es ist dringend.**	ehss ist **dring**ernt
Hurry up!	**Beeilen Sie sich!**	ber**igh**lern zee zikh

It is/There is ... *Es ist/Es gibt ...*

| It is ... | **Es ist ...** | ehss ist |
| Is it ...? | **Ist es ...?** | ist ehss |

It isn't ...	**Es ist nicht ...**	ehss ist nikht
Here it is.	**Hier ist es.**	heer ist ehss
Here they are.	**Hier sind sie.**	heer zint zee
There it is.	**Dort ist es.**	dort ist ehss
There they are.	**Dort sind sie.**	dort zint zee
There is/are ...	**Es gibt ...**	ehss gipt
Is there/Are there ...?	**Gibt es ...?**	gipt ehss
There isn't (any) ...	**Es gibt keinen/Es gibt keine/Es gibt kein ...**	ehss gipt kighnern/ehss gipt kighner/ehss gipt kighn
There aren't (any) ...	**Es gibt keine ...**	ehss gipt kighner

Adjectives *Eigenschaftswörter*

big/small	**groß/klein**	groass/klighn
quick/slow	**schnell/langsam**	shnehl/**lahng**zaam
cheap/expensive	**billig/teuer**	**bil**likh/**toy**err
hot/cold	**heiß/kalt**	highss/kahlt
full/empty	**voll/leer**	fol/layr
easy/difficult	**leicht/schwierig**	lighkht/**shwee**rikh
heavy/light	**schwer/leicht**	shvayr/lighkht
open/shut	**offen/geschlossen**	offern/gershlossern
right/wrong	**richtig/falsch**	**rikh**tikh/fahlsh
old/new	**alt/neu**	ahlt/noy
old/young	**alt/jung**	ahlt/yung
next/last	**nächste/letzte**	naikhster/**lehts**ter
beautiful/ugly	**schön/häßlich**	shurn/**hehs**likh
free (vacant)/ occupied	**frei/besetzt**	frigh/berzehtst
good/bad	**gut/schlecht**	goot/shlehkht
better/worse	**besser/schlechter**	behsserr/**shlehkh**terr
early/late	**früh/spät**	frew/shpait
near/far	**nah/weit**	naa/vight
left/right	**linke/rechte**	linker/**rehkh**ter

Quantities *Mengen*

a little	**ein wenig**	ighn **vay**nikh
a lot	**eine Menge**	**igh**ner **meh**nger
few/a few	**wenige/einige**	**vay**nigger/**igh**nigger
much/many	**viel/viele**	feel/**fee**ler
more (than)	**mehr (als)**	mayr (ahlss)
less (than)	**weniger (als)**	**vay**niggerr (ahlss)
enough/too (much)	**genug/zu (viel)**	ger**nook**/tsu (feel)
some/any (sing.)	**etwas**	**eht**vahss
some/any (pl.)	**einige**	**igh**nigger

A few more useful words *Weitere nützliche Wörter*

at	**an/bei**	ahn/bigh
on	**an/auf**	ahn/owf
in	**in**	in
to	**zu**	tsoo
after	**nach**	naakh
before	**vor**	foar
for	**für**	fewr
from	**von**	fon
with	**mit**	mit
without	**ohne**	**oa**ner
through	**durch**	doorkh
towards	**gegen**	**gay**gern
until	**bis**	biss
during	**während**	**vai**rernt
next to	**neben**	**nay**bern
behind	**hinter**	**hin**terr
between	**zwischen**	**tsvi**shern
since	**seit**	zight
above	**oben**	**oa**bern
below	**unten**	**un**tern
over	**über**	**ew**berr
under	**unter**	**un**terr

inside	**drinnen**	drinnern
outside	**draußen**	drowssern
up	**hinauf**	hinnowf
down	**hinunter**	hinnunterr
here	**hier**	heer
there	**dort**	dort
and	**und**	unt
or	**oder**	oaderr
but	**aber**	aaberr
not	**nicht**	nikht
never	**nie**	nee
nothing	**nichts**	nikhts
none	**kein**	kighn
very	**sehr**	zayr
too (also)	**auch**	owkh
yet	**noch**	nokh
soon	**bald**	bahlt
now	**jetzt**	yehtst
only	**nur**	noor
then	**dann**	dahn
perhaps	**vielleicht**	feelighkht

Pronunciation of the German alphabet						
A	aa	**H**	haa	**Ö**	ur	
Ä	ai	**I**	ee	**P**	pay	
B	bay	**J**	yot	**Q**	koo	
C	tsay	**K**	kaa	**R**	ehr	
D	day	**L**	ehl	**S**	ehss	
E	ay	**M**	ehm	**T**	tay	
F	ehf	**N**	ehn	**U**	oo	
G	gay	**O**	oa	**Ü**	ew	

						V	fow
						W	vay
						X	eeks
						Y	ewpsillon
						Z	tseht

In addition to these letters there is the ß sign, a combination of
s and z. It is pronounced exactly like **ss**.

Arrival

| | **PASSKONTROLLE**
PASSPORT CONTROL | |

Here's my passport.	**Hier ist mein Paß.**	heer ist mighn pahss
I'll be staying ...	**Ich bleibe ...**	ikh blighber
a few days	**ein paar Tage**	ighn paar **taa**ger
a week	**eine Woche**	**igh**ner **vokher**
a month	**einen Monat**	**igh**nern **moa**naht
I don't know yet.	**Ich weiß es noch nicht.**	ikh vighss ehss nokh nikht
I'm here on holiday.	**Ich bin auf Urlaub hier.**	ikh bin owf **oor**lowp heer
I'm here on business.	**Ich bin geschäftlich hier.**	ikh bin ger**shehft**likh heer
I'm just passing through.	**Ich bin nur auf der Durchreise.**	ikh bin noor owf derr **doorkh**righzer

If things become difficult:

I'm sorry, I don't understand.	**Es tut mir leid, ich verstehe nicht.**	ehss toot meer light ikh fehr**shtay**er nikht
Is there anyone here who speaks English?	**Spricht hier jemand Englisch?**	shprikht heer **yay**mahnt **ehng**lish

Customs *Zoll*

After collecting your baggage at the airport (*der Flughafen*—derr **floog**haafern) you have a choice: use the green exit if you have nothing to declare. Or leave via the red exit if you have items to declare (in excess of those allowed).

| **ANMELDEFREIE WAREN**
NOTHING TO DECLARE | Zoll Customs | Zoll Customs | **ANMELDEPFLICHTIGE WAREN**
GOODS TO DECLARE |

The chart below shows what you can bring in duty-free.

		Cigarettes		Cigars		Tobacco	Spirits (Liquor)	Wine
Germany	1)	200	or	50	or	250 g.	1 l. and 2 l.	
	2)	800	or	200	or	1 kg.	10 l. and 90 l.	
	3)	400	or	100	or	500 g.	1 l. and 2 l.	
Austria		200	or	50	or	250 g.	1 l. and 2 l.	
Switzerland		200	or	50	or	250 g.	1 l. and 2 l.	

1) Visitors arriving from EC countries with tax-free items, and visitors from other European countries
2) Visitors arriving from EC countries with non-tax-free items
3) Visitors arriving from countries outside Europe

I've nothing to declare.	Ich habe nichts zu verzollen.	ikh **haaber** nikhts tsoo fehrt**soll**ern
I've ...	Ich habe ...	ikh **haaber**
a carton of cigarettes	eine Stange Zigaretten	**ighner shtahng**er tsigga**reht**ern
a bottle of gin	eine Flasche Gin	**ighner flahsh**er ''gin''
It's for my personal use.	Es ist für meinen persönlichen Gebrauch.	ehss ist fewr **migh**nern pehr**zurn**likhern ger**browkh**
This is a gift.	Das ist ein Geschenk.	dahss ist ighn ger**shenk**

Ihren Paß, bitte.	Your passport, please.
Haben Sie etwas zu verzollen?	Do you have anything to declare?
Bitte öffnen Sie diese Tasche.	Please open this bag.
Dies ist zollpflichtig.	You'll have to pay duty on this.
Haben Sie noch mehr Gepäck?	Do you have any more luggage?

Baggage—Porters   *Gepäck—Gepäckträger*

These days porters are only available at airports or the railway stations of large cities. Where no porters are available you'll find luggage trolleys for the use of the passengers.

Porter!	**Gepäckträger!**	gerpehktraigerr
Please take this luggage.	**Nehmen Sie bitte dieses Gepäck.**	naymern zee bitter deezerss gerpehk
That's mine.	**Das gehört mir.**	dahss gerhurrt meer
That's my suitcase/ (travelling) bag.	**Das ist mein Koffer/ meine (Reise)tasche.**	dahss ist mighn kofferr/ mighner (righzer)tahsher
There is one piece missing.	**Es fehlt ein Gepäck-stück.**	ehss faylt ighn gerpehk-shtewk
Please take this to the ...	**Bringen Sie das bitte ...**	bringern zee dahss bitter
bus/taxi	**zum Bus/Taxi**	tsum buss/tahksi
luggage lockers	**zu den Schließ-fächern**	tsoo dayn shleesfehkherrn
How much is that?	**Wieviel macht das?**	veefeel mahkht dahss
Where are the luggage trolleys (carts)?	**Wo sind die Koffer-kulis?**	voa zint dee kofferr-kooliss

Changing money   *Geldwechsel*

Where's the nearest currency exchange office?	**Wo ist die nächste Wechselstube?**	voa ist dee naikhster vehkserlshtoober
Can you change these traveller's cheques (checks)?	**Können Sie diese Reiseschecks einlösen?**	kurnern zee deezer righzershehks ighnlurzern
I want to change some dollars/pounds.	**Ich möchte Dollar/ Pfund wechseln.**	ikh murkhter dollahr/pfunt vehkserln
Can you change this into ...?	**Können Sie das in ... umwechseln?**	kurnern zee dahss in ... umvehkserln
Austrian shillings	**Schilling**	shilling
German marks	**D-Mark**	day-mahrk
Swiss francs	**Schweizer Franken**	shvightserr frahnkern
What's the exchange rate?	**Wie ist der Wechselkurs?**	vee ist derr vehkserlkoors

BANK—CURRENCY, see page 129

Where is ...? *Wo ist ...?*

Where is the ...?	**Wo ist ...?**	voa ist
booking office	**der Reservierungs-schalter**	derr rehzerr**vee**rungs-shahlterr
car hire	**der Autoverleih**	derr **ow**toffehrligh
duty-free shop	**der Duty-free-Shop**	derr "duty-free-shop"
newsstand	**der Zeitungsstand**	derr **tsight**ungsshtahnt
restaurant	**das Restaurant**	dahss rehstor**rahng**
shopping gallery	**die Einkaufsgalerie**	dee **ighn**kowfsgahlehree
How do I get to Stuttgart?	**Wie komme ich nach Stuttgart?**	vee **kom**mer ikh nakh **shtut**gahrt
How do I get to the ... Hotel?	**Wie komme ich zum Hotel ...?**	vee **kom**mer ikh tsum hot**tehl**
Is there a bus into town?	**Fährt ein Bus ins Stadtzentrum?**	fairt ighn buss ins **shtaht**tsehntrum
Where can I get a taxi?	**Wo finde ich ein Taxi?**	voa **fin**der ikh ighn **tahk**si
Where can I hire (rent) a car?	**Wo kann ich ein Auto mieten?**	voa kahn ikh ighn **ow**to **mee**tern

Hotel reservation *Hotelreservierung*

Do you have a hotel guide?	**Haben Sie ein Hotel-verzeichnis?**	**haa**bern zee ighn hot**tehl**-fehrtsighkhniss
Could you reserve a room for me at a hotel/boarding house?	**Können Sie mir bitte ein Hotel-/Pensions-zimmer reservieren?**	**kur**nern zee meer **bit**ter ighn hot**tehl**/pehn**zioans**-tsimmerr rehzerr**vee**rern
in the centre	**im Zentrum**	im **tsehn**trum
near the railway station	**beim Bahnhof**	bighm **baan**hoaf
a single room	**ein Einzelzimmer**	ighn **ighn**tserltsimmerr
a double room	**ein Doppelzimmer**	ighn **dopp**erltsimmerr
not too expensive	**nicht zu teuer**	nikht tsu **toy**err
Where is the hotel/boarding house?	**Wo liegt das Hotel/die Pension?**	voa leegt dahss hot**tehl**/dee pehn**zioan**
Do you have a street map?	**Haben Sie einen Stadtplan?**	**haa**bern zee **igh**nern **shtaht**plaan

HOTEL/ACCOMMODATION, see page 22

Car hire (rental) *Autoverleih*

To hire a car you must produce a valid driving licence (held for at least one year) and your passport. Some firms set a minimum age at 21, other 25. Holders of major credit cards are normally exempt from deposit payments, otherwise you must pay a substantial (refundable) deposit for a car. Third-party insurance is usually automatically included.

I'd like to hire (rent) a car.	**Ich möchte ein Auto mieten.**	ikh **murkh**ter ighn **ow**to **mee**tern
small/medium-sized/ large automatic	**ein kleines/mittleres/ großes mit Automatik**	ighn **kligh**nerss/**mit**lrerss **groasserss** mit **ow**tommaatik
I'd like it for a day/a week.	**Ich möchte es für einen Tag/eine Woche.**	ikh **murkh**ter ehss fewr **igh**nern taag/**igh**ner **vokh**er
Are there any week-end arrangements?	**Gibt es Wochenend-pauschalen?**	gipt ehss **vokh**ernehnt-**pow**shaalern
Do you have any special rates?	**Haben Sie Sonder-tarife?**	**haa**bern zee **zon**derr-tahreefer
How much does it cost per day/week?	**Wieviel kostet es pro Tag/Woche?**	vee**feel kos**tert ehss proa taag/**vokh**er
Is mileage included?	**Ist das Kilometer-geld inbegriffen?**	ist dahss killom**may**terr-gehlt **in**bergriffern
What's the charge per kilometer?	**Wieviel kostet es pro Kilometer?**	vee**feel kos**tert ehss proa killom**may**terr
I want to hire the car here and leave it in ...	**Ich möchte den Wagen hier mieten und in ... zurück-geben.**	ikh **murkh**ter dayn **vaa**gern heer **mee**tern unt in ... tsoorewk**gay**bern
I want full insurance.	**Ich möchte eine Vollkasko-versicherung.**	ikh **murkh**ter **igh**ner **fol**kahskoffehrzikherrung
What's the deposit?	**Wieviel muß ich hinterlegen?**	vee**feel** muss ikh hinterr**lay**gern
I've a credit card.	**Ich habe eine Kreditkarte.**	ikh **haa**ber **igh**ner krehd**it**kahrter
Here's my driving licence.	**Hier ist mein Führerschein.**	heer ist mighn **few**rerrshighn

CAR, see page 75

Taxi *Taxi*

A taxi is usually caught at a rank (*der Taxistand*—der **tahk**si-shtahnt). You can also phone for a taxi wherever you are; numbers are listed on a separate page in front of the phone books. All taxis have meters.

English	German	Pronunciation
Where can I get a taxi?	**Wo finde ich ein Taxi?**	voa **fin**der ikh ighn **tahk**si
Please get me a taxi.	**Besorgen Sie mir bitte ein Taxi.**	berz**or**gern zee meer **bitter** ighn **tahk**si
What's the fare to ...?	**Was kostet es bis ...?**	vahss **kos**tert ehss biss
How far is it to ...?	**Wie weit ist es bis ...?**	vee vight ist ehss biss
Take me to ...	**Bringen Sie mich ...**	**bring**ern zee mikh
this address	zu dieser Adresse	tsoo **dee**zerr ah**dreh**sser
the airport	zum Flughafen	tsum **floog**haafern
the railway station	zum Bahnhof	tsum **baan**hoaf
the town centre	ins Stadtzentrum	ins **shtahtt**sehntrum
the ... Hotel	zum Hotel ...	tsum ho**tehl**
Turn ... at the next corner.	**Biegen Sie an der nächsten Ecke ... ab.**	**bee**gern zee ahn derr **naikh**stern **ehk**er ... ahp
left/right	links/rechts	links/**rehkhts**
Go straight ahead.	Geradeaus.	gerr**aa**der**rowss**
Please stop here.	**Halten Sie hier, bitte.**	**hahl**tern zee heer **bitter**
I'm in a hurry.	**Ich habe es eilig.**	ikh **haa**ber ehss **igh**likh
Could you drive more slowly?	**Bitte fahren Sie langsamer.**	**bitter faa**rern zee **lahng**zaamerr
Could you help me carry my luggage?	**Könnten Sie mir bitte beim Gepäcktragen helfen?**	**kurn**tern zee meer **bitter** bighm ger**pehk**traagern **hehl**fern
Will you wait for me, please?	**Würden Sie bitte auf mich warten?**	**vewr**dern zee **bitter** owf mikh **vahr**tern
I'll be back in 10 minutes.	**Ich bin in 10 Minuten zurück.**	ikh bin in 10 min**noo**tern tsoo**rewk**

TIPPING, see inside back-cover

Hotel—Other accommodation

Early reservation and confirmation are essential in most major tourist centres during the high season. Most towns and arrival points have a tourist information office (*Fremdenverkehrsbüro*—**frehm**dernfehrkayrsbewroa), and that's the place to go if you're stuck without a room.

Hotel
(hottehl)

Hotel; simple or fancy, your room will be spotless. You'll probably sleep under a quilt filled with duck or goose down. *Hotel garni* means that only a room and breakfast are offered, no other meals.

Schloßhotel
(shloshottehl)

Castle or palace converted into a hotel; often located in the countryside.

Rasthof
(rahsthoaf)

Wayside lodge, motel; most are located just off a motorway (expressway) or principal route.

Gasthaus/Gasthof
(gahsthowss/gahsthoaf)

Inn

Pension/Fremdenheim
(pehnzioan/frehm-
dernhighm)

Boarding-house; offers full or half board. *Zimmer frei* will tell you there's a room to let, sometimes also in a private home.

Jugendherberge
(yoogernthehrbehrger)

Youth hostel

Ferienwohnung
(fayriernvoanung)

Furnished flat (apartment) found in holiday resorts; you'll probably have to reserve it in advance. Otherwise, contact the local tourist office.

Can you recommend a hotel/pension?	**Können Sie mir ein Hotel/eine Pension empfehlen?**	kurnern zee meer ighn hottehl/ighner pehnzioan ehmpfaylern
Do you have a hotel guide?	**Haben Sie ein Hotelverzeichnis?**	haabern zee ighn hottehlfehrtsighkhniss
Are there any flats (apartments) vacant?	**Gibt es noch freie Ferienwohnungen?**	gipt ehss nokh frigher fayriernvoanungern

CAMPING, see page 32

Checking in—Reception *Empfang*

My name is …	Mein Name ist …	mighn naamer ist
I've a reservation.	Ich habe reservieren lassen.	ikh haaber rehzerrveeerern lahssern
We've reserved two rooms, a single and a double.	Wir haben zwei Zimmer reservieren lassen – ein Einzelzimmer und ein Doppelzimmer.	veer haabern tsvigh tsimmerr rehzerrveeerern lahssern—ighn ighntserltsimmerr unt ighn dopperltsimmerr
Here's the confirmation.	Hier ist die Bestätigung.	heer ist dee bershtaitiggung
Do you have any vacancies?	Haben Sie noch freie Zimmer?	haabern zee nokh frigher tsimmerr
I'd like a…	Ich hätte gern ein …	ikh hehter gehrn ighn
single room	Einzelzimmer	ighntserltsimmerr
double room	Doppelzimmer	dopperltsimmerr
A room …	Ein Zimmer …	ighn tsimmerr
with twin beds	mit zwei Einzelbetten	mit tsvigh ighntserlbehtern
with a double bed	mit einem Doppelbett	mit ighnerm dopperlbeht
with a bath	mit Bad	mit baat
with a shower	mit Dusche	mit dusher
with a balcony	mit Balkon	mit bahlkoan
with a view	mit Aussicht	mit owssikht
facing the lake/ the mountains	mit Blick auf den See/ auf die Berge	mit blik owf dayn zay/ owf dee behrger
in the front	zur Straße	tsoor shtraasser
at the back	zum Hof	tsum hoaf
It must be quiet.	Es muß ruhig sein.	ehss muss rooikh zighn
Is there …?	Gibt es …?	gipt ehss
air conditioning	Klimaanlage	kleemahnlaager
a radio/a television in the room	Radio/Fernsehen im Zimmer	raadio/fehrnzayern im tsimmerr
laundry service	einen Wäschedienst	ighnern vehsherdeenst
room service	Zimmerbedienung	tsimmerrberdeenung
hot water	warmes Wasser	vahrmerss vahsserr
running water	fließendes Wasser	fleessernderss vahsserr
a private toilet	eine eigene Toilette	ighner ighgener toahlehter
Could you put an extra bed in the room?	Könnten Sie ein zusätzliches Bett ins Zimmer stellen?	kurntern zee ighn tsoozehtslikherss beht ins tsimmerr shtehlern

CHECKING OUT, see page 31

How much? *Wieviel?*

What's the price ...?	**Wieviel kostet es ...?**	veefeel kostert ehss
per night	**pro Nacht**	proa nahkht
per week	**pro Woche**	proa vokher
for bed and breakfast	**für Übernachtung mit Frühstück**	fewr ewbernahkhtung mit frewshtewk
excluding meals	**ohne Mahlzeiten**	oaner maaltsightern
for full board (A.P.)	**mit Vollpension**	mit folpehnzioan
for half board (M.A.P.)	**mit Halbpension**	mit hahlppehnzioan
Does that include ...?	**Ist ... inbegriffen?**	ist ... inbegriffern
breakfast	**Frühstück**	frewshtewk
service	**Bedienung**	berdeenung
Value-Added Tax (VAT) *	**Mehrwertsteuer**	mayrvayrtshtoyerr
Is there any reduction for children?	**Gibt es Ermäßigung für Kinder?**	gipt ehss ehrmaissigung fewr kinderr
Do you charge for the baby?	**Berechnen Sie etwas für das Baby?**	berrehkhnern zee ehtvahss fewr dahss ''baby''
That's too expensive.	**Das ist zu teuer.**	dahss ist tsu toyerr
Haven't you anything cheaper?	**Haben Sie nichts Billigeres?**	haabern zee nihkts billiggerrerss

Decision *Entscheidung*

May I see the room?	**Kann ich das Zimmer sehen?**	kahn ikh dahss tsimmerr zayern
That's fine. I'll take it.	**Gut, ich nehme es.**	goot ikh naymer ehss
No, I don't like it.	**Nein, es gefällt mir nicht.**	nighn ehss gerfehlt meer nikht
It's too ...	**Es ist zu ...**	ehss ist tsu
cold/hot	**kalt/warm**	kahlt/vahrm
dark/small	**dunkel/klein**	dunkerl/klighn
noisy	**laut**	lowt
I asked for a room with a bath.	**Ich wollte ein Zimmer mit Bad.**	ikh volter ighn tsimmerr mit baat

---

* Americans note: a type of sales tax in Germany and Austria

NUMBERS, see page 147

Do you have anything ...?	**Haben Sie etwas ...?**	haabern zee ehtvahss
better/bigger	**Besseres/Größeres**	behsserrerss/grurserrerss
cheaper/quieter	**Billigeres/Ruhigeres**	billiggerrerss/rooiggerrerss
higher up/lower down	**weiter oben/weiter unten**	vighterr oabern/vighterr untern
Do you have a room with a better view?	**Haben Sie ein Zimmer mit einer besseren Aussicht?**	haabern zee ighn tsimmerr mit ighnerr behsserrern owssikht

Registration *Anmeldung*

Upon arrival at a hotel or boarding-house you may be asked to fill in a registration form. (*Anmeldeschein*—**ahn**mehldershighn).

Name/Vorname	Name/First name
Wohnort/Straße/Nr.	Home address/Street/Number
Nationalität/Beruf	Nationality/Profession
Geburtsdatum/Geburtsort	Date/Place of birth
Letzter Aufenthaltsort/ Reiseziel	Coming from/Going to
Paßnummer	Passport number
Kraftfahrzeugnummer	Car number
Ort/Datum	Place/Date
Unterschrift	Signature

| What does this mean? | **Was bedeutet das?** | vahss berdoytert dahss |

🖝	👉
Kann ich Ihren Paß sehen?	May I see your passport?
Würden Sie bitte den Anmeldeschein ausfüllen?	Would you mind filling in the registration form?
Unterschreiben Sie hier, bitte.	Please sign here.
Wie lange bleiben Sie?	How long will you be staying?

We'll be staying ...	Wir bleiben ...	veer blighbern
overnight only	nur eine Nacht	noor ighner nahkht
a few days	einige Tage	ighnigger taager
a week (at least)	(mindestens) eine Woche	(mindersterns) ighner vokher
I don't know yet.	Ich weiß es noch nicht.	ikh vighss ehss nokh nikht

Hotel staff *Hotelpersonal*

hall porter	der Portier	derr portyayr
maid	das Zimmermädchen	dahss tsimmermaitkhern
manager	der Direktor	derr dirrehktor
page (bellboy)	der Page	derr paazher
porter	der Hausdiener	derr howsdeenerr
receptionist	der Empfangschef	derr empfahngsshehf
switchboard operator	die Telefonistin	dee taylayfoanistin
waiter	der Kellner	derr kehlnerr
waitress	die Kellnerin	dee kehlnerrin

If you want to address members of the staff, don't say *Herr, Frau* or *Fräulein,* but use an introductory phrase such as:

| Excuse me. Could you please ...? | Entschuldigung. Könnten Sie bitte ...? | ehntshuldiggung. kurntern zee bitter |

General requirements *Allgemeine Fragen*

What's my room number?	Welche Zimmernummer habe ich?	vehlkher tsimmerrnummerr haaber ikh
The key, please.	Den Schlüssel, bitte.	dayn shlewsserl bitter
Where can I park my car?	Wo kann ich meinen Wagen parken?	voa kahn ikh mighnern vaagern pahrkern
Does the hotel have a garage?	Gibt es eine Hotelgarage?	gipt ehss ighner hottehlgahraazher
Will you have our luggage sent up?	Bitte schicken Sie unser Gepäck hinauf.	bitter shikkern zee unzerr gerpehk hinnowf
I'd like to leave this in your safe.	Ich möchte dies in Ihrem Safe lassen.	ikh murkhter deess in eererm "safe" lahssern

TELLING THE TIME, see page 153

Is there a bath on this floor?	Gibt es ein Bad auf dieser Etage?	gipt ehss ighn baat owf deezerr aytaazher
What's the voltage here?	Welche Strom-spannung haben Sie hier?	vehlkher shtroam-shpahnung haabern zee heer
Where's the outlet for the shaver?	Wo ist die Steckdose für den Rasierapparat?	voa ist dee shtehkdoazer fewr dayn rahzeerahpahraat
Would you please wake me at ...?	Würden Sie mich bitte um ... Uhr wecken?	vewrdern zee mikh bitter um ... oor vehkern
Can we have break-fast in our room?	Können wir im Zim-mer frühstücken?	kurnern veer im tsimmerr frewshtewkern
Can you find me a ...?	Können Sie mir ... besorgen?	kurnern zee meer ... berzorgern
babysitter	einen Babysitter	ighnern "babysitter"
secretary	eine Sekretärin	ighner zaykraytairin
typewriter	eine Schreibmaschine	ighner shrighpmahsheener
May I have a/an/some ...?	Kann ich ... haben?	kahn ikh ... haabern
ashtray	einen Aschenbecher	ighnern ahshernbehkherr
bath towel	ein Badetuch	ighn baadertookh
(extra) blanket	eine (extra) Decke	ighner (ekstraa) dehker
envelopes	Briefumschläge	breefumshlaiger
(more) hangers	(noch) einige Kleiderbügel	(nokh) ighnigger klighderrbewgerl
hot-water bottle	eine Wärmflasche	ighner vehrmflahsher
ice cubes	Eiswürfel	ighsvewrferl
needle and thread	eine Nadel und etwas Faden	ighner naaderl unt ehtvahss faadern
(extra) pillow	ein (extra) Kopfkissen	ighn(ekstraa) kopfkissern
reading-lamp	eine Leselampe	ighner layzerlahmper
soap	Seife	zighfer
writing-paper	Schreibpapier	shrighppahpeer
Where's the ...?	Wo ist ...?	voa ist
bathroom	das Bad	dahss baat
dining-room	der Speisesaal	derr shpighzerzaal
emergency exit	der Notausgang	derr noatowsgahng
hairdresser's	der Friseur	derr frizurr
lift (elevator)	der Fahrstuhl	derr faarshtool
television room	der Fernsehraum	derr fehrnzayrowm
toilet	die Toilette	dee toahlehter

Telephone—Post (mail) *Telefon – Post*

Can you put me through to Vienna 1 23 4 56?	**Können Sie mich mit Wien 12 34 56 verbinden?**	kurnern zee mikh mit veen 12 34 56 fehr**bin**dern
Do you have stamps?	**Haben Sie Briefmarken?**	**haa**bern zee **breef**mahrkern
Would you post this for me, please?	**Würden Sie das bitte für mich aufgeben?**	vew**r**dern zee dahss **bit**ter fewr mikh **owf**gaybern
Is there any mail for me?	**Ist Post für mich da?**	ist post fewr mikh daa
Are there any messages for me?	**Hat jemand eine Nachricht für mich hinterlassen?**	haht **yay**mahnt **igh**ner **naak**hrikht fewr mikh hinter**lahs**sern
How much are my telephone charges?	**Wie hoch ist meine Telefonrechnung?**	vee hoakh ist **migh**ner taylay**foan**rehkhnung

Difficulties *Schwierigkeiten*

The ... doesn't work.	**... funktioniert nicht.**	... funktsion**neert** nikht
air conditioner	**die Klimaanlage**	dee **klee**mahahnlaager
fan	**der Ventilator**	derr **vehn**tillaator
heating	**die Heizung**	dee **hight**sung
light	**das Licht**	dahss likht
radio	**das Radio**	dahss **raa**dio
television	**der Fernseher**	derr **fehrn**zayerr
The tap (faucet) is dripping.	**Der Wasserhahn tropft.**	derr **vahs**serrhaan tropft
There's no hot water.	**Es gibt kein warmes Wasser.**	ehs gipt kighn **vahr**mers **vahs**serr
The wash-basin is blocked.	**Das Waschbecken ist verstopft.**	dahss **vahsh**behkern ist fehr**shtopft**
The window/The door is jammed.	**Das Fenster/Die Tür klemmt.**	dahss **fehn**sterr/dee tewr klehmt
The curtain is stuck.	**Der Vorhang klemmt.**	derr **foar**hahng klehmt
The bulb is burned out.	**Die Birne ist kaputt.**	dee **beer**ner ist kah**put**
My room has not been made up.	**Mein Zimmer ist nicht gemacht.**	mighn **tsim**merr ist nikht ger**mahkht**

POST OFFICE AND TELEPHONE, see page 132

The ... is broken.	... ist kaputt.	... ist kahput
blind	das Rollo	dahss rollo
lamp	die Lampe	dee lahmper
plug	der Stecker	derr shtehkerr
shutter	der Fensterladen	derr fehnsterrlaadern
switch	der Schalter	derr shahlterr
Can you get it repaired?	Können Sie es reparieren lassen?	kurnern zee ehss rehpahreerern lahssern

Laundry—Dry cleaner's *Wäscherei – Reinigung*

I want these clothes ...	Ich möchte diese Kleider ... lassen.	ikh murkhter deezer klighderr ... lahssern
cleaned	reinigen	righniggern
ironed	bügeln	bewgerln
pressed	dampfbügeln	dahmpfbewgerln
washed	waschen	vahshern
When will they be ready?	Wann sind sie fertig?	vahn zint zee fehrtikh
I need them ...	Ich brauche sie ...	ikh browkher zee
today	heute	hoyter
tonight	heute abend	hoyter aabernt
tomorrow	morgen	morgern
before Friday	vor Freitag	foar frightaag
Can you ... this?	Können Sie das ...?	kurnern zee dahss
mend	ausbessern	owsbehsserrn
patch	flicken	flikkern
stitch	nähen	naiern
Can you sew on this button?	Können Sie diesen Knopf annähen?	kurnern zee deezern knopf ahnnaiern
Can you get this stain out?	Können Sie diesen Fleck entfernen?	kurnern zee deezern flehk ehntfehrnern
Is my laundry ready?	Ist meine Wäsche fertig?	ist mighner vehsher fehrtikh
This isn't mine.	Das gehört nicht mir.	dahss gerhurrt nikht meer
There's one piece missing.	Es fehlt ein Stück.	ehss faylt ighn shtewk
There's a hole in this.	Da ist ein Loch drin.	daa ist ighn lokh drin

DAYS OF THE WEEK, see page 151

Hairdresser's—Barber's *Damen- und Herrenfriseur*

Is there a hairdresser/beauty salon in the hotel?	**Gibt es einen Friseur/Kosmetiksalon im Hotel?**	gipt ehss ighnern frizurr/kosmaytikzahlong im hottehl
Can I make an appointment for sometime on Thursday?	**Kann ich mich für Donnerstag anmelden?**	kahn ikh mikh fewr donnerrstaag ahnmehldern
I'd like it cut and shaped.	**Schneiden und Legen, bitte.**	shnighdern unt laygern bitter
The parting (part) left/right, please.	**Den Scheitel links/rechts, bitte.**	dayn shighterl links/rehkhts bitter
I want a haircut, please.	**Haare schneiden, bitte.**	haarer shnighdern bitter
bleach	**eine Aufhellung**	ighner owfhehlung
blow-dry	**fönen**	furnern
colour rinse	**eine Farbspülung**	ighner fahrpshpewlung
dye	**färben**	fehrbern
face-pack	**eine Gesichtsmaske**	ighner gerzikhtsmahsker
manicure	**eine Maniküre**	ighner mahnikkewrer
permanent wave	**eine Dauerwelle**	ighner dowerrvehler
setting lotion	**ein Haarfestiger**	ighn haarfehstiggerr
shampoo and set	**Waschen und Legen**	vahshern unt laygern
with a fringe (bangs)	**mit Ponyfransen**	mit ponnifrahnzern
I'd like a shampoo for ... hair.	**Ein Haarwaschmittel für ... Haar, bitte.**	ighn haarvahshmitterl fewr ... haar bitter
normal/dry/greasy (oily)	**normales/trockenes/fettiges**	normaalerss/trokkernerss/fehtiggerss
Do you have a colour chart?	**Haben Sie eine Farbtabelle?**	haabern zee ighner fahrptahbehler
Don't cut it too short.	**Nicht zu kurz schneiden.**	nikht tsu koorts shnighdern
A little more off the ...	**Bitte ... etwas kürzer.**	bitter ... ehtvahss kewrtserr
back	**hinten**	hintern
neck	**im Nacken**	im nahkern
sides	**an den Seiten**	ahn dayn zightern
top	**oben**	oabern
I don't want any hairspray.	**Kein Haarspray, bitte.**	kighn haarshpray bitter
I'd like a shave.	**Rasieren, bitte.**	rahzeerern bitter

DAYS OF THE WEEK, see page 151

Would you please trim my ...?	Stutzen Sie mir bitte ...	shtutsern zee meer bitter
beard	den Bart	dayn baart
moustache	den Schnurrbart	dayn shnoorbaart
sideboards (sideburns)	die Koteletten	dee kotlehtern

Checking out *Abreise*

May I please have my bill?	Kann ich bitte die Rechnung haben?	kahn ikh bitter dee rehkhnung haabern
I'm leaving early tomorrow. Please have my bill ready.	Ich reise morgen früh ab. Bereiten Sie bitte meine Rechnung vor.	ikh righzer morgern frew ahp. berrightern zee bitter mighner rehkhnung foar
I must leave at once.	Ich muß sofort abreisen.	ikh muss zoafort ahprighzern
Is everything included?	Ist alles inbegriffen?	ist ahlerss inbergriffern
Can I pay by credit card?	Kann ich mit Kreditkarte bezahlen?	kahn ikh mit krehditkahrter bertsaalern
You've made a mistake in this bill, I think.	Ich glaube, Sie haben sich verrechnet.	ikh glowber zee haabern zikh fehrrehkhnert
Can you get us a taxi?	Können Sie uns ein Taxi bestellen?	kurnern zee uns ighn tahksi bershtehlern
Could you have our luggage brought down, please?	Würden Sie bitte unser Gepäck herunterbringen lassen?	vewrdern zee bitter unzerr gerpehk hehrunterrbringern lahssern
We're in a great hurry.	Wir haben es sehr eilig.	veer haabern ehss zayr ighlikh
Here's the forwarding address.	Hier ist meine Nachsendeadresse.	heer ist mighner naakhzehnderahdrehsser
You have my home address.	Sie haben meine Wohnadresse.	zee haabern mighner voanahdrehsser
It's been a very enjoyable stay.	Es war ein sehr angenehmer Aufenthalt.	ehss vaar ighn zayr ahngernaymerr owfehnthahlt

TIPPING, see inside back-cover

Camping

There are plenty of authorized camp sites in Germany, many with excellent facilities. Austria and Switzerland also have well-equipped camp sites, some of them high up in the mountains. For information apply to any Tourist Office.

Is there a camp site near here?	**Gibt es hier in der Nähe einen Campingplatz?**	gipt ehss heer in derr naier ighnern kehmpingplahts
Can we camp here?	**Können wir hier zelten?**	kurnern veer heer tsehltern
Have you room for a tent/caravan (trailer)?	**Haben Sie Platz für ein Zelt/einen Wohnwagen?**	haabern zee plahts fewr ighn tsehlt/ighnern voanvaagern
Is there/Are there (a) ...?	**Gibt es ...?**	gipt ehss
drinking water	**Trinkwasser**	trinkvahsserr
electricity	**Stromanschluß**	shtroamahnshluss
playground	**einen Spielplatz**	ighnern shpeelplahts
restaurant	**ein Restaurant**	ighn rehstorrahng
shopping facilities	**Einkaufs-möglichkeiten**	ighnkowfsmurglikhkightern
swimming pool	**ein Schwimmbad**	ighn shvimbaat
What's the charge ...?	**Wie hoch sind die Gebühren ...?**	vee hoakh zint dee gerbewrern
per day	**pro Tag**	proa taag
per person	**pro Person**	proa pehrzoan
for a car	**für ein Auto**	fewr ighn owto
for a caravan (trailer)	**für einen Wohn-wagen**	fewr ighnern voan-vaagern
for a tent	**für ein Zelt**	fewr ighn tsehlt
Is the tourist tax included?	**Ist die Kurtaxe inbegriffen?**	ist dee koortahkser inbergriffern
Where are the showers/toilets?	**Wo sind die Duschen/die Toiletten?**	voa zint dee dushern/dee toahlehtern
Where can I get butane gas?	**Wo kann ich Butan-gas bekommen?**	voa kahn ikh buttaangaass berkommern
Is there a youth hostel near here?	**Gibt es hier irgend-wo eine Jugend-herberge?**	gipt ehss heer eergerntvoa ighner yoogerrnthehrbehrger

CAMPING EQUIPMENT, see page 106

Eating out

There are many types of places where you can eat and drink in Germany, Austria and Switzerland.

Beisel
(bighzerl)

The Austrian equivalent to a *Gasthaus*.

Bierhalle
(beerhahler)

Beer hall; besides beer served from huge barrels, you'll also be able to order hot dishes, sausages, salads and pretzels. The best-known beer halls are those in Munich which has a giant beer festival *(Oktoberfest)* annually in late September.

Bierstube
(beershtoober)

The nearest equivalent to an English pub or an American tavern though the atmosphere may be very different; usually only serves a few "dishes of the day".

Café
(kahfay)

Coffee shop; besides coffee, you'll be able to get pastries, snacks and drinks. There's a small dance floor in a *Tanzcafé*.

Gasthaus/Gasthof
(gahsthowss/gahsthoaf)

Inn, usually in the country. It offers home-cooking and a folksy atmosphere.

Gaststätte
(gahstshtehter)

Another word for *Restaurant*.

Kaffeehaus
(kahfayhowss)

The Austrian equivalent to a *Café*.

Konditorei
(kondeetoarigh)

A pastry shop; will often have a salon for coffee and pastries.

Milchbar
(milkhbaar)

A bar serving mainly plain and flavoured milk drinks with pastries. Also called a *Milchstübl*.

Raststätte
(rahstshtehter)

Roadside restaurant; also called a *Rasthof* in Austria; it's usually found on a motorway (expressway). Lodging and service-station facilities are on the premises.

Ratskeller
(rahtskehlerr)

A restaurant in the cellar of the town-hall (often a very historic, old building); food is generally excellent.

Restaurant
(rehstorrahng)

These are generally found only in urban areas. Menus often cater to foreign visitors as well as offering numerous local specialities.

Schnellbuffet (**shnehl**bewfay)	A snack bar; often with counter service.
Schnellimbiß (**shnehl**imbiss)	Snack bar; the English term is also seen. The principal fare is beer and sausages. A sausage stand *(Würstchenstand)* is often quite similar.
Tea-room ("tea-room")	The Swiss equivalent to a *Café*.
Weinstube (**vighn**shtoober)	A cozy type of restaurant found in wine-producing districts where you can sample new wine with simple hot dishes and snacks. In Austria, it's called a *Heuriger* and is identified by a wreath hanging over the portal.

Meal times   *Essenszeiten*

Breakfast (*das Frühstück*—dahss **frew**shtewk) is served from 7 a.m. to 10 a.m. and is generally included in the hotel arrangement.

Lunch (*das Mittagessen*—dahss **mit**tahgehssern) is generally served from 11.30 a.m. until 2 p.m.

Dinner (*das Abendessen*—dahss **aa**berntehssern) is served from 6.30 to 8.30 p.m., in large restaurants to 10 or 11 p.m. After this it's usually a case of cold snacks or hot sausages only.

Eating habits   *Eßgewohnheiten*

Germans start the day early with a meal that is somewhat more substantial than the typical "continental" breakfast, and they like to eat their main meal in the middle of the day. Supper is generally a slightly more copious version of breakfast—cold meat and cheese, with the addition of a salad. Most restaurants will, however, serve a three course dinner in the evening.

On weekends Germans often eat an afternoon snack. It can be either coffee or tea with pastries, or cold meat and cheese.

Fellow diners usually wish each other *"Mahlzeit"* or *"Guten Appetit"*.

German cuisine   *Die deutsche Küche*

German cuisine has undergone many changes in the postwar years. Non-fattening, healthy fare has become more popular, and the influence of French, Italian, Greek, Chinese and other cuisines is remarkable. However, rich hearty dishes, mostly with pork and potatoes, are still served. Each region has its own specialities, and almost each town its own beer (or wine), but everywhere you'll find an extraordinary range of sausages, smoked ham, soused fish and many kinds of good bread. Not to mention *Sauerkraut, Schnitzel, Spätzle, Frankfurter, Frikadellen, Rollmops* ... And if you like game, Germany is the place.

Möchten Sie etwas essen?	Would you like to eat something?
Was nehmen Sie?	What would you like?
Ich empfehle Ihnen ...	I recommend ...
Was trinken Sie?	What would you like to drink?
Möchten Sie ...?	Do you want ...?
... haben wir nicht.	We haven't got ...

Hungry?   *Hungrig?*

I'm hungry/I'm thirsty.	**Ich habe Hunger/ Ich habe Durst.**	ikh **haaber** hunger/ikh **haaber** doorst
Can you recommend a good restaurant?	**Können Sie mir ein gutes Restaurant empfehlen?**	**kurnern** zee meer ighn **gooterss** rehstor**rahng** ehmp**faylern**
Is there an inexpensive restaurant around here?	**Gibt es in der Nähe ein preiswertes Restaurant?**	gibt ehss in derr **naier** ighn **prighs**vehrterss rehstor**rahng**

If you want to be sure of getting a table in well-known restaurants, it may be better to telephone in advance.

I'd like to reserve a table for 4.	Ich möchte einen Tisch für 4 Personen reservieren lassen.	ikh murkhter ighnern tish fewr 4 pehrzoanern rehzehrveerern lahssern
We'll come at 8.	Wir kommen um 8 Uhr.	veer kommern um 8 oor
Could we have a table ...?	Können wir einen Tisch ... haben?	kurnern veer ighnern tish ... haabern
in the corner	in der Ecke	in derr ehker
by the window	am Fenster	ahm fehnsterr
outside	im Freien	im frighern
on the terrace	auf der Terrasse	owf derr tehrahsser
in a nonsmoking area	in der Nichtraucher-ecke	in derr nikhtrowkherr-ehker

Asking and ordering *Fragen und Bestellen*

Waiter/Waitress!	Herr Ober/Fräulein, bitte!	hehr oaberr/froylighn bitter
I'd like something to eat/drink.	Ich möchte gerne essen/etwas trinken.	ikh murkhter gehrner ehssern/ehtvahss trinkern
May I have the menu, please?	Kann ich bitte die Speisekarte haben?	kahn ikh bitter dee shpighzerkahrter haabern
Do you have a set menu/local dishes?	Haben Sie ein Gedeck/hiesige Gerichte?	haabern zee ighn gerdehk/heezigger gerrikhter
What do you recommend?	Was würden Sie mir empfehlen?	vahss vewrdern zee meer ehmpfaylern
I'd like ...	Ich hätte gern ...	ikh hehter gehrn
Could we have a/an ..., please?	Könnten wir bitte ... haben?	kurntern veer bitter ... haabern
ashtray	einen Aschenbecher	ighnern ahshernbehkherr
cup	eine Tasse	ighner tahsser
fork	eine Gabel	ighner gaaberl
glass	ein Glas	ighn glaass
knife	ein Messer	ighn mehsserr
napkin (serviette)	eine Serviette	ighner sehrviehter
plate	einen Teller	ighnern tehlerr
spoon	einen Löffel	ighnern lurferl
May I have some ...?	Könnte ich etwas ... haben?	kurnter ikh ehtvahss ... haabern
bread	Brot	broat
butter	Butter	butterr

lemon	**Zitrone**	tsitroaner
mustard	**Senf**	zehnf
pepper	**Pfeffer**	pfehferr
salt	**Salz**	zahlts
seasoning	**Würze**	vewrtser
sugar	**Zucker**	tsukkerr

Some useful expressions for dieters and special requirements:

I'm on a diet.	**Ich muß Diät leben.**	ikh muss deeait laybern
I don't drink alcohol.	**Ich trinke keinen Alkohol.**	ikh trinker kighnern ahlkohoal
I mustn't eat food containing ...	**Ich darf nichts essen, was ... enthält.**	ikh dahrf nikhts ehssern vahss ... ehnthehlt
flour/fat	**Mehl/Fett**	mayl/feht
salt/sugar	**Salz/Zucker**	zahlts/tsukkerr
Do you have ... for diabetics?	**Haben Sie ... für Diabetiker?**	haabern zee ... fewr deeahbaytikkerr
cakes	**Kuchen**	kookhern
fruit juice	**Fruchtsaft**	frukhtzahft
special menu	**ein Spezialmenü**	ighn shpehtsiahlmaynew
Do you have vegetarian dishes?	**Haben Sie vegetarische Gerichte?**	haabern zee vehgehtaarisher gerrikhter
Could I have cheese/fruit instead of the dessert?	**Könnte ich statt der Süßspeise Käse/Obst haben?**	kurnter ikh shtaht derr zewsshpighzer kaizer/opst haabern
Can I have an artificial sweetener?	**Kann ich Süßstoff haben?**	kahn ikh zewsshtof haabern

And ...

I'd like some more.	**Ich möchte etwas mehr.**	ikh murkhter ehtvahss mayr
Can I have more ..., please.	**Kann ich noch ... haben, bitte?**	kahn ikh nokh ... haabern bitter
Just a small portion.	**Nur eine kleine Portion.**	noor ighner klighner portsioan
Nothing more, thanks.	**Nichts mehr, danke.**	nikhts mayr dahnker
Where are the toilets?	**Wo ist die Toilette?**	voa ist dee toahlehter

Breakfast   *Frühstück*

A German breakfast is a rather substantial meal. You may be served cold meat, cheese, a variety of breads—*Schwarzbrot, Vollkornbrot, Roggenbrot, Weißbrot* (black, wholegrain, rye, white)—and rolls *(Brötchen* or *Semmeln)* or croissants *(Hörnchen)* with butter and jam, accompanied by coffee or tea.

I'd like breakfast, please.	**Ich möchte frühstücken, bitte.**	ikh murkhter frewshtewkern bitter
I'll have a/an/some …	**Ich hätte gern …**	ikh hehter gehrn
bacon and eggs	**Spiegeleier mit Speck**	shpeegerligherr mit shpehk
boiled egg	**ein gekochtes Ei**	ighn gerkokhterss igh
soft/hard	**weich/hartgekocht**	vighkh/hahrtgerkokht
cereal	**Getreideflocken**	gertrighderflokkern
cheese	**Käse**	kaizer
eggs	**Eier**	igherr
fried eggs	**Spiegeleier**	shpeegerligherr
scrambled eggs	**Rühreier**	rewrigherr
grapefruit juice	**Grapefruitsaft**	grehpfrootzahft
ham and eggs	**Spiegeleier mit Schinken**	shpeegerligherr mit shinkern
jam	**Marmelade**	mahrmehlaader
marmalade	**Apfelsinenmarmelade**	ahpferlzeenernmahrmehlaader
orange juice	**Orangensaft**	orrahngzhernzahft
toast	**Toast**	toast
May I have some …?	**Kann ich … haben?**	kahn ikh … haabern
bread	**Brot**	broat
butter	**Butter**	butterr
(hot) chocolate	**(heiße) Schokolade**	(highsser) shokkollaader
coffee	**Kaffee**	kahfay
decaffeinated	**koffeinfreien Kaffee**	koffeheenfrighern kahfay
black	**schwarzen Kaffee**	shvahrtsern kahfay
with milk	**Milchkaffee**	milkhkahfay
honey	**Honig**	hoanikh
milk	**Milch**	milkh
hot/cold	**heiße/kalte**	highsser/kahlter
rolls	**Brötchen**	brurtkhern
tea	**Tee**	tay
with milk/lemon	**mit Milch/Zitrone**	mit milkh/tsitroaner
(hot) water	**(heißes) Wasser**	(highsserss) vahsserr

What's on the menu? *Was steht auf der Speisekarte?*

Most restaurants display a menu *(Speisekarte)* outside. Besides the à la carte menu, they'll usually offer one or more set menus *(Menü* or *Gedeck)*. Value-added tax—a type of sales tax *(Mehrwertsteuer* or *Mwst)*—and a service charge *(Bedienung)* are usually included.

Under the headings below you'll find alphabetical lists of dishes that might be offered on a German menu, with their English equivalent. You can simply show the book to the waiter. If you want some cheese, for instance, let *him* point to what's available on the appropriate list. Use pages 36 and 37 for ordering in general.

Gaststätten

Reading the menu *Die Speisekarte lesen*

Tagesgedeck	Set menu of the day
Tagesgericht	Dish of the day
Spezialität des Hauses	Speciality of the house
Unser Küchenchef empfiehlt ...	The chef recommends ...
Nach ... art	... style
Hausgemacht	Home-made
Dasselbe mit ...	The same served with ...
Nur auf Bestellung	Made to order
Alle Preise sind inklusive Bedienung und Mehrwertsteuer	Service charge and VAT (sales tax) included
... im Preis inbegriffen	... included in the price
Nach Wahl	At your choice
Extraaufschlag	Extra charge

Beilagen	**bigh**laagern	accompaniments
Eierspeisen	**igh**ershpigh**zern	egg dishes
Eintopfgerichte	**igh**ntopfgerrikhter	stews
Eis	**igh**ss	ice-cream
Fischgerichte	**fish**gerrikhter	fish
Fleischgerichte	**fligh**shgerrikhter	meat
Glace	**glah**sser	ice-cream
Gemüse	**ger**mewzer	vegetables
Geflügel	ger**flew**gerl	poultry
Getränke	ger**train**ker	drinks
Hauptgerichte	**howpt**gerrikhter	main course
Käse	**kai**zer	cheese
Meeresfrüchte	**may**rersfrewkhter	seafood
Nachspeisen/ Nachtisch	**naakh**shpigh**zern**/ **naakh**tish	desserts
Obst	**oapst**	fruit
Reisgerichte	**righs**gerrikhter	rice
Salate	**zah**laater	salads
Suppen	**zup**pern	soups
Süßspeisen	**zews**shpighzern	desserts
Teigwaren	**tighk**vaarern	pasta
Vom Rost	fom roast	grilled (broiled)
Vorspeisen	**foar**shpighzern	first course
Wein	**vighn**	wine
Wild	**vilt**	game

Appetizers *Vorspeisen*

If you feel like something to whet your appetite, choose
carefully, for the German appetizer can be filling. Starters
may also be listed on the menu under *Kleine Gerichte* or
Kalte Platten.

I'd like an appetizer.	Ich hätte gern eine Vorspeise.	ikh **hehter** gehrn **ighner** foarsh**pigh**zer
Aal (in Gelee)	aal in zherlay	(jellied) eel
Appetithäppchen	ahpeh**teet**hehpkhern	canapés
Artischocken	ahrtishokkern	artichoke
Austern	owsterrn	oysters
Bündnerfleisch	bewndnerrflighsh	cured, dried beef served in thin slices
Bückling	bewkling	bloater, kipper
Fleischpastete	flighshpahstayter	meat loaf
Froschschenkel	froshshehnkerl	frog's legs
Gänseleberpastete	gehnzerlayberr-pahstayter	pâté, goose liver purée
Hering	hayring	herring
Hummer	hummerr	lobster
Hummerkrabben	hummerrkrahbern	large prawns
Käsehäppchen	kaizer**hehp**khern	cheese sticks
Krabben	krahbern	prawns, shrimps
Krebs	krayps	river crayfish
Lachs	lahks	salmon
Languste	lahng**gus**ter	spiny lobster
Makrele	mah**kray**ler	mackerel
Muscheln	musherln	mussels
Pilze	**pil**tser	mushrooms
Räucheraal	roykherraal	smoked eel
Räucherhering	roykherrhayring	smoked herring
Rollmops	rolmops	soused herring
Rohschinken	roashinkern	cured ham
Russische Eier	russisher igherr	hard-boiled eggs with mayonnaise
Sardellen	zahr**dehl**lern	anchovies
Sardinen	zahr**dee**nern	sardines
Schinken	shinkern	ham
Schnecken	shnehkern	snails
Spargelspitzen	shpaargerlshpitsern	asparagus tips
Thunfisch	toonfish	tunny, tuna
Wurst	voorst	sausage
Wurstplatte	**voorst**plahter	assorted cold cuts

Bismarckhering
(bismahrkhayring)

soused herring with onions

Frisch geräucherte Gänsebrust auf Toast
(frish gerroykherrter gehnzerbrust owf toast)

freshly smoked breast of goose on toast

Hoppel-Poppel
(hopperl-popperl)

scrambled eggs with diced sausages or bacon

Königinpastete
(kurnigginpahstayter)

puff-pastry shell filled with diced meat and mushrooms

Matjeshering
(mahtyehshayring)

salted young herring

Matjesfilet nach Hausfrauenart
(mahtyehsfillay nahkh howsfrowernahrt)

fillets of herring with apples and onions

Hausgemachte Rehpastete
(howsgermakhkter raypahstayter)

home-made venison meatloaf

Schinkenröllchen mit Spargel
(shinkernrurlkhern mit shpahrgerl)

rolled ham with asparagus filling

Strammer Max
(shtrahmerr mahkss)

slice of bread with highly spiced minced pork served with fried eggs and onions

Soups and stews *Suppen und Eintopfgerichte*

German soup can be hearty fare and particularly welcome on a cold day. *Eintopf* is a stew and will usually be a meal in itself.

I'd like some soup.	**Ich möchte gern eine Suppe.**	ikh murkhter gehrn ighner zupper
Aalsuppe	aalzupper	eel soup
Bauernsuppe	bowerrnzupper	cabbage and frankfurter soup
Bohnensuppe	boanernzupper	bean soup with bacon
Bouillon	boolyong	clear soup
Erbsensuppe	ehrpzernzupper	pea soup
Fischsuppe	fishzupper	fish soup
Fischbeuschelsuppe	fishboysherlzupper	fish roe and vegetable soup
Fridattensuppe	friddahternzupper	broth with pancake strips

Frühlingssuppe	frewlingszupper	spring vegetable soup
Grießnockerlsuppe	greesnokkerrlzupper	semolina-dumpling soup
Gulaschsuppe	goolahshzupper	spiced soup of stewed beef
Hühnerbrühe	hewnerrbrewer	chicken broth
Kartoffelsuppe	kahrtofferlzupper	potato soup
(Semmel-) Knödelsuppe	(zehmerl-) knurderlzupper	dumpling soup
Königinsuppe	kurnigginzupper	soup with beef, sour cream and almonds
Kraftbrühe	krahftbrewer	beef consommé
mit Ei	mit igh	with raw egg
mit Einlage	mit ighnlaager	with a garnish
Leberknödelsuppe	layberrknurderlzupper	liver-dumpling soup
Linsensuppe	linzernzupper	lentil soup
Nudelsuppe	nooderlzupper	noodle soup
Ochsenschwanz-suppe	oksernshvahntszupper	oxtail soup
Pichelsteiner Eintopf	pikherlshtighnerr ighntopf	meat and vegetable stew
Schildkrötensuppe	shiltkrurternzupper	turtle soup
Serbische Bohnensuppe	zehrbisher boanernzupper	spiced bean soup
Tomatensuppe	tommaaternzupper	tomato soup
Zwiebelsuppe	tsveeberlzupper	onion soup

Backerbsensuppe (bahkehrpsernzupper)	broth served with pea-sized balls of pasta
Basler Mehlsuppe (baaslerr maylzupper)	flour soup with grated cheese (Swiss)
Labskaus (laapskowss)	thick stew of minced and marinated meat with mashed potatoes

Fish and seafood *Fisch und Meeresfrüchte*

I'd like some fish.	**Ich hätte gern Fisch.**	ikh hehter gehrn fish
What kind of seafood do you have?	**Welche Meeres-früchte haben Sie?**	vehlkher mayrersfrewkhter haabern zee
Aal	aal	eel
Austern	owsterrn	oysters
Barsch	bahrsh	freshwater perch
Brasse/Brachse	brahsser/brahkser	bream

Dorsch	dorsh	cod
Egli	ehglee	perch
Felchen	fehlkhern	kind of trout
Fischfrikadellen	fishfrikkahdehlern	fish croquettes
Forelle	forehler	trout
Flunder	flunderr	flounder
Garnelen	gahrnaylern	prawns/shrimps
Hecht	hehkht	pike
Heilbutt	highlbut	halibut
Hering	hayring	herring
Hummer	hummerr	lobster
Jakobsmuscheln	yaakopsmusherln	scallops
Kabeljau	kaaberlyow	cod
Kaisergranate	kighzerrgrahnahter	kind of scampi
Karpfen	kahrpfen	carp
Krebs	krayps	river crayfish
Lachs	lahks	salmon
Languste	lahnggooster	spiny lobster
Makrele	mahkrayler	mackerel
Muscheln	musherln	clams/mussels
Rotbarsch	roatbahrsh	red sea-bass
Salm	zahlm	salmon
Schellfisch	shehlfish	haddock
Scholle	sholler	plaice
Seebarsch	zaybahrsh	sea bass
Seebutt	zaybut	brill
Seezunge	zaytsunger	sole
Sprotten	shprottern	sprats
Steinbutt	shtighnbut	turbot
Stint	shtint	smelt
Stör	shturr	sturgeon
Zander	tsahnderr	(giant) pike-perch

baked	**gebacken**	gerbahkern
boiled in bouillon	**blau**	blow
breaded	**paniert**	pahneert
fried	**gebraten**	gerbraatern
deep-fried	**im schwimmenden**	im shvimmerndern
	Fett gebacken	feht gerbahkern
grilled	**gegrillt**	gergrilt
marinated	**mariniert**	mahrinneert
sautéed (in butter)	**(in Butter)**	(in butterr)
	geschwenkt	gershvehnkt
smoked	**geräuchert**	gerroykhert
steamed	**gedämpft**	gerdehmpft

Meat *Fleisch*

Bear in mind that the Germans most often write in one word what would take us two or more. For example, *Rindszunge* is *Rinds-* (beef) and *-zunge* (tongue) or *Kalbsbrust* is breast of veal. So you may have to look under two entries in the following lists to fully understand what's on the menu.

I'd like some ...	Ich hätte gern ...	ikh **heh**ter gehrn
beef	**Rindfleisch**	**rint**flighsh
lamb	**Lammfleisch**	**lahm**flighsh
mutton	**Hammelfleisch**	**hahm**erlflighsh
pork	**Schweinefleisch**	**shvigh**nerflighsh
veal	**Kalbfleisch**	**kahlp**flighsh

Bauernomelett	bowerrnomleht	diced bacon and onion omelet
(deutsches) Beefsteak	(doytsherss) beef-stayk	hamburger
Beuschel	boysherl	veal offal with lemon sauce
-braten	-braatern	joint, roast
-brust	-brust	breast
Eisbein	**ighs**bighn	pickled pig's knuckle
Faschiertes	fah**sheer**terss	minced meat
Filetsteak	**fillay**stayk	beef steak
Fleischkäse	**flighsh**kaizer	type of bologna sausage
Frikadellen	frikkah**dehl**ern	meat patties
Geschnetzeltes	ger**shneht**serlterss	chipped veal served in wine sauce
Geselchtes	ger**zehlkht**erss	smoked or salted meat usually pork
Gulasch	**goo**lahsh	gulash; chunks of beef stewed in a rich paprika gravy
Hackbraten	**hahk**braatern	meatloaf
-hachse/haxe	-**hahk**ser	shank
-herz	-**hehrts**	heart
Kasseler Rippenspeer	**kahs**sehlerr **rippern**shpayr	smoked pork chops
-klößchen	-**klurs**khern	meatballs
-kotelett	-**kot**leht	cutlet, chop
Krenfleisch	**krayn**flighsh	pork, usually brawn, served with shredded vegetables and horseradish

Kutteln	kutterln	tripe
Leber	layberr	liver
Leberkäse	layberrkaizer	type of meatloaf
Lenden-	lehndern	fillet of beef (tenderloin)
Nieren	neerern	kidneys
Nierenstück	neerernshtewk	loin
-plätzli	-plehtslee	escalope
Pökelfleisch	purkerlflighsh	marinated meat
Rippensteak	rippernshtayk	rib steak
Rostbraten	roastbraatern	rumpsteak
Rouladen	roolaadern	slices of beef or veal filled, rolled and braised (in brown gravy)
Sauerbraten	zowerrbraatern	marinated, brased beef
Schinken	shinkern	ham
Schlachtplatte	shlahkhtplahter	platter of various sausages and cold meats
Schnitzel	shnitserl	escalope
Spanferkel	shpaanfehrkerl	suck(l)ing pig
Speck	shpehk	bacon
-spießchen	-shpeeskhern	skewered meat
Sülze	zewltser	brawn (headcheese)
Wiener Schnitzel	veenerr shnitserl	breaded veal escalope
-zunge	-tsunger	tongue

Here are some hearty dishes you'll certainly want to try:

Bauernschmaus (bowerrnshmowss)	sauerkraut garnished with boiled bacon, smoked pork, sausages, dumplings, potatoes (Austrian)
Berner Platte (behrnerr plahter)	sauerkraut (or green beans) liberally garnished with pork chops, boiled bacon and beef, sausages, tongue and ham (Swiss)
Holsteiner Schnitzel (holshtighnerr shnitserl)	breaded veal escalope topped with fried egg, garnished with vegetables and usually accompanied by bread and butter, anchovies, mussels and smoked salmon
Kohlroulade (koalroolaader)	cabbage leaves stuffed with minced meat
Königsberger Klopse (kurnigsbehrgerr klopser)	Meatballs in white caper sauce

boiled	**gekocht**	gerkokht
braised	**geschmort**	gershmoart
fried	**(in der Pfanne)**	(in derr pfahner)
	gebraten	gerbraatern
grilled (broiled)	**gegrillt**	gergrilt
roasted	**(im Ofen)**	(im oafern)
	gebraten	gerbraatern
stewed	**gedämpft**	gerdehmpft
stuffed	**gefüllt**	gerfewlt
underdone (rare)	**blutig**	blootikh
medium	**mittel**	mitterl
well-done	**gut durchgebraten**	goot **doorch**gerbraatern

Sausages *Würste*

Sausages are produced in dozens of different varieties.
Some with more garlic or spices than others. One of the
mildest is the Frankfurter.

Bierwurst	beervoorst	smoked, pork and beef
Blutwurst	blootvoorst	black pudding (blood sausage)
Bockwurst	bokvoorst	large frankfurter
Bratwurst	braatvoorst	fried, pork
Jagdwurst	yaagtvoorst	smoked, with garlic and mustard
Leberwurst	layberrvoorst	liver sausage
Katenrauchwurst	kaaternrowkhvoorst	country-style, smoked
Nürnberger Bratwurst	newrnbehrgerr **braat**voorst	fried, veal and pork
Regensburger	raygernsburgerr	highly spiced, smoked
Rotwurst	roatvoorst	black pudding (blood sausage)
Weißwurst	vighsvoorst	veal and bacon with parsley and onion
Wienerli	veenerrli	Vienna-style frankfurter
Zervelat(wurst)	zehrvehlaat(voorst)	seasoned, smoked, pork, beef and bacon
Zungenwurst	tsungernvoorst	blood sausage with pieces of tongue and diced fat
Zwiebelwurst	tsveeberlvoorst	liver and onion

Game and poultry *Wild und Geflügel*

German cuisine is often said to be unimaginative, but this certainly doesn't apply to game. The venison is usually carefully marinated till tender and served with sweet raisin or red currant sauce or a purée of chestnuts *(Maronenpüree)*.

If your meal is prepared *nach Jägerart* (in the hunter's style), it's likely sautéed with mushrooms and root vegetables and served in a wine gravy *(Weinsoße*—**vighn**zoasser).

Back-	bahk-	fried
Brat-	braat-	roast
-braten	-braatern	joint, roast
Ente	ehnter	duck
Fasan	fahzaan	pheasant
Gans	gahns	goose
Hähnchen	hainkhern	chicken
Hase	haazer	hare
-hendl	-hehndl	chicken
gespickter Hirsch	gershpikterr heersh	larded venison
Huhn	hoon	chicken
Kaninchen	kahneenkhern	rabbit
Kapaun	kahpown	capon
-keule	-koyler	haunch
Masthühnchen	mahsthewnkhern	pullet chicken
-pfeffer	-pfehferr	jugged game
Poulet	poolay	chicken
Rebhuhn	rehphoon	partridge
Reh	ray	venison
-rücken	-rewkern	saddle
Schnepfe	shnehpfer	woodcock
Taube	towber	pigeon, squab
Truthahn	troothaan	turkey
Wachtel	vahkhterl	quail
Wildschwein	viltshvighn	wild boar

Potatoes *Kartoffeln*

The Germans' favourite accompaniment *(Beilage)* is undoubtedly the potato which can be prepared in a seemingly endless variety of ways.

Bratkartoffeln	braatkahrtofferln	fried potatoes
Geröstete	gerrursterter	hashed-brown potatoes

Kartoffel(n)	kahrtofferl(n)	potato(es)
-bälle	-behler	balls
-brei	-brigh	mashed
-klöße	-klursser	dumplings
-kroketten	-kroakehtern	croquettes
-mus	-mooss	mashed
-puffer	-pufferr	fritters
-stock	-shtok	mashed
Kartoffelsalat	kahrtofferlzahlaat	potato salad
Pellkartoffeln	pehlkahrtofferln	potatoes boiled in their jackets
Petersilienkartoffeln	payterrzeeliern-kahrtofferln	parsley potatoes
Pommes frites	pom frit	chips (french fries)
Reibekuchen	righberkookhern	potato pancake
Rösti	rurshtee	hashed-brown potatoes
Röstkartoffeln	rurstkahrtofferln	fried potatoes
Salzkartoffeln	zahltskahrtofferln	boiled potatoes

Rice and noodles *Reis und Nudeln*

Butterreis	butterrighss	buttered rice
Curryreis	kurreerighss	curried rice
Knöpfli	knurpflee	kind of gnocchi
Mehlnockerln	maylnokkerrln	small dumplings
Nudeln	nooderln	noodles
Reis	righss	rice
Spätzle	shpehtsler	kind of gnocchi
Teigwaren	tighgvaarern	pasta

Vegetables and salads *Gemüse und Salate*

What vegetables do you recommend?	**Welches Gemüse empfehlen Sie?**	vehlkhers germewzer ehmpfaylern zee
I'd prefer some salad.	**Ich nehme lieber Salat.**	ikh naymer leeberr zahlaart
Auberginen	oaberrzheenern	aubergines (eggplant)
Blaukraut	blowkrowt	red cabbage
Blumenkohl	bloomernkoal	cauliflower
Bohnen	boanern	beans
grüne	grewner	French (green) beens
weiße	vighsser	haricot beans, white kidney beans
Brokkoli	brokkollee	broccoli

Champignons	shahmpinyong	button mushrooms
Chicorée	sheekorray	endive (Am. chicory)
Endivien	ehndeeviern	chicory (Am. endives)
Erbsen	ehrpsern	peas
Essiggurken	ehssikhgoorkern	gherkins (pickles)
Fenchel	fehnkherl	fennel
Fisolen	feezoalern	french (green) beans
Gemüse	germewzer	vegetables
gemischtes	germishterss	mixed vegetables
grüner Salat	grewnerr zahlaat	green salad
Grünkohl	grewnkoal	kale
Gurken	goorkern	cucumber
Häuptlsalat	hoyptlzahlaat	lettuce salad
Karfiol	kahrfioal	cauliflower
Karotten	kahrottern	carrots
Kohl	koal	cabbage
Kohlrabi	koalraabee	turnips
Kopfsalat	kopfzahlaat	lettuce salad
Krautstiel	krowtshteel	white beet
Kürbis	kewrbiss	pumpkin
Lattich	lahtikh	lettuce
Lauch	lowkh	leeks
Leipziger Allerlei	lighptseegerr ahlerrligh	peas, carrots, asparagus
Mais	mighss	sweet corn
Mohrrüben	moarrewbern	carrots
Paradeiser	pahrahdighzerr	tomatoes
Pfifferlinge	pfifferrlinger	chanterelle mushrooms
Pilze	piltser	mushrooms
Radieschen	rahdeeskhern	radishes
Rettich	rehtikh	black radish
Rosenkohl	roazernkoal	Brussels sprouts
rote Beete/Rüben	roater bayter/rewbern	beetroot
Rotkohl	roatkoal	red cabbage
Rüebli	rewblee	carrots
Salat	zahlaat	salad
Sauerkraut	zowerrkrowt	sauerkraut
Schwarzwurzeln	shvahrtsvoortserln	salsify
Sellerie	zehlerree	celery
Spargel	shpaargerl	asparagus
Spargelspitzen	shpaargerlshpitsern	asparagus tips
Spinat	shpeenaat	spinach
Tomaten	tommaatern	tomatoes
Weißkohl	vighskoal	cabbage
Zwiebeln	tsveeberln	onions
Zucchetti	tsuggehtee	courgette (zucchini)

Vegetables may be served ...

oven-browned	**überbacken**	ewberr**bah**kern
boiled	**gekocht**	ger**kokht**
creamed	-**püree**	-**pew**ray
diced	**gehackt**	ger**hahkt**
stewed	**gedämpft**	ger**dehmpft**

As for the seasoning ...

Anis	ah**nees**	aniseed
Basilikum	bah**zee**likkum	basil
Dill	dil	dill
Essig	**ehs**sikh	vinegar
Estragon	**ehs**trahgon	tarragon
Gewürz	ger**vewrts**	spice
Ingwer	**ing**verr	ginger
Kapern	**kaa**pernn	capers
Knoblauch	**knop**lowkh	garlic
Kräuter	**kroy**terr	mixture of herbs
Kren	krayn	horseradish
Kresse	**kreh**sser	cress
Kümmel	**kew**merl	caraway
Lorbeer	**loar**bayr	bay leaf
Majoran	mahyo**raan**	marjoram
Meerrettich	**mayr**rehtikh	horseradish
Muskatnuß	mus**kaht**nuss	nutmeg
Nelke	**nehl**ker	clove
Öl	url	oil
Petersilie	**pay**terr**zee**lier	parsley
Pfeffer	**pfeh**ferr	pepper
Pfefferminz	**pfeh**ferrmints	mint
Rosmarin	ros**mah**reen	rosemary
Safran	**zah**fraan	saffron
Salbei	**zahl**bigh	sage
Salz	**zahl**ts	salt
Schnittlauch	**shnit**lowkh	chives
Senf	**zehnf**	mustard
Süßstoff	**zews**shtof	artificial sweetener
Thymian	**tew**miaan	thyme
Tomatenketchup	tom**maa**ternkehtshup	ketchup
Wacholder	**vahk**holderr	juniper
Würze	**vewr**tser	seasoning
Zimt	**tsimt**	cinnamon
Zucker	**tsuk**kerr	sugar

Cheese *Käse*

Most of the cheese produced in Germany, Austria and Switzerland is mild. You may see *Käseteller* (**kai**zertehlerr) on the menu. This means you'll get a plate of three or four varieties of cheese, doubtless including the renowned *Emmentaler* (**eh**merntaalerr), which we call simply Swiss cheese. If you are looking for curd cheese, ask for *Frischkäse*.

What sort of cheese do you have?	**Welche Käsesorten haben Sie?**	**vehl**kher **kai**zerzoartern **haa**bern zee
A piece of that one, please.	**Ein Stück von dem da, bitte.**	ighn shtewk fon daym daa bitter

mild	Allgäuer Bergkäse (like Swiss cheese), Allgäuer Rahmkäse, Altenburger (made of goat's milk), Appenzeller, Greyerzer, Kümmelkäse (made with caraway seeds), Quark, Räucherkäse (smoked cheese), Schichtkäse, Sahnekäse, Tilsiter, Topfen, Weißkäse.
sharp	Handkäse, Harzer Käse, Schabzieger.

curd	**frisch**	frish
hard	**hart**	hahrt
mild	**mild**	millt
ripe	**reif**	righf
sharp	**scharf**	shahrf
soft	**weich**	vighkh

The following dish in Switzerland makes a meal in itself:

fondue (fong**dew**)	a hot, bubbly mixture of melted cheese, white wine, a drop of kirsch and a hint of garlic; each guest dips a bite-size piece of bread on a fork into the pot of cheese.

And for a cheesy snack try one of the following specialities:

Käsewähe (**kai**zervaier)	a hot cheese tart
Käseschnitte (**kai**zershnitter)	an open-faced melted cheese sandwich

Fruit and nuts *Obst und Nüsse*

Do you have (fresh) fruit?	**Haben Sie (frisches) Obst?**	haabern zee (frisherss) oapst
I'd like a fruit cocktail.	**Ich hätte gern einen Obstsalat.**	ikh hehter gehrn ighnern oapstzahlaat
Ananas	ahnahnahss	pineapple
Apfel	ahpferl	apple
Apfelsine	ahpferlzeener	orange
Aprikosen	ahprekkoazern	apricots
Backpflaumen	bahkpflowmern	prunes
Banane	bahnaaner	banana
Birne	beerner	pear
Blaubeeren	blowbayrern	blueberries
Brombeeren	brombayrern	blackberries
Datteln	dahterln	dates
Erdbeeren	ehrtbayrern	strawberries
Erdnüsse	ehrdnewsser	peanuts
Feigen	fighgern	figs
Haselnüsse	haazerlnewsser	hazelnuts
Heidelbeeren	highderlbayrern	blueberries
Himbeeren	himbayrern	raspberries
Johannisbeeren	yohhahnisbayrern	currants
rote/schwarze	roater/shvahrtser	red/black
Kirschen	keershern	cherries
Kokosnuß	kokkosnuss	coconut
Mandarine	mahndahreener	tangerine
Mandeln	mahnderln	almonds
Marillen	mahrillern	apricots
Melone	mayloaner	melon (cantaloupe)
Mirabellen	meerahbehlern	a variety of plums
Nüsse	newsser	nuts
Pampelmuse	pahmperlmoozer	grapefruit
Pfirsich	pfeerzikh	peach
Pflaumen	pflowmern	plums
Preiselbeeren	prighzerlbayrern	cranberries
Quitte	kvitter	quince
Rhabarber	rahbahrberr	rhubarb
Ribisel	reebeezl	currants
Rosinen	rozeenern	raisins
Stachelbeeren	stahkherlbayrern	gooseberries
Walnüsse	vahlnewsser	walnuts
Wassermelone	vahsserrmayloaner	watermelon
Weintrauben	vighntrowbern	grapes
Zitrone	tsitroaner	lemon
Zwetsch(g)en	tsvehtsh(g)ern	plums

Dessert–Pastries *Nachtisch–Gebäck*

Desserts may also be listed on the menu under *Nachspeisen* or *Süßspeisen*. If you want an ice-cream, look under *Eis* in Germany and Austria and under *Glace* in Switzerland. The German waiter may ask you if you want your dessert served with *Schlagsahne*, the Austrian will say *Schlagobers* or simply *Schlag* and the Swiss *Schlagrahm*. Wherever you are it means whipped cream.

I'd like a dessert, please.	**Ich hätte gern eine Nachspeise.**	ikh **heh**ter gehrn **ighn**er **naakh**shpighzer
Something light, please.	**Etwas Leichtes, bitte.**	**ehtvahss lighkh**terss **bitter**
Just a small portion.	**Nur eine kleine Portion.**	noor **ighn**er **kligh**ner **port**sioan
Nothing more, thanks.	**Nein danke, nichts mehr.**	nighn **dahn**ker **nikhts mayr**
Götterspeise	gurterrshpighzer	fruit jelly (Jell-O)
Kaltschale	**kahlt**shaaler	chilled fruit soup
Obstsalat	**oapst**zahlaat	fruit cocktail

Here are some basic words you'll need to know if you want to order a dessert. Remember that Germans often write in one word what would take us two. The words below may be combined with a fruit or a flavour, e.g. *Apfelauflauf*, *Erdbeereis*, etc.

-auflauf	-owflowf	soufflé
-creme	-kraym	pudding
-eis, -glace	-ighss -glahsser	ice-cream
-kompott	-kompot	compote
-kuchen	-kookhern	cake
-pudding	-pudding	pudding
-torte	-torter	layer cake

These flavours of ice-cream are very popular:

Erdbeer-	ehrtbayr-	strawberry
Karamel-	kahrahmehl-	caramel
Mokka-	mokkah-	coffee
Schokoladen-	shokkollaadern-	chocolate
Vanille-	vahniller-	vanilla
Zitronen-	tsitroanern-	lemon

If you'd like to try something more filling with your coffee, we'd recommend ...

Apfelstrudel
(ahpferlshtrooderl)
paper-thin layers of pastry filled with apple slices, nuts, raisins and jam

Berliner
(behrleenerr)
jam doughnut

Bienenstich
(beenernshtikh)
honey-almond cake

Cremeschnitte
(kraymshnitter)
millefeuille (napoleon)

Gugelhupf
(googerlhupf)
a moulded cake with a hole in the centre, usually filled with raisins and almonds

Hefekranz
(hayferkrahnts)
ring-shaped cake of yeast dough, with almonds and sometimes candied fruit

Kaiserschmarren
(kighzerrshmahrern)
shredded pancake with raisins served with syrup (Austrian)

Mohrenkopf
(moarernkopf)
chocolate meringue with whipped-cream filling

Palatschinken
(pahlahtshinkern)
when listed under desserts, pancakes with a jam or white cheese filling, otherwise they are a savoury dish

Schillerlocke
(shillerrlokker)
pastry cornet with vanilla cream filling

Schwarzwälder Kirschtorte
(shvahrtsvehlderr keershtorter)
chocolate layer cake filled with cream and cherries, flavoured with cherry brandy

Topfenstrudel
(topfernshtrooderl)
flaky pastry with creamed, vanilla-flavoured white cheese, rolled and baked

Windbeutel
(vintboyterl)
cream puff

Here are the names of some favourite biscuits (cookies):

Honigkuchen	hoanikhkookhern	honey biscuits
Leckerli	lehkerrli	ginger biscuits
Makronen	mahkroanern	macaroons
Printen	printern	honey biscuits
Spekulatius	shpehkoolaatsiuss	almond biscuits

Beer *Bier*

Needless to say, beer is the Germans' favourite drink. Almost every town with a sizable population has at least one brewery. You'll want to try some of the local brews. However, Dortmund and Bavarian beer are found throughout the country. *Bier vom Faß* (draught or draft beer) is considered to have a better taste and is less expensive, too, than bottled beer.

I'd like a beer.	**Ich hätte gern ein Bier.**	ikh **hehter** gehrn ighn beer
a dark beer	**ein Dunkles**	ighn **dunk**lerss
a light beer	**ein Helles**	ighn **heh**lerss
I'd like a ... of beer.	**Ich hätte gern ... Bier.**	ikh **hehter** gehrn ... beer
bottle	**eine Flasche**	**igh**ner **flah**sher
glass	**ein Glas**	ighn glaass
a small one	**ein kleines**	ighn **kligh**nerss
a large one	**ein großes**	ighn **groa**serss
mug (a quart)	**eine Maß**	**igh**ner maass
Waiter! Another beer, please!	**Herr Ober, noch ein Bier, bitte!**	hehr **oa**berr nokh ighn beer **bit**ter

Altbier
(**ahlt**beer)

a bitter beer with a high hops content

Bockbier, Doppelbock, Märzen, Starkbier
(**bok**beer, **dop**perlbok, **mehrt**sern, **shtahrk**beer)

these are beers with a high alcoholic and malt content

Malzbier
(**mahlts**beer)

a dark, sweetish beer with a low alcoholic content but high in calories

Pilsener
(**pil**zernerr)

has a particularly strong aroma of hops

Radlermaß
(**raad**lerrmaass)

a light beer to which a bit of lemonade is added; in north Germany it's called *Alsterwasser* (**ahl**sterrvahsserr)

Weißbier
(**vighs**beer)

a light beer brewed from wheat grain; Berliners love a *Berliner Weiße mit Schuß—Weißbier* with a shot of raspberry juice.

Wine *Wein*

The best wine-producing regions of Germany are those round the Rhine and Moselle rivers—the northernmost wine-producing areas of Europe.

More so than French vintners to the west, German wine producers are at the mercy of the vagaries of the country's climatic conditions. One type of wine can have a quite different character from one year to the next depending upon the weather. For this reason, you'll have to learn to recognize a few basic terms on German labels which will tell you something about how you can likely expect a certain wine to taste.

In good years wine may be labeled *naturrein* or *Naturwein* which just means it's been produced under ordinary methods. In a bad year, sugar is sometimes added to increase the alcoholic content. If this is done, *verbessert* (improved) is euphemistically printed on the label.

There are four other words commonly found on German wine labels which you should know. They indicate the ripeness of the grapes when they were picked—or the degree of dryness or sweetness of the wine.

Spätlese (**spait**layzer)	gathered late after the normal harvesting; dry wine
Auslese (**ows**layzer)	selected gathering of particularly ripe bunches of grapes; slightly dry wine
Beerenauslese (**bayrern**owslayzer)	selected overripe grapes, slightly sweet wine
Trockenbeerenauslese (**trokkern**bayrern-owslayzer)	selected dried or raisin-like grapes; one drop of nectar can be squeezed out of each grape; a sweet or dessert wine is produced.

In neighbouring German-speaking Switzerland, mostly red wine is produced. Austria's Wachau region along the fabled Danube riverbanks produces white wine while Burgenland to the south of Vienna has red wine.

Gaststätten

Type of wine	Examples	Accompanies
sweet white wine	Rheinpfalz is noted for wine in this category; bottles labeled *Trockenbeerenauslese* also fall into this section.	desserts, especially puddings and cake
dry white wine	The Rheingau region produces extraordinary white wine in good vintage years; Moselle wine can usually be counted on to be very dry; wine labelled *Spätlese* or *Auslese* can go into this category as well as those with the term *naturrein* or *Naturwein*.	cold meat or shellfish, fish, boiled meat, egg dishes, first courses, fowl, veal, dishes served with sauerkraut, sausages
rosé	Sometimes referred to as *Schillerwein*	goes with almost anything but especially cold dishes, eggs, pork, lamb
light-bodied red wine	Most local red wine fits into this category, particularly the wine of Austria's Burgenland, German-speaking Switzerland, the Ahr region (look for the names *Ahrweiler*, *Neuenahr* and *Walporzheim* on the label) and Baden-Württemberg.	roast chicken, turkey, veal, lamb, beef steak, ham, liver, quail, pheasant, stews, dishes served with gravy
full-bodied red wine	A difficult wine to find but a *Spätburgunder* from the Ahr Valley is a good example.	duck, goose, kidneys, most game, goulash, in short, any strong-flavoured preparations
sparkling wine	German *Sekt* comes into this category; some of it rivals French champagne in quality.	if it's dry, it goes with anything; may be drunk as an aperitif or as the climax to the dinner; goes well with shellfish, nuts and dried fruit; if it's sweet, it'll go nicely with dessert and pastry like *Strudel*

May I please have the wine list?	Die Weinkarte, bitte.	dee **vighn**kahrter **bitter**
I want a bottle of white wine/red wine/sparkling wine.	**Ich möchte eine Flasche Weißwein/ Rotwein/Schaum-wein.**	ikh **murkhter ighner** flahsher **vighs**vighn/ **roat**vighn/**showm**vighn
I'd like a glass/carafe of ...	**Ich hätte gern ein Glas/eine Karaffe ...**	ikh **hehter** gehrn ighn glaass/**ighner** kah**rah**fer
Please bring me another ...	**Bitte bringen Sie mir noch ...**	**bitter** bringern zee mir nokh
Where does this wine come from?	**Woher kommt dieser Wein?**	voa**hayr** komt **deezerr** vighn

red/white/rosé	**rot/weiß/rosé**	roat/vighss/**rozay**
(very) dry/sweet	**(sehr) trocken/süß**	(zayr) **trokkern**/zewss
light	**leicht**	lighkht
full-bodied	**vollmundig**	**vol**mundig

A refreshing highball for the ladies is sparkling wine and orange juice, *Damengedeck* (**daa**merngerdehk) or for the men, *Herrengedeck* (**heh**rerngerdehk), which is sparkling wine and beer. The German champagne (*Sekt*—sehkt) is also worth trying.

Other alcoholic drinks *Andere alkoholische Getränke*

I'd like a/an/some ...	**Ich hätte gern ...**	ikh **hehter** gehrn
aperitif	**einen Aperitif**	**ighnern** ahpayri**teef**
brandy	**einen Weinbrand**	**ighnern vighn**brahnt
cider	**Apfelwein**	**ahpferl**vighn
cognac	**einen Kognak**	**ighnern** konyahk
liqueur	**einen Likör**	**ighnern** likkurr
mulled wine	**Glühwein**	**glew**vighn
port	**Portwein**	**port**vighn
rum	**einen Rum**	**ighnern** rum
vermouth	**einen Wermut**	**ighnern vayr**moot
vodka	**einen Wodka**	**ighnern** votkah
whisky	**einen Whisky**	**ighnern** "whisky"
neat (straight)	**pur**	poor
on the rocks	**mit Eis**	mit ighss

You'll certainly want to take the occasion to sip a liqueur or brandy after your meal. The names of some well-known wine-distilled brandies are *Asbach-Uralt, Chantré* and *Dujardin*. Here are some other after-dinner drinks:

Are there any local specialities?	Haben Sie hiesige Spezialitäten?	haabern zee heezigger shpehtsiahlitaitern
I'd like to try a glass of ..., please.	Ich möchte ein Glas ... probieren.	ikh murkhter ighn glaass ... proabeerern
Apfelschnaps	ahpferlshnahps	apple brandy
Aprikosenlikör	ahprikkoazernlikkurr	apricot liqueur
Birnenschnaps	beernernshnahps	pear brandy
Bommerlunder	bommerrlunderr	caraway-flavoured brandy
Doornkaat	dornkaat	German gin, juniper-berry brandy
Eierlikör	igherrlikkurr	eggflip, eggnog
Heidelbeergeist	highderlbayrgighst	blueberry brandy
Himbeergeist	himbayrgighst	raspberry brandy
Himbeerlikör	himbayrlikkurr	raspberry liqueur
Kirschlikör	kirshlikkurr	cherry liqueur
Kirschwasser	kirshvahsserr	cherry brandy
(Doppel)Korn	(dopperl)korn	grain-distilled liquor, akin to whisky
Kümmel	kewmerl	caraway-flavoured liquor
Obstler	oapstlerr	fruit brandy
Pflümli(wasser)	pflewmli(vahsserr)	plum brandy
Steinhäger	shtighnhaigerr	juniperberry brandy, akin to gin
Träsch	traish	pear and apple brandy
Weizenkorn	vightsernkorn	wheat-distilled liquor, akin to whisky
Zwetschgenwasser	tsvehtshgernvahsserr	plum brandy

ZUM WOHL / PROST!

(tsum voal / proast)

YOUR HEALTH / CHEERS!

Nonalcoholic drinks *Alkoholfreie Getränke*

I'd like a/an ...	Ich hätte gern ...	ikh **hehter** gehrn
apple juice	einen Apfelsaft	**ighnern** ahpferlzahft
currant juice (red or black)	einen Johannisbeersaft	**ighnern** yohhahnisbayrzaft
fruit juice	einen Fruchtsaft	**ighnern** frukhtzahft
grape juice	einen Traubensaft	**ighnern** trowbernzahft
herb tea	einen Kräutertee	**ighnern** kroyterrtay
iced tea	einen Eistee	**ighnern** ighstay
lemonade	eine Limonade	**ighner** limmonnaader
(glass of) milk	(ein Glas) Milch	(ighn glaass) milkh
milkshake	ein Milchmixgetränk	ighn **milkh**miksgertrehnk
mineral water	ein Mineralwasser	ighn minnerraalvahsserr
fizzy (carbonated)	mit Kohlensäure	mit koalernzoyrer
still	ohne Kohlensäure	oaner koalernzoyrer
orange juice	einen Orangensaft	**ighnern** orrahngzhernzahft
orangeade	eine Orangeade	**ighner** orahngzhaader
tomato juice	einen Tomatensaft	**ighnern** tommaaternzahft
tonic water	ein Tonic	ighn **tonnik**

Hot beverages *Warme Getränke*

Perhaps you'd like a coffee after dinner. In Austria, you can't ask for just ''a cup of coffee''; the varieties are endless. There, you can ask for anything from a *Nußschwarzer* (**nuss**hvahrtserr) or *Neger* (**nay**gerr)—strong black coffee—to an *Einspänner* (**ighn**shpehnerr)—topped with whipped cream—or a *Melange* (may**lahng**zher)—coffee and hot milk.

I'd like a/an ...	Ich hätte gern ...	ikh **hehter** gehrn
(hot) chocolate	eine (heiße) Schokolade	**ighner** (**highss**er) shokkollaader
coffee	einen Kaffee	**ighnern** kahfay
with cream	mit Sahne	mit zaaner
with milk	einen Milchkaffee	**ighnern** milkhkahfay
black/decaffeinated coffee	einen schwarzen/ koffeinfreien Kaffee	**ighnern** shvahrtsern/ koffeheenfrighern kahfay
espresso coffee	einen Expresso	**ighnern** ehksprehsoa
mokka	einen Mokka	**ighnern** mokkah
tea	einen Tee	**ighnern** tay
cup of tea	eine Tasse Tee	**ighner** tahsser tay
with milk/lemon	mit Milch/Zitrone	mit milkh/tsitroaner

Complaints   *Reklamationen*

There is a plate/glass missing.	Es fehlt ein Teller/ein Glas.	ehss faylt ighn **tehlerr**/ighn glaass
I have no knife/fork/spoon.	Ich habe kein Messer/keine Gabel/keinen Löffel.	ikh **haaber** kighn **mehsserr**/kighner **gaaberl**/**kighnern lurferl**
That's not what I ordered.	Das habe ich nicht bestellt.	dahss **haaber** ikh nikht berstehlt
I asked for ...	Ich wollte ...	ikh **volter**
There must be some mistake.	Es muß ein Irrtum sein.	ehss muss ighn **irtoom** zighn
May I change this?	Können Sie mir dafür etwas anderes bringen?	kurnern zee meer daafewr **ehtvahss ahnderrerss bringern**
I asked for a small portion (for the child).	Ich wollte eine kleine Portion (für das Kind).	ikh **volter ighner klighner portsioan** (fewr dahss kint)
The meat is ...	Das Fleisch ist ...	dahss **flighsh** ist
overdone	zu stark gebraten	tsu **shtahrk** gerbraatern
underdone (too rare)	zu roh	tsu roa
too tough	zu zäh	tsu tsai
This is too ...	Das ist zu ...	dahss ist tsu
bitter/sour	bitter/sauer	**bitter**/**zowerr**
salty/sweet	salzig/süß	**zahl**tsikh/**zewss**
I don't like this.	Das schmeckt mir nicht.	dahs **shmehkt** meer nikht
The food is cold.	Das Essen ist kalt.	dahss **ehssern** ist kahlt
This isn't fresh.	Das ist nicht frisch.	dahss ist nikht frish
What's taking you so long?	Weshalb dauert es so lange?	veh**shahlp** dowerrt ehss zoa **lahng**er
Have you forgotten our drinks?	Haben Sie unsere Getränke vergessen?	**haabern** zee **un**zerrer ger**trehn**ker fehr**geh**ssern
The wine is corked.	Der Wein schmeckt nach Korken.	derr vighn shmehkt naakh **koar**kern
This isn't clean.	Das ist nicht sauber.	dahss ist nikht **zow**berr
Would you ask the head waiter to come over?	Würden Sie bitte den Oberkellner rufen?	**vewr**dern zee **bit**ter dayn **oaberrkehl**nerr **roo**fern

The bill (check) *Die Rechnung*

A service charge is generally included automatically in restaurant bills. Anything extra for the waiter is optional. Credit cards may be used in an increasing number of restaurants.

I'd like to pay.	**Ich möchte zahlen.**	ikh murkhter tsaalern
We'd like to pay separately.	**Wir möchten getrennt bezahlen.**	veer murkhtern gehtrehnt bertsaalern
I think you made a mistake in this bill.	**Ich glaube, Sie haben sich verrechnet.**	ikh glowber zee haabern zikh fehrrehkhnert
What is this amount for?	**Wofür ist dieser Betrag?**	voafewr ist deezerr bertraakh
Is service included?	**Ist die Bedienung inbegriffen?**	ist dee berdeenung inbergriffern
Do you accept traveller's cheques?	**Nehmen Sie Reiseschecks?**	naymern zee righzershehks
Can I pay with this credit card?	**Kann ich mit dieser Kreditkarte bezahlen?**	kahn ikh mit deezerr krayditkahrter bertsaalern
That was a very good meal.	**Das Essen war sehr gut.**	dahss ehssern vaar zayr goot

> **BEDIENUNG INBEGRIFFEN**
> SERVICE INCLUDED

Snacks—Picnic *Imbiß – Picknick*

A *Café* (in Austria *Kaffeehaus*) will serve anything from simple pastries to luscious, monumental sweet delicacies and often snacks. For a fast meal the German *Schnellimbiß* (snack bar) is the place. Ordering is easy since most of the snacks are on display. And if you are in a hurry have a sausage at a *Würstchenstand*.

Give me two of these and one of those.	**Geben Sie mir davon zwei und davon eins.**	gaybern zee meer daafon tsvigh unt daafon ighns
to the left/right	**links/rechts**	links/rehkhts
above/below	**darüber/darunter**	dahrewberr/dahrunterr
It's to take away.	**Es ist zum Mitnehmen.**	ehss ist tsum mitnaymern

TIPPING, see inside back-cover

I'd like a piece of cake.	Ich hätte gern ein Stück Kuchen.	ikh **heh**ter gehrn ighn shtewk **koo**khern
fried sausage	eine Bratwurst	**igh**ner **braat**voorst
omelet	ein Omelett	ighn om**leht**
open sandwich	ein belegtes Brot	ighn ber**layg**terss broat
with ham	mit Schinken	mit **shin**kern
with cheese	mit Käse	mit **kai**zer
potato salad	Kartoffelsalat	kahr**tof**ferlzahlaat
sandwich	ein Sandwich	ighn **sehnd**vitsh

Here's a basic list of food and drink that might come in useful when shopping for a picnic.

I'd like a/an/ some ...	Ich hätte gern ...	ikh **heh**ter gehrn
apples	Äpfel	**ehp**ferl
bananas	Bananen	bah**naa**nern
biscuits (Br.)	Kekse	**kayk**ser
beer	Bier	beer
bread	ein Brot	ighn broat
butter	Butter	**butt**err
cheese	Käse	**kai**zer
chips (Am.)	Kartoffelchips	kahr**tof**ferlcheeps
chocolate bar	eine Tafel Schoko-lade	**igh**ner **taaf**erl shokkol-**laa**der
coffee	Kaffee	kah**fay**
cold cuts	Aufschnitt	**owf**shnit
cookies	Kekse	**kayk**ser
crisps	Kartoffelchips	kahr**tof**ferlcheeps
eggs	Eier	**igh**err
gherkins (pickles)	Essiggurken	**ehss**ikhgoorkern
grapes	Trauben	**trow**bern
ice-cream	ein Eis	ighn ighss
milk	Milch	milkh
mustard	Senf	zehnf
oranges	Orangen	or**rahng**zhern
pepper	Pfeffer	**pfeh**ferr
rolls	Brötchen	**brurt**khern
salt	Salz	zahlts
sausage	eine Wurst	**igh**ner voorst
soft drink	ein alkoholfreies Getränk	ighn ahlko**hoal**frigherss ger**trehnk**
sugar	Zucker	**tsuk**kerr
tea	Tee	tay
yoghurt	Joghurt	**yoa**goort

Travelling around

Plane *Flugzeug*

Is there a flight to Vienna?	**Gibt es einen Flug nach Wien?**	gipt ehss **igh**nern floog naakh veen
Is it a direct flight?	**Ist es ein Direktflug?**	ist ehss ighn dir**rehkt**floog
When's the next flight to Hamburg?	**Wann ist der nächste Flug nach Hamburg?**	vahn ist derr **naikh**ster **floog** nahkh **hahm**boorg
Do I have to change planes?	**Muß ich umsteigen?**	muss ikh **um**shtighgern
Can I make a connection to Cologne?	**Habe ich Anschluß nach Köln?**	**haab**err ikh **ahn**shluss nahkh kurln
I'd like a ticket to Zurich.	**Bitte ein Flugticket nach Zürich.**	**bitt**er ighn **floog**tikkert naakh **tsew**rikh
single (one-way)	**Hinflug**	**hin**floog
return (roundtrip)	**Hin- und Rückflug**	hin unt **rewk**floog
What time does the plane take off?	**Wann ist der Abflug?**	vahn ist derr **ahp**floog
What time do I have to check in?	**Wann muß ich einchecken?**	vahn muss ikh **ighn**shehkern
Is there an airport-bus?	**Gibt es einen Flughafenbus?**	gipt ehss **igh**nern **floog**haafernbuss
What's the flight number?	**Welche Flugnummer ist es?**	**vehl**kher **floog**nummerr ist ehss
What time do we arrive?	**Wann landen wir?**	vahn **lahn**dern veer
I'd like to ... my reservation.	**Ich möchte meine Reservierung ...**	ikh **murkh**ter **migh**ner rehzer**vee**rung
cancel	**annullieren**	ahnul**lee**rern
change	**umbuchen**	**um**bookhern
confirm	**bestätigen**	ber**shtai**tiggern

| **ANKUNFT** ARRIVAL | **FLUGSTEIG** GATE | **ABFLUG** DEPARTURE |

Train *Eisenbahn*

Travel on the main railway lines is generally fast, and the trains run on time. First-class coaches are comfortable; second-class, more than adequate.

EuroCity (oyroa"city")	International express trains; first and second class
Intercity ("intercity")	Long distance inter-city trains; some only first, others with first and second class, with surcharge; in Switzerland the equivalent of the Austrian *Städteschnellzug*
City-D-Zug ("city"-**day**-tsoog)	Short-distance inter-city trains, with few stops at major points only; first and second class with surcharge on trips of less than 50 kilometres (Germany)
D-Zug (**day**-tsoog)	Intermediate- to long-distance trains (Germany)
Schnellzug (**shnehl**tsoog)	Fast trains, stop at big and medium towns (Austria, Switzerland)
Städteschnellzug (**shteht**ershnehltsoog)	Fast trains, connecting the biggest towns (Austria)
Expreßzug (**ayksprehst**soog)	Fast trains, stop at big and medium towns (Austria)
Eilzug (**ight**soog)	Medium-distance trains, not stopping at small stations (Germany, Austria)
Nahverkehrszug (**naafehrkayrst**soog)	Local trains, stopping at all stations; in Austria called *Personenzug* and in Switzerland *Regionalzug*
Triebwagen (**treep**vaagern)	Small diesel coach used for short runs (Austria, Germany); in Germany sometimes *Schienenbus*

Here are a few more useful terms:

Speisewagen (**shpighzer**vaagern)	Dining-car
Schlafwagen (**shlaaf**vaagern)	Sleeping-car, compartments with wash basins and 1, 2 or 3 berths
Liegewagen (**leeger**vaagern)	Coach containing berths with sheets, blankets and pillows

To the railway station *Unterwegs zum Bahnhof*

Where's the railway station?	**Wo ist der Bahnhof?**	voa ist derr **baan**hoaf
Taxi, please!	**Taxi bitte!**	tahksi bitter
Take me to the ...	**Fahren Sie mich ...**	faarern zee mikh
main railway station	**zum Hauptbahnhof**	tsum **howpt**baanhoaf
railway station	**zum Bahnhof**	tsum **baan**hoaf
What's the fare?	**Was macht das?**	vahss mahkht dahss

EINGANG	ENTRANCE
AUSGANG	EXIT
ZU DEN BAHNSTEIGEN	TO THE PLATFORMS
AUSKUNFT	INFORMATION

Where's the ...? *Wo ist ...?*

Where is/are the ...?	**Wo ist/sind ...?**	voa ist/zint
booking office	**die Platz-reservierung**	dee **plahts**rehzerrveerung
currency-exchange office	**die Wechselstube**	dee **wehk**zerlshtoober
left-luggage office (baggage check)	**die Gepäckauf-bewahrung**	dee ger**pehk**owfbervaarung
lost property (lost-and-found) office	**das Fundbüro**	dahss **funt**bewroa
luggage lockers	**die Schließfächer**	dee **shlees**fehkherr
newsstand	**der Zeitungsstand**	derr **tsight**ungsshtahnt
platform 3	**Bahnsteig 3**	**baan**shtighg 3
reservations office	**die Platz-reservierung**	dee **plahts**rehzerrveerung
restaurant	**das Restaurant**	dahss rehstor**rahng**
snack bar	**der Schnellimbiß**	derr **shnehl**imbiss
ticket office	**der Fahrkarten-schalter**	derr **faar**kahrternshahlterr
track 7	**Gleis 7**	**glighss** 7
waiting room	**der Wartesaal**	derr **vahr**terzaal
Where are the toilets?	**Wo sind die Toiletten?**	voa zint dee toah**leh**tern

TAXI, see page 21

Inquiries *Auskunft*

When is the ... train to Kiel?	**Wann fährt der ... Zug nach Kiel?**	vahn fairt derr ... tsoog naakh keel
first/last/next	**erste/letzte/nächste**	ehrster/lehtster/naikhster
What's the fare to Basle?	**Was kostet die Fahrt nach Basel?**	vahss kostert dee faart naakh baazerl
Is it a through train?	**Ist es ein durch-gehender Zug?**	ist ehss ighn doorkhgayernderr tsoog
Must I pay a surcharge?	**Muß ich einen Zu-schlag bezahlen?**	muss ikh ighnern tsu-shlaag bertsahlern
Is there a connection to ...?	**Gibt es einen Anschluß nach ...?**	gipt ehss ighnern ahnshluss naakh
Do I have to change trains?	**Muß ich umsteigen?**	muss ikh umshtighgern
Is there sufficient time to change?	**Reicht die Zeit zum Umsteigen?**	righkht dee tsight tsum umshtighgern
Will the train leave on time?	**Fährt der Zug pünktlich ab?**	fairt derr tsoog pewnktlikh ahp
What time does the train arrive at Münster?	**Wann kommt der Zug in Münster an?**	vahn komt derr tsoog in mewnsterr ahn
Is there a dining-car/ sleeping-car on the train?	**Führt der Zug einen Speisewagen/ Schlafwagen?**	fewrt derr tsoog ighnern shpighzervaagern/ shlaafvaagern
Does the train stop at Ingolstadt?	**Hält der Zug in Ingolstadt?**	hehlt derr tsoog in ingolshtaht
What platform does the train for Bonn leave from?	**Auf welchem Bahn-steig fährt der Zug nach Bonn ab?**	owf vehlkherm baan-shtighg fairt derr tsoog naakh bon ahp
What track does the train from Hamburg arrive at?	**Auf welchem Gleis kommt der Zug aus Hamburg an?**	owf vehlkherm glighss komt derr tsoog owss hahmboorg ahn
I'd like a time-table.	**Ich hätte gern einen Fahrplan.**	ikh hehter gehrn ighnern faarplaan

ANKUNFT ARRIVAL	**ABFAHRT** DEPARTURE

Es ist ein durchgehender Zug.	It's a through train.
Sie müssen in ... umsteigen.	You have to change at ...
Steigen Sie in Heidelberg in einen Nahverkehrszug um.	Change at Heidelberg and get a local train.
Bahnsteig 7 ist ...	Platform 7 is ...
dort drüben/oben/unten links/rechts	over there/upstairs/downstairs on the left/on the right
Es gibt einen Zug nach Bonn um ...	There's a train to Bonn at ...
Ihr Zug fährt auf Gleis ... ab.	Your train will leave from track ...
Der Zug hat ... Minuten Verspätung.	There'll be a delay of ... minutes.
Erste Klasse an der Spitze/in der Mitte/ am Ende des Zuges.	First class at the front/ in the middle/at the end.

Tickets *Fahrkarten*

I want a ticket to ...	Ich möchte eine Fahrkarte nach ...	ikh murkhter ighner faarkahrter naakh
single (one-way)	einfach	ighnfahkh
return (roundtrip)	hin und zurück	hin unt stoorewk
first class	erste Klasse	ehrster klahsser
second class	zweite Klasse	tsvighter klahsser
half price	zum halben Preis	tsum hahlbern prighss

Reservation *Reservierung*

I want to book a ...	Ich möchte ... reservieren lassen.	ikh murkhter ... rehzerrveerern lahssern
seat (by the window)	einen (Fenster)platz	ighnern (fehnsterr)plahts
berth	einen Platz im Liegewagen	ighnern plahts im leegervaagern
upper	oben	oabern
middle	in der Mitte	in derr mitter
lower	unten	untern
berth in the sleeping car	einen Platz im Schlafwagen	ighnern plahts im shlaafvaagern

NUMBERS, see page 147

Reisen im Lande

All aboard *Einsteigen bitte*

Is this the right platform for the train to Vienna?	**Ist das der richtige Bahnsteig für den Zug nach Wien?**	ist dahss derr **rikh**tigger **baan**shtighg fewr dayn tsoog naakh veen
Is this the right train to Graz?	**Ist das der Zug nach Graz?**	ist dahss derr tsoog naakh graats
Excuse me. May I get by?	**Verzeihung. Kann ich vorbei?**	**fehrt**sighung. kahn ikh forbigh
Is this seat taken?	**Ist dieser Platz besetzt?**	ist **dee**zerr plahts berzehtst

RAUCHER	NICHTRAUCHER
SMOKER	NONSMOKER

I think that's my seat.	**Ich glaube, das ist mein Platz.**	ikh **glow**ber dahss ist mighn plahts
Would you let me know before we get to Bamberg?	**Sagen Sie mir bitte, wenn wir in Bamberg ankommen?**	**zaa**gern zee mir **bit**ter vehn veer in **bahm**behrg **ahn**kommern
What station is this?	**Wie heißt dieser Ort?**	vee highst **dee**zerr ort
How long does the train stop here?	**Wie lange hält der Zug hier?**	vee **lahng**er hehlt derr tsoog heer
When do we get to Cologne?	**Wann kommen wir in Köln an?**	vahn **kom**mern veer in kurln ahn

Sleeping *Im Schlafwagen*

Are there any free compartments in the sleeping-car?	**Sind im Schlafwagen noch Abteile frei?**	zint im **shlaaf**vaagern nokh **ahp**tighler frigh
Where's the sleeping-car?	**Wo ist der Schlafwagen?**	voa ist derr **shlaaf**vaagern
Where's my berth?	**Wo ist mein Schlafplatz?**	voa ist mighn **shlaaf**plahts
I'd like a lower berth.	**Ich möchte unten schlafen.**	ikh **murkh**ter **un**tern **shlaa**fern

Would you make up our berths?	**Würden Sie unsere Schlafplätze machen?**	vewrdern zee unzerrer shlaafplehtser mahkhern
Would you call me at 7 o'clock?	**Würden Sie mich um 7 Uhr wecken?**	vewrdern zee mikh um 7 oor vehkern
Would you bring me coffee in the morning?	**Würden Sie mir bitte morgen früh Kaffee bringen?**	vewrdern zee meer bitter morgern frew kahfay bringern

Eating   *Im Speisewagen*

You can get snacks and drinks in the buffet-car and in the dining-car when it isn't being used for main meals. On some trains an attendant comes around with a cart with snacks, tea, coffee and soft drinks.

| Where's the dining-car? | **Wo ist der Speisewagen?** | voa ist derr shpighzer-vaagern |

Baggage—Porters   *Gepäck – Gepäckträger*

Porter!	**Gepäckträger!**	gerpehktraiger
Can you help me with my luggage?	**Können Sie mir mit meinem Gepäck helfen?**	kurnern zee mir mit mighnerm gerpehk hehlfern
Where are the luggage trolleys (carts)?	**Wo sind die Koffer-kulis?**	voa zint dee kofferr-kooliss
Where are the luggage lockers?	**Wo sind die Schließfächer?**	voa zint dee shleesfehkherr
Where's the left-luggage office (baggage check)?	**Wo ist die Gepäck-aufbewahrung?**	voa ist dee gerpehk-owfbervaarung
I'd like to leave my luggage, please.	**Ich möchte mein Gepäck einstellen.**	ikh murkhter mighn gerpehk ighnshtehlern
I'd like to register (check) my luggage.	**Ich möchte mein Gepäck aufgeben.**	ikh murkhter mighn gerpehk owfgaybern

> **GEPÄCKAUFGABE**
> REGISTERING (CHECKING) BAGGAGE

PORTERS, see also page 18

Coach (long-distance bus) *Überlandbus*

To reach out-of-the-way places, you'll find frequent bus services available including the *Kraftpost* or *Postauto*. You'll find information on destinations and timetables at the coach terminals, usually situated near railway stations.

When's the next coach to ...?	**Wann fährt der nächste Bus nach ...?**	vahn fairt derr naikhster buss naakh
Does the coach stop at ...?	**Hält der Bus in ...?**	hehlt derr buss in
How long does the journey (trip) take?	**Wie lange dauert die Fahrt?**	vee lahnger dowerrt dee faart

Note: Most of the phrases on the previous pages can be used or adapted for travelling on local transport.

Bus—Tram (streetcar) *Bus – Straßenbahn*

In most cities you'll find automatic ticket dispensers at each stop enabling you to buy your ticket in advance. In major cities it may be worthwhile to get a pass or a booklet of tickets.

I'd like a pass/booklet of tickets.	**Ich möchte eine Mehrfahrkarte/ein Fahrscheinheft.**	ikh murkhter ighner mayrfaarkahrter/ighn faarshighnhehft
Which tram (streetcar) goes to the centre of town?	**Welche Straßenbahn fährt ins Stadtzentrum?**	vehlkher shtraassernbaan fairt ins shtahttsehntrum
Where can I get a bus into town?	**Wo hält der Bus, der ins Stadtzentrum fährt?**	voa hehlt derr buss derr ins shtahttsehntrum fairt
What bus do I take for ...?	**Welchen Bus muß ich nach ... nehmen?**	vehlkhern buss muss ikh naakh ... naymern
Where's the ...?	**Wo ist ...?**	voa ist
bus stop terminus	**die Bushaltestelle die Endstation**	dee busshahltershtehler dee ehntshtahtsioan
When is the ... bus to ...?	**Wann fährt der ... Bus nach ...?**	vahn fairt derr ... buss naakh
first/last/next	**erste/letzte/nächste**	ehrster/lehtster/naikhster

How often do the buses to the airport run?	**Wie oft fahren die Busse zum Flughafen?**	vee oft faarern dee busser tsum flooghaafern
How much is the fare to ...?	**Was kostet es nach ...?**	vahss kostert ehss naakh
Do I have to change buses?	**Muß ich umsteigen?**	muss ikh umshtighgern
How many bus stops are there to ...?	**Wie viele Haltestellen sind es bis ...?**	vee feeler hahltershtehlern zint ehss biss
Will you tell me when to get off?	**Können Sie mir bitte sagen, wann ich aussteigen muß?**	kurnern zee meer bitter zaagern vahn ikh owsshtighgern muss
I want to get off at the next stop.	**Ich möchte an der nächsten Haltestelle aussteigen.**	ikh murkhter ahn derr naikhstern hahltershtehler owsshtighgern

| **BUSHALTESTELLE** | REGULAR BUS STOP |
| **BEDARFSHALTESTELLE** | STOPS ON REQUEST |

Underground (subway) *U-Bahn*

The *U-Bahn* (**oo**-baan) in Berlin, Bonn, Düsseldorf, Cologne, Frankfurt, Hamburg and Munich corresponds to the London underground or the New York subway. A map showing the various lines and stations is displayed outside every station.

Where's the nearest underground station?	**Wo ist die nächste U-Bahnstation?**	voa ist dee naikhster oo-baanshtahtsioan
Does this train go to ...?	**Fährt dieser Zug nach ...?**	fairt deezerr tsoog naakh
Where do I change for ...?	**Wo muß ich nach ... umsteigen?**	voa muss ikh naakh ... umshtighgern
Is the next station ...?	**Ist die nächste Station ...?**	ist dee naikhster shtahtsioan
Which line should I take for ...?	**Welche Linie fährt nach ...?**	vehlkher leenier fairt naakh

Boat service *Auf dem Schiff*

When does a boat for ... leave?	**Wann fährt ein Schiff nach ...?**	vahn fairt ighn shif naakh
Where's the embarkation point?	**Wo ist der Anlegeplatz?**	voa ist derr **ahn**layger-plahts
When do we call at Cologne?	**Wann legen wir in Köln an?**	vahn **lay**gern veer in kurln ahn
I'd like to take a harbour roundtour.	**Ich möchte eine Hafenrundfahrt machen.**	ikh **murkh**ter **ighner** haa-fernruntfaart **mah**khern
boat	**das Schiff/das Boot**	dahss shif/dahss boat
cabin	**die Kabine**	dee **kah**beener
single	**Einzelkabine**	**ighnt**serlkahbeener
double	**Zweierkabine**	**tsvigher**rkahbeener
cruise	**die Kreuzfahrt**	dee **kroyts**faart
crossing	**die Überfahrt**	dee **ew**berrfaart
deck	**das Deck**	dahss dehk
ferry	**die Fähre**	dee **fair**er
hydrofoil	**das Tragflächenboot**	dahss **traag**flehkhernboat
life belt	**der Rettungsring**	derr **reh**tungsring
life boat	**das Rettungsboot**	dahss **reh**tungsboat
port	**der Hafen**	derr **haa**fern
river cruise	**die Flußfahrt**	dee **flus**faart
ship	**das Schiff**	dahss shif
steamer	**das Dampfschiff**	dahss **dahmpf**shif

Bicycle hire *Fahrradverleih*

Many railway stations provide a bicycle-hire service.

I'd like to hire a bicycle.	**Ich möchte ein Fahrrad mieten.**	ikh **murkh**ter ighn **faar**raat **mee**tern

Other means of transport *Weitere Transportmittel*

cable car	**die Seilbahn**	dee **zighl**baan
helicopter	**der Hubschrauber**	derr **hoop**shrowberr
moped	**das Moped**	dahss **mo**apeht
motorbike	**das Motorrad**	dahss **mo**atorraat
scooter	**der Motorroller**	derr **mo**atorrollerr

Or perhaps you prefer:

to hike	**wandern**	**vahn**derrn
to hitchhike	**trampen**	**treh**mpern
to walk	**zu Fuß gehen**	tsoo fuss **gay**ern

Car *Das Auto*

In general roads are good in Germany, Austria and Switzerland. Motorways (expressways) are free in Germany. In Austria some Alpine roads and tunnels charge tolls *(die Maut).* If you use the motorways in Switzerland you must purchase a sticker *(die Vignette)* to be displayed on the windscreen.

A red reflector warning triangle must be carried for use in case of a breakdown, and seat-belts *(der Sicherheitsgurt)* are obligatory. In winter snow tyres or chains are compulsory on Alpine passes.

Where's the nearest filling station?	**Wo ist die nächste Tankstelle?**	voa ist dee **naikh**ster **tahnk**shtehler
Full tank, please.	**Volltanken, bitte.**	**volt**ahnkern **bit**ter
Give me ... litres of petrol (gasoline).	**Geben Sie mir ... Liter Benzin.**	**gay**bern zee mir ... **lee**terr behn**tseen**
super (premium)/ regular/lead-free/ diesel	**Super/Normal/ bleifreies Benzin/ Diesel**	**zoo**perr/nor**maal**/ **bligh**frigherss behn**tseen**/ **dee**zerl
Please check the ...	**Kontrollieren Sie bitte ...**	kontrol**leer**ern zee **bit**ter
battery	**die Batterie**	dee bahte**hree**
brake fluid	**die Bremsflüssigkeit**	dee **brehms**flewssikhkight
oil	**das Öl**	dahss url
water	**das Wasser**	dahss **vahss**err
Would you check the tyre pressure?	**Würden Sie bitte den Reifendruck prüfen?**	**vewr**dern zee **bit**ter dayn **righ**ferndruk **prew**fern
1.6 front, 1.8 rear.	**Vorne 1,6, hinten 1,8.**	**for**ner ighns zehks **hin**tern ighns ahkht
Please check the spare tyre, too.	**Prüfen Sie auch den Ersatzreifen, bitte.**	**prew**fern zee owkh dayn ehr**zahts**righfern **bit**ter
Can you mend this puncture (fix this flat)?	**Können Sie diesen Reifen flicken?**	**kur**nern zee **dee**zern **righ**fern **flik**kern
Would you please change the ...?	**Würden Sie bitte ... wechseln?**	**vewr**dern zee **bit**ter ... **vehk**serln
bulb	**die Glühbirne**	dee **glewb**irner
fan belt	**den Keilriemen**	dayn **kighl**reemern

CAR HIRE, see page 20

spark(ing) plugs	die Zündkerzen	dee **tsewntkehrtsern**
tyre	den Reifen	dayn **righfern**
wipers	die Scheibenwischer	dee **shighbernvisherr**
Would you clean the windscreen (windshield)?	Würden Sie bitte die Windschutzscheibe reinigen?	vewrdern zee bitter dee **vintshutsshighber righniggern**

Asking the way—Street directions   *Nach dem Weg fragen*

Can you tell me the way to ...?	Können Sie mir sagen, wie ich nach ... komme?	kurnern zee meer **zaagern** vee ikh naakh ... **kommer**
How do I get to ...?	Wie komme ich nach ...?	vee **kommer** ikh naakh ...
Are we on the right road for ...?	Sind wir auf der richtigen Straße nach ...?	zint veer owf derr **rikhtiggern shtraasser** naakh
How far is the next village?	Wie weit ist es bis zum nächsten Dorf?	vee vight ist ehss biss tsum **nehkhstern** dorf
How far is it to ... from here?	Wie weit ist es von hier nach ...?	vee vight ist ehss fon heer naakh
Is there a motorway (expressway)?	Gibt es eine Autobahn?	gipt ehss **ighner owtobbaan**
Is there a road with little traffic?	Gibt es eine wenig befahrene Straße?	gipt ehss **ighner vaynikh** berfaarerner **shtraasser**
How long does it take by car/on foot?	Wie lange dauert es mit dem Auto/zu Fuß?	vee **lahnger dowerrt** ehss mit daym **owto**/tsoo fuss
Can I drive to the centre of town?	Kann ich bis ins Stadtzentrum fahren?	kahn ikh biss ins **shtahttsehntrum faarern**
Can you tell me, where ... is?	Können Sie mir sagen, wo ... ist?	kurnern zee meer **zaagern** voa ... ist
Where can I find this address/place?	Wie komme ich zu dieser Adresse/diesem Ort?	vee **kommer** ikh tsoo **deezerr ahdrehsser**/**deezerr** ort
Where's this?	Wo ist das?	voa ist dahss
Can you show me on the map where I am?	Können Sie mir auf der Karte zeigen, wo ich bin?	kurnern zee meer owf derr **kahrter tsighgern** voa ikh bin

Sie sind auf der falschen Straße.	You're on the wrong road.
Fahren Sie geradeaus.	Go straight ahead.
Es ist dort vorne ...	It's down there on the ...
links/rechts gegenüber/hinter ... neben/nach ...	left/right opposite/behind ... next to/after ...
Nord/Süd/Ost/West	north/south/east/west
Fahren Sie bis zur ersten/ zweiten Kreuzung.	Go to the first/second crossroad (intersection).
Biegen Sie bei der Ampel links ab.	Turn left at the traffic lights.
Biegen Sie bei der nächsten Ecke rechts ab.	Turn right at the next corner.
Nehmen Sie die Straße nach ...	Take the road for ...
Sie müssen zurück nach ...	You have to go back to ...

Parking *Parken*

In town centres there are blue zones for which you need a parking disk (*eine Parkscheibe*—**igh**nerr **pahrk**shighber). You set it to show when you arrived and when you must leave. The disk can be obtained from tourist offices, petrol stations and hotels.

Where can I park?	**Wo kann ich parken?**	voa kahn ikh **pahrk**ern
Is there a car park nearby?	**Gibt es einen Park- platz hier in der Nähe?**	gipt ehss **igh**nern **pahrk**- plahts heer in derr **naier**
May I park here?	**Darf ich hier parken?**	dahrf ikh heer **pahrk**ern
How long can I park here?	**Wie lange kann ich parken?**	vee **lahng**er kahn ikh heer **pahrk**ern
What's the charge per hour?	**Wieviel kostet es pro Stunde?**	veefeel kostert ehss proa **shtun**der
Do you have some change for the parking meter?	**Haben Sie Kleingeld für die Parkuhr?**	**haab**ern zee **kligh**ngehlt fewr dee **pahrk**oor

Breakdown—Road assistance   *Panne – Pannendienst*

Where's the nearest garage?	**Wo ist die nächste Reparaturwerkstatt?**	voa ist dee **naikh**ster raypahrah**toor**vehrkshtaht
Excuse me. My car has broken down.	**Entschuldigung, mein Wagen hat eine Panne.**	ehnt**shul**diggung mighn **vaa**gern haht **igh**ner **pah**ner
I've had a breakdown.	**Ich habe eine Panne.**	ikh **haa**ber **igh**ner **pah**ner
Can you send a mechanic?	**Können Sie einen Mechaniker schicken?**	**kur**nern zee **igh**nern meh**khah**nikkerr **shik**kern
My car won't start.	**Mein Auto springt nicht an.**	mighn **ow**to shpringt nikht ahn
The battery is dead.	**Die Batterie ist leer.**	dee bah**teh**ree ist layr
I've run out of petrol (gasoline).	**Ich habe eine Benzinpanne.**	ikh **haa**ber **igh**ner behnt**seen**pahner
I have a flat tyre.	**Ich habe einen Platten.**	ikh **haa**ber **igh**nern **plah**tern
The engine is overheating.	**Der Motor läuft heiß.**	derr **moa**tor loyft highss
There is something wrong with ...	**... ist/sind nicht in Ordnung.**	... ist/zint nikht in **ort**nung
brakes	**die Bremsen**	dee **brehm**zern
carburettor	**der Vergaser**	derr fehr**gaa**zerr
exhaust pipe	**der Auspuff**	derr **ows**puf
radiator	**der Kühler**	derr **kew**lerr
a wheel	**ein Rad**	ighn roat
Can you send a breakdown van (tow truck)?	**Können Sie einen Abschleppwagen schicken?**	**kur**nern zee **igh**nern ahp**shlehp**vaagerr **shik**kern
How long will you be?	**Wie lange dauert es?**	vee **lahn**ger **dow**errt ehss

Accident—Police   *Verkehrsunfall – Polizei*

Please call the police.	**Rufen Sie bitte die Polizei.**	**roo**fern zee **bit**ter dee **pol**litsigh
There's been an accident. It's about 2 km. from ...	**Es ist ein Unfall passiert, ungefähr 2 Kilometer von ...**	ehss ist ighn **un**fahl pahs**seert un**ger**fair 2 kill**oam**mayterr fon

Where's the nearest telephone?	Wo ist das nächste Telefon?	voa ist dahss naikhster taylayfoan
Call a doctor/an ambulance, quickly.	Rufen Sie schnell einen Arzt/einen Krankenwagen.	roofern zee shnehl ighnern ahrtst/ighnern krahnkernvaagern
There are people injured.	Es hat Verletzte gegeben.	ehss haht fehrlehtster gergaybern
Here's my driving licence.	Hier ist mein Führerschein.	heer ist mighn few-rerrshighn
What's your name and address?	Ihr Name und Ihre Anschrift, bitte?	eer naamer unt eerer ahnshrift bitter
What's your insurance company?	Ihre Versicherungsgesellschaft, bitte?	eerer fehrzeekherrungs-gerzehlshahft bitter

Road signs *Verkehrszeichen*

AUSFAHRT	Exit (motorway)
AUTOBAHNKRENZ	Motorway junction
DURCHGANGSVERKEHR	Through traffic
EINBAHNSTRASSE	One-way street
EINORDNEN	Get in lane
FROSTSCHÄDEN	Ice damage
FUSSGÄNGER	Pedestrians
GEFÄHRLICHES GEFÄLLE	Steep descent
GLATTEIS	Icy road
HALT, POLIZEI	Stop, police
HUPEN VERBOTEN	No honking
KURZPARKZONE	Limited parking zone
LANGSAM FAHREN	Slow down
LAWINENGEFAHR	Avalanche area
LKW	Heavy vehicles
NUR FÜR ANLIEGER	Access to residents only
PARKEN VERBOTEN	No parking
RECHTS FAHREN	Keep right
SCHLECHTE FAHRBAHN	Bad road surface
SCHULE	School
STAU	Traffic jam
STEINSCHLAG	Falling rocks
STRASSENARBEITEN	Road works ahead
UMLEITUNG	Diversion (detour)
... VERBOTEN	No ...
VORFAHRT GEWÄHREN	Give way (yield)
VORSICHT	Caution

Sightseeing

Where's the tourist office?	Wo ist das Fremdenverkehrsbüro?	voa ist dahss **frehmdern**fehrkayrsbewroa
What are the main points of interest?	Was sind die Hauptsehenswürdigkeiten?	vahss zint dee **howpt**zayernsvewrdikhkightern
We're here for ...	Wir sind für ... hier.	veer zint fewr ... heer
a few hours	ein paar Stunden	ighn paar **shtundern**
a day	einen Tag	**ighnern** taag
a week	eine Woche	**ighner** vokher
Can you recommend a sightseeing tour/an excursion?	Können Sie eine Stadtrundfahrt/einen Ausflug empfehlen?	kurnern zee **ighner shtaht**runtfaart/**ighnern** owsfloog ehmpfaylern
What's the point of departure?	Von wo fahren wir ab?	fon voa **fahrern** veer ahp
Will the bus pick us up at the hotel?	Holt uns der Bus vorm Hotel ab?	hoalt uns derr buss foarm **hottehl** ahp
How much does the tour cost?	Was kostet die Rundfahrt?	vahss kostert dee **runtfaart**
What time does the tour start?	Wann beginnt die Rundfahrt?	vahn berg**int** dee **runtfaart**
Is lunch included?	Ist das Mittagessen inbegriffen?	ist dahss **mittaagehssern** inbergriffern
What time do we get back?	Wann werden wir zurück sein?	vahn **vayrdern** veer tsoo**rewk** zighn
Do we have free time in ...?	Haben wir in ... Zeit zu freier Verfügung?	**haabern** veer in ... tsight tsoo **frigherr** fehrfewgung
Is there an English-speaking guide?	Gibt es einen englischsprechenden Fremdenführer?	gipt ehss **ighnern** ehnglishshprehkherndern frehmdernfewrerr
I'd like to hire a private guide for ...	Ich möchte einen Fremdenführer für ...	ikh **murchter ighnern** frehmdernfewrerr fewr
half a day	einen halben Tag	**ighnern hahl**bern taag
a full day	einen Tag	**ighnern** taag

Where is/Where are the ...?	Wo ist/Wo sind ...?	voa ist/voa zint
abbey	die Abtei	dee ahptigh
alley	die Gasse	dee gahsser
amusement park	der Vergnügungspark	derr fehrgnewgungspahrk
art gallery	die Kunstgalerie	dee kunstgahlehree
botanical gardens	der Botanische Garten	derr bottaanisher gahrtern
building	das Gebäude	dahss gerboyder
business district	das Geschäftsviertel	dahss gershehftsfeerterl
cathedral	die Kathedrale/der Dom	dee kahtehdraaler/derr doam
cave	die Höhle	dee hurler
cemetery	der Friedhof	derr freethoaf
chapel	die Kapelle	dee kahpehler
church	die Kirche	dee keerkher
city walls	die Stadtmauern	dee shtahtmowerrn
concert hall	die Konzerthalle	dee kontsehrthahler
convent	das Kloster	dahss kloasterr
convention hall	die Kongreßhalle	dee kongrehshahler
court house	das Gericht	dahss gerrikht
downtown area	die Innenstadt	dee innernshtaht
exhibition	die Ausstellung	dee owsshtehlung
factory	die Fabrik	dee fahbrik
fair	die Messe	dee mehsser
flea market	der Flohmarkt	derr floamahrkt
fortress	die Festung	dee fehstung
fountain	der Brunnen/ Springbrunnen	derr brunnern/ shpringbrunnern
gardens	die Grünanlagen	dee grewnahnlaagern
harbour	der Hafen	derr haafern
lake	der See	derr zay
library	die Bibliothek	dee bibliotayk
market	der Markt	derr mahrkt
memorial	das Denkmal	dahss dehnkmaal
monastery	das Kloster	dahss kloasterr
monument	das Denkmal	dahss dehnkmaal
museum	das Museum	dahss muzayum
old town	die Altstadt	dee ahltshtaht
opera house	das Opernhaus	dahss oaperrnhowss
palace	der Palast/das Schloß	derr pahlahst/dahss shloss
park	der Park	derr pahrk
parliament building	das Parlaments- gebäude	dahss pahrlahmehnts- gerboyder
ruins	die Ruinen	dee rueenern
shopping area	das Geschäftsviertel	dahss gershehftsfeerterl

square	**der Platz**	derr plahts
stadium	**das Stadion**	dahss shtaadion
statue	**die Statue**	dee shtaatuer
stock exchange	**die Börse**	dee burrzer
street	**die Straße**	dee shtrahsser
theatre	**das Theater**	dahss tayaaterr
tomb	**das Grab**	dahss graap
tower	**der Turm**	derr toorm
town hall	**das Rathaus**	dahss raathowss
university	**die Universität**	dee unnivehrzitait
wall	**die Mauer**	dee mowerr
zoo	**der Zoo**	derr tsoa

Admission *Eintritt*

Is ... open on Sundays?	**Ist ... sonntags geöffnet?**	ist ... zontaags gerurfnert
What are the opening hours?	**Welches sind die Öffnungszeiten?**	vehlkherss zint dee urfnungstsightern
When does it close?	**Wann schließt es?**	vahn shleest ehss
How much is the entrance fee?	**Was kostet der Eintritt?**	vahss kostert derr ighntrit
Is there any reduction for ...?	**Gibt es Ermäßigung für ...?**	gipt ehss ehrmaissiggung fewr
children	**Kinder**	kinderr
disabled	**Behinderte**	berhinderrter
groups	**Gruppen**	gruppern
pensioners	**Rentner**	rehntnerr
students	**Studenten**	shtuddehntern
Have you a guide book (in English)?	**Haben Sie einen Reiseführer (in Englisch)?**	haabern zee ighnern righzerfewrerr (in ehnglish)
Can I buy a catalogue?	**Kann ich einen Katalog kaufen?**	kahn ikh ighnern kahtahloag kowfern
Is it all right to take pictures?	**Darf man fotografieren?**	dahrf mahn fottografeerern

---

EINTRITT FREI ADMISSION FREE
FOTOGRAFIEREN VERBOTEN NO CAMERAS ALLOWED

Who—What—When? *Wer – Was – Wann?*

What's that building?	**Was für ein Gebäude ist das?**	vahss fewr ighn gerboyder ist dahss
Who was the ...?	**Wer war der ...?**	vayr vaar derr
architect	**Architekt**	ahrkhittehkt
artist	**Künstler**	kewnstlerr
painter	**Maler**	maalerr
sculptor	**Bildhauer**	bilthowerr
Who built it?	**Wer hat es gebaut?**	vayr haht ehss gerbowt
Who painted that picture?	**Wer hat das Bild gemalt?**	vayr haht dahss bilt germaalt
When did he live?	**Wann hat er gelebt?**	vahn haht ehr gerlaybt
When was it built?	**Wann wurde es erbaut?**	vahn voorder ehss ehrbowt
Where's the house where ... lived?	**Wo ist das Haus, in dem ... wohnte?**	voa ist dahss howss in daym ... voanter
We're interested in ...	**Wir interessieren uns für ...**	veer intehrehsseerern uns fewr
antiques	**Antiquitäten**	ahntikvittaitern
archaeology	**Archäologie**	ahrkhehollogee
art	**Kunst**	kunst
botany	**Botanik**	bottaanik
ceramics	**Keramik**	kehrraamik
coins	**Münzen**	mewntsern
fine arts	**bildende Künste**	bildernder kewnster
furniture	**Möbel**	murberl
geology	**Geologie**	gayollogee
handicrafts	**Kunsthandwerk**	kunsthahntvehrk
history	**Geschichte**	gershikhter
medicine	**Medizin**	mehditseen
music	**Musik**	muzeek
natural history	**Naturkunde**	nahtoorkunder
ornithology	**Vogelkunde**	foagerlkunder
painting	**Malerei**	maalehrigh
pottery	**Töpferei**	turpfehrigh
religion	**Religion**	rayliggioan
sculpture	**Bildhauerei**	bilthowerrigh
zoology	**Zoologie**	tsoaollogee
Where's the ... department?	**Wo ist die ...-Abteilung?**	voa ist dee ... ahptighlung

It's ...	Es ist ...	ehss ist
amazing	erstaunlich	ehrshtownlikh
awful	scheußlich	shoysslikh
beautiful	schön	shurn
gloomy	düster	dewsterr
impressive	eindrucksvoll	ighndruksfol
interesting	interessant	intehrehssahnt
lovely	wunderschön	voonderrshurn
magnificent	großartig	groassahrtikh
overwhelming	überwältigend	ewberrvehltiggernt
pretty	hübsch	hewpsh
romantic	romantisch	rommahntish
sinister	unheimlich	unhighmlikh
strange	seltsam	zehltzaam
superb	prächtig	prehkhtikh
terrible	schrecklich	shrehklikh
tremendous	außerordentlich	owsserrorderntlikh
ugly	häßlich	hehsslikh

Churches—Religious services *Kirchen – Gottesdienste*

Most churches and cathedrals are open to the public except, of course, when a service is being conducted.

Services are conducted in English in many towns. Ask the local tourist office for further details.

Is there a ... near here?	Gibt es eine ... in der Nähe?	gipt ehss ighner ... in derr naier
Catholic church	katholische Kirche	kahtoalisher keerkher
Protestant church	evangelische/protestantische Kirche	ehvahngaylisher/protteh-shtahntisher keerkher
synagogue	Synagoge	zewnahgoager
mosque	Moschee	moshay
At what time is ...?	Wann beginnt ...?	vahn bergint
mass	die Messe	dee mehsser
the service	der Gottesdienst	derr gottersdeenst
Where can I find a ... who speaks English?	Wo finde ich einen ..., der Englisch spricht?	voa finder ikh ighnern ... derr ehnglish shprikht
priest/minister rabbi	Priester/Pfarrer Rabbiner	preesterr/pfahrerr/ rahbeenerr
I'd like to visit the church.	Ich möchte die Kirche besichtigen.	ikh murkhter dee kirkherr berzikhtiggern

In the countryside *Auf dem Lande*

Is there a scenic route to ...?	**Gibt es eine landschaftlich schöne Straße nach ...?**	gipt ehss **ighner lahnt**shahftlikh **shurner shtraasser** naakh
How far is it to ...?	**Wie weit ist es bis ...?**	vee vight ist ehss biss
Can we walk?	**Können wir zu Fuß gehen?**	kurnern veer tsoo fooss **gayern**
How high is that mountain?	**Wie hoch ist dieser Berg?**	vee hoakh ist **deezerr** behrg
What kind of ... is that?	**Was für ... ist das?**	vahss fewr ... ist dahss
animal/bird	**ein Tier/ein Vogel**	ighn teer/ighn **foagerl**
flower/tree	**eine Blume/ein Baum**	**ighner bloomer**/ighn bowm

Landmarks *Zur Orientierung*

bridge	**die Brücke**	dee **brewker**
castle	**das Schloß/die Burg**	dahss shloss/dee boorg
farm	**der Bauernhof**	derr **bowerrnhoaf**
field	**das Feld**	dahss fehlt
footpath	**der Fußweg**	derr **foosvayg**
forest/wood	**der Wald**	derr vahlt
garden	**der Garten**	derr **gahrtern**
heath	**die Heide**	dee **highder**
hill	**der Hügel**	derr **hewgerl**
house	**das Haus**	dahss howss
lake	**der See**	derr zay
meadow	**die Wiese**	dee **veezer**
path	**der Weg**	derr vayg
mountain pass	**der Paß**	derr pahss
peak	**die Bergspitze**	dee **behrgshpitser**
pond	**der Teich**	derr tighkh
river	**der Fluß/der Strom**	derr fluss/derr **shtroam**
rock	**der Felsen**	derr **fehlzern**
road	**die Straße**	dee **shtraasser**
sea	**die See/das Meer**	dee zay/dahss mayr
spring	**die Quelle**	dee **kvehler**
valley	**das Tal**	dahss taal
village	**das Dorf**	dahss dorf
vineyard	**der Weinberg**	derr **vighnbehrg**
waterfall	**der Wasserfall**	derr **vahsserfahl**
well	**der Brunnen**	derr **brunnern**

ASKING THE WAY, see page 76

Besichtigungen

Relaxing

Cinema (movies) — Theatre   *Kino – Theater*

Foreign films are usually dubbed into German, though some cinemas also screen them in the original, with German subtitles, at certain times on certain days. Since cinema showings are seldom continuous you can buy your tickets in advance. Theatre curtain time is about 8 p.m. Advance booking is advisable.

You can find out what's playing from newspapers and billboards. In most large towns you can buy a publication of the type "This Week in ...".

What's showing at the cinema tonight?	**Was gibt es heute abend im Kino zu sehen?**	vahss gipt ehss **hoyter aabernt** im **keen**o tsoo **zay**ern
What's playing at the ... theatre?	**Was wird im ...theater gegeben?**	vahss veert im ... tayaaterr gergaybern
What sort of play is it?	**Was für ein Stück ist es?**	vahss fewr ighn shtewk ist ehss
Who's it by?	**Von wem ist es?**	fon vaym ist ehss
Can you recommend a ...?	**Können Sie mir ... empfehlen?**	kurnern zee meer ... ehmpfaylern
good film comedy musical	**einen guten Film eine Komödie ein Musical**	ighnern gootern film ighner kommurdier ighn "musical"
Where's that new film by ... being shown?	**Wo läuft der neue Film von ...?**	voa loyft derr noyer film fon
Who's in it?	**Mit welchen Schauspielern?**	mit vehlkhern showshpeelerrn
Who's playing the lead?	**Wer spielt die Hauptrolle?**	vayr shpeelt dee howptroller
Who's the director?	**Wer ist der Regisseur?**	vayr ist derr rehzhissurr
At what theatre is that new play by ... being performed?	**In welchem Theater wird das neue Stück von ... gespielt?**	in vehlkherm tayaaterr veert dahss noyer shtewk fon ... gershpeelt

English	German	Pronunciation
What time does the show begin?	**Wann beginnt die Vorstellung?**	vahn bergint dee foarshtehlung
What time does the performance end?	**Wann ist die Vorstellung zu Ende?**	vahn ist dee foarshtehlung tsoo ehnder
Are there any tickets for tonight?	**Gibt es noch Karten für heute abend?**	gipt ehss nokh kahrtern fewr hoyter aabernt
How much are the tickets?	**Wie teuer sind die Karten?**	vee toyerr zint dee kahrtern
I want to reserve 2 tickets for the show on Friday evening.	**Ich möchte 2 Karten für Freitag abend vorbestellen.**	ikh murkhter 2 kahrtern fewr frightaag aabernt foarbershtehlern
Can I have a ticket for the matinée on ...?	**Kann ich eine Karte für die Nachmittagsvorstellung am ... bekommen?**	kahn ikh ighner kahrter fewr dee nahkhmittaags-foarshtehlung ahm ... berkommern
I want a seat in the stalls (orchestra).	**Ich hätte gern einen Platz im Parkett.**	ikh hehter gehrn ighnern plahts im pahrkeht
Not too far back.	**Nicht zu weit hinten.**	nikht tsu vight hintern
Somewhere in the middle.	**Irgendwo in der Mitte.**	eergerntvoa in derr mitter
How much are the seats in the circle (mezzanine)?	**Wie teuer sind die Plätze im Rang?**	vee toyer zint dee plehtser im rahng
May I please have a programme?	**Kann ich bitte ein Programm haben?**	kahn ikh bitter ighn programh haabern
Where's the cloakroom?	**Wo ist die Garderobe?**	voa ist dee gahrderroaber

---

Bedaure, es ist alles ausverkauft.	I'm sorry, we're sold out.
Es gibt nur noch ein paar Plätze im Rang.	There are only a few seats left in the circle (mezzanine).
Darf ich Ihre Eintrittskarte sehen?	May I see your ticket?
Hier ist Ihr Platz.	This is your seat.

Unterhaltung

DAYS OF THE WEEK, see page 151

Opera—Ballet—Concert   *Oper – Ballett – Konzert*

Can you recommend a ...?	**Können Sie mir ... empfehlen?**	kurnern zee meer ehmpfaylern
ballet	**ein Ballett**	ighn bah**leht**
concert	**ein Konzert**	ighn kont**sehrt**
opera	**eine Oper**	**igh**ner **oa**perr
operetta	**eine Operette**	**igh**ner oppe**reh**ter
Where's the opera house/the concert hall?	**Wo ist das Opernhaus/die Konzerthalle?**	voa ist dahss **oa**pernhowss/ dee kont**sehrt**hahler
What's on at the opera tonight?	**Was wird heute abend in der Oper gegeben?**	vahss veert **hoy**ter **aa**bernt in derr **oa**perr ger**gay**bern
Who's singing/ dancing?	**Wer singt/tanzt?**	vayr zingt/tahntst
What orchestra is playing?	**Welches Orchester spielt?**	**vehl**khers or**keh**sterr shpeelt
What are they playing?	**Was wird gespielt?**	vahss veert ger**shpeelt**
Who's the conductor/ soloist?	**Wer ist der Dirigent/ der Solist?**	vayr ist derr dirri**geh**nt/ derr sollist

Nightclubs   *Nachtlokale*

Can you recommend a good nightclub?	**Können Sie mir ein gutes Nachtlokal empfehlen?**	kurnern zee meer ighn **goo**terss **nahkht**lokkaal ehmpfaylern
Is there a floor show?	**Gibt es Attraktionen?**	gipt ehss ahtrahk**tsio**anern
Is evening dress necessary?	**Wird Abendgarderobe verlangt?**	veert **aa**berntgahrdehroaber fehr**lahngt**

Discos   *Diskotheken*

Where can we go dancing?	**Wo können wir tanzen gehen?**	voa kurnern veer **tahnt**sern **gay**ern
Is there a disco- theque in town?	**Gibt es hier eine Diskothek?**	gipt ehss heer **igh**ner diskot**tayk**
Would you like to dance?	**Möchten Sie tanzen?**	murkhtern zee **tahnt**sern

Sports *Sport*

You name the sport, and you'll doubtless be able to find it in Germany, Austria and Switzerland. The most popular spectator sport is by far football (soccer).

Is there a football (soccer) game anywhere this Saturday?	**Findet diesen Samstag irgendwo ein Fußballspiel statt?**	findert deezern zahmstaag irgerntvoa ighn foosbahlshpeel shtaht
Which teams are playing?	**Welche Mannschaften spielen?**	vehlkher mahnshahftern shpeelern
Can you get me a ticket?	**Können Sie mir eine Karte besorgen?**	kurnen zee meer ighner kahrter berzorgern

basketball	**Basketball**	baaskertbahl
boxing	**Boxen**	boksern
car racing	**Autorennen**	owtorrehnern
cycling	**Radfahren**	raatfaarern
football (soccer)	**Fußball**	foosbahl
horse racing	**Pferderennen**	pfayrderrehnern
horseback riding	**Reiten**	rightern
mountaineering	**Bergsteigen**	behrgshtighgern
skiing	**Skifahren**	sheefaarern
swimming	**Schwimmen**	shvimmern
tennis	**Tennis**	tehniss
volleyball	**Volleyball**	vollibbahl

I'd like to see a boxing match.	**Ich möchte gern einen Boxkampf sehen.**	ikh murkhter gehrn ighnern bokskahmpf zayern
What's the admission charge?	**Was kostet der Eintritt?**	vahss kostert derr ighntrit
Where's the nearest golf course?	**Wo ist der nächste Golfplatz?**	voa ist derr naikhster golfplahts
Where are the tennis courts?	**Wo sind die Tennisplätze?**	voa zint dee tehnisplehtser
Can I hire (rent) rackets?	**Kann ich Tennisschläger mieten?**	kahn ikh tehnisshlaigerr meetern
What's the charge per ...?	**Wieviel kostet es pro ...**	veefeel kostert ehss proa
day/round/hour	**Tag/Spiel/Stunde**	taag/shpeel/shtunder

DAYS OF THE WEEK, see page 151

Where's the nearest race course (track)?	**Wo ist die nächste Pferderennbahn?**	voa ist dee **naikhs**ter **pfehr**derrehnbaan
Is there any good fishing around here?	**Kann man hier in der Nähe angeln?**	kahn mahn heer in derr **nai**er **ahng**erln
Do I need a permit?	**Brauche ich einen Angelschein?**	**brow**kher ikh **igh**nern **ahng**erlshighn
Where can I get one?	**Wo bekomme ich einen?**	voa ber**kom**mer ikh **igh**nern
Can one swim in the lake/river?	**Kann man im See/Fluß baden?**	kahn mahn im zay/fluss **baa**dern
Is there a swimming pool here?	**Gibt es hier ein Schwimmbad?**	gipt ehss heer ighn **shvim**baat
Is it open-air or indoor?	**Ist es ein Freibad oder ein Hallenbad?**	ist ehss ighn **frigh**baat **oa**derr ighn **hah**lernbaat
Is it heated?	**Ist es geheizt?**	ist ehss ger**highst**
What's the temperature of the water?	**Welche Temperatur hat das Wasser?**	**vehl**kher tehmperrah**toor** haht dahss **vah**sser
Is there a sandy beach?	**Gibt es einen Sandstrand?**	gipt ehss **igh**nern **zahnt**shtrahnt

On the beach *Am Strand*

The sea is very calm.	**Das Meer ist sehr ruhig.**	dahss mayr ist zayr **rooikh**
There are some big waves.	**Das Meer hat hohen Wellengang.**	dahss mayr haht **hoa**ern **vehl**lerngahng
Is it safe for swimming?	**Kann man hier gefahrlos schwimmen?**	kahn mahn heer ger**faar**loass **shvim**mern
Is there a lifeguard?	**Gibt es einen Rettungsdienst?**	gipt ehss **igh**nern **reh**tungsdeenst
Is it safe for children?	**Ist es für Kinder ungefährlich?**	ist ehss fewr **kin**derr **un**gerfairlikh
Are there any dangerous currents?	**Gibt es gefährliche Strömungen?**	gipt ehss ger**fair**likher **shtrur**mungern
What time is high tide/low tide?	**Wann ist Flut/Ebbe?**	vahn ist floot/**ehb**er

I want to hire (rent) a/an/some ...	Ich möchte ... mieten.	ikh murkhter ... meetern
bathing hut (cabana)	eine Badekabine	ighner baaderkahbeener
deck-chair	einen Liegestuhl	ighnern leegershtool
motorboat	ein Motorboot	ighn moatorboat
rowing-boat	ein Ruderboot	ighn rooderrboat
sailboard	einen Windsurfer	ighnern vintsurrferr
sailing-boat	ein Segelboot	ighn zaygerlboat
skin-diving equipment	eine Taucherausrüstung	ighner towkherrowsrewstung
sunshade (umbrella)	einen Sonnenschirm	ighnern zonnernsheerm
surfboard	ein Surfbrett	ighn surfbreht
water-skis	Wasserski	vahssershee

PRIVATSTRAND	PRIVATE BEACH
BADEN VERBOTEN	NO SWIMMING

Winter sports *Wintersport*

Is there a skating-rink near here?	Gibt es hier in der Nähe eine Eisbahn?	gipt ehss heer in derr naier ighner ighsbaan
I'd like to ski.	Ich möchte skifahren.	ikh murkhter sheefaarern
downhill/cross-country skiing	Abfahrtslauf/ Langlauf	ahpfahrtslowf/ lahnglowf
Are there any ski runs for ...?	Gibt es Skipisten für ...?	gipt ehss sheepistern fewr
beginners	Anfänger	ahnfaingerr
good skiers	Fortgeschrittene	fortgershritterner
Can I take skiing lessons?	Kann ich Skiunterricht nehmen?	kahn ikh sheeunterrrikht naymern
Are there ski lifts?	Gibt es Skilifte?	gipt ehss sheelifter
I want to hire a/ some ...	Ich möchte ... mieten.	ikh murkhter ... meetern
poles	Skistöcke	sheeshturker
skates	Schlittschuhe	shlitshooer
ski boots	Skischuhe	sheeshooer
skiing equipment	eine Skiausrüstung	ighner sheeowsrewstung
skis	Skier	sheeerr

Making friends

Introductions *Vorstellen*

May I introduce ...?	**Darf ich ... vorstellen?**	dahrf ikh ... foarshtehlern
John, this is ...	**John, das ist ...**	John dahss ist
My name is ...	**Ich heiße ...**	ikh highsser
Glad to know you.	**Sehr erfreut.**	zayr ehrfroyt
What's your name?	**Wie heißen Sie?**	vee highssern zee
How are you?	**Wie geht es Ihnen?**	vee gayt ehss eenern
Fine, thanks. And you?	**Danke, gut. Und Ihnen?**	dahnker goot. unt eenern

Follow-up *Näheres Kennenlernen*

How long have you been here?	**Wie lange sind Sie schon hier?**	vee lahnger zint zee shoan heer
We've been here a week.	**Wir sind seit einer Woche hier.**	veer zint zight ighnerr vokher heer
Is this your first visit?	**Sind Sie zum ersten Mal hier?**	zint zee tsum ehrstern maal heer
No, we came here last year.	**Nein, wir waren schon letztes Jahr hier.**	nighn veer vaarern shoan lehtsterss yaar heer
Are you enjoying your stay?	**Gefällt es Ihnen hier?**	gerfehlt ehss eenern heer
Yes, I like it very much.	**Ja, mir gefällt es sehr gut.**	yaa meer gerfehlt ehss zayr goot
I like the landscape a lot.	**Die Landschaft gefällt mir sehr.**	dee lahntshahft gerfehlt meer zayr
What do you think of the country/ the city?	**Wie gefällt Ihnen das Land/die Stadt?**	vee gerfehlt eenern dahss lahnt/dee shtaht
Where do you come from?	**Woher kommen Sie?**	voahayr kommern zee
I'm from ...	**Ich bin aus ...**	ikh bin owss

COUNTRIES, see page 146

I'm ...	**Ich bin ...**	ikh bin
American	**Amerikaner(in)**	ahmehrikkaanerr(in)
British	**Brite (Britin)**	britter (brittin)
Canadian	**Kanadier(in)**	kahnaadierr(rin)
English	**Engländer(in)**	ehnglehnderr(in)
Irish	**Ire (Irin)**	eerer (eerin)
Where are you staying?	**Wo wohnen Sie?**	voa voanern zee
Are you on your own?	**Sind Sie allein hier?**	zint zee ahlighn heer
I'm with my ...	**Ich bin mit ... hier.**	ikh bin mit ... heer
wife	**meiner Frau**	mighnerr frow
husband	**meinem Mann**	mighnerm mahn
family	**meiner Familie**	mighnerr fahmeelier
parents	**meinen Eltern**	mighnern ehlterrn
boyfriend	**meinem Freund**	mighnerm froynt
girlfriend	**meiner Freundin**	mighnerr froyndin

father/mother	**der Vater/die Mutter**	derr faaterr/dee mutterr
son/daughter	**der Sohn/die Tochter**	derr zoan/dee tokhterr
brother/sister	**der Bruder/die Schwester**	derr brooderr/dee shvehsterr
uncle/aunt	**der Onkel/die Tante**	derr onkerl/dee tahnter
nephew/niece	**der Neffe/die Nichte**	derr nehfer/dee neekhter
cousin	**der Cousin/die Cousine**	derr kuzehng/dee kuzeener

Are you married/single?	**Sind Sie verheiratet/ledig?**	zint zee fehrhighraatert/laydikh
Do you have children?	**Haben Sie Kinder?**	haarbern zee kinderr
What's your occupation?	**Was machen Sie beruflich?**	vahss mahkhern zee berrooflikh
I'm a student.	**Ich bin Student(in).**	ikh bin shtuddehnt(in)
What are you studying?	**Was studieren Sie?**	vahss shtuddeerern zee
I'm here on a business trip.	**Ich bin auf einer Geschäftsreise hier.**	ikh bin owf ighnerr gershehftsrighzer heer
Do you travel a lot?	**Reisen Sie viel?**	righzern zee feel
Do you play cards/chess?	**Spielen Sie Karten/Schach?**	shpeelern zee kahrtern/shahkh

The weather   Das Wetter

What a lovely day!	Was für ein herrlicher Tag!	vahss fewr ighn hehrlikherr taag
What awful weather!	Was für ein scheußliches Wetter!	vahss fewr ighn shoysslikherss vehterr
Isn't it cold/hot today?	Welche Kälte/Hitze heute!	vehlkher kehlter/hitser hoyter
Is it usually as warm as this?	Ist es immer so warm?	ist ehss immerr zoa vahrm
Do you think it's going to ... tomorrow?	Glauben Sie, es wird morgen ...?	glowbern zee ehss veert morgern
be a nice day	schön sein	shurn zighn
rain	regnen	raygnern
snow	schneien	shnighern
What is the weather forecast?	Was sagt der Wetterbericht?	vahss zahgt derr vehterrberrikht

cloud	die Wolke	dee volker
fog	der Nebel	derr nayberl
frost	der Frost	derr frost
ice	das Eis	dahss ighss
lightning	der Blitz	derr blits
moon	der Mond	derr moant
rain	der Regen	derr raygern
sky	der Himmel	derr himmerl
snow	der Schnee	derr shnay
star	der Stern	derr shtehrn
sun	die Sonne	dee zonner
thunder	der Donner	derr donnerr
thunderstorm	das Gewitter	dahss gervitterr
wind	der Wind	derr vint

Invitations   Einladungen

| Would you like to have dinner with us on ...? | Möchten Sie am ... mit uns zu Abend essen? | murkhtern zee ahm ... mit uns tsoo aabernt ehssern |
| May I invite you for lunch? | Darf ich Sie zum Mittagessen einladen? | dahrf ikh zee tsum mittaagehssern ighnlaadern |

DAYS OF THE WEEK, see page 151

Can you come over for a drink this evening?	**Kommen Sie heute abend auf ein Gläschen zu uns?**	kommern zee **hoyter** aabernt owf ighn glaiskhern tsoo uns
There's a party. Are you coming?	**Es gibt eine Party. Kommen Sie auch?**	ehss gipt ighner **paartee.** kommern zee owkh
That's very kind of you.	**Das ist sehr nett von Ihnen.**	dahss ist zayr neht fon **eenern**
Great. I'd love to come.	**Prima, ich komme sehr gerne.**	preemaa ikh **kommer** zayr **gehrner**
What time shall we come?	**Wann sollen wir da sein?**	vahn **zollern** veer daa zighn
May I bring a friend/ a girlfriend?	**Kann ich einen Freund/eine Freundin mitbringen?**	kahn ikh **ighnern** froynt/**ighnerr froyndin** mitbringern
I'm afraid we've got to leave now.	**Leider müssen wir jetzt gehen.**	**lighderr mewssern** veer yehtst **gayern**
Next time you must come to visit us.	**Nächstes Mal müssen Sie uns besuchen.**	**naikhsterss** maal **mewssern** zee uns berzookhern
Thanks for the evening. It was great.	**Vielen Dank für den schönen Abend.**	feelern dahnk fewr dayn **shurnern** aabernt

Dating *Verabredung*

Do you mind if I smoke?	**Stört es Sie, wenn ich rauche?**	shturt ehss zee vehn ikh **rowkher**
Would you like a cigarette?	**Möchten Sie eine Zigarette?**	**murkhtern** zee **ighner** tsiggahrehter
Do you have a light, please?	**Können Sie mir bitte Feuer geben?**	kurnern zee meer **bitter foyerr** gaybern
Why are you laughing?	**Warum lachen Sie?**	vahroom lahkhern zee
Is my German that bad?	**Ist mein Deutsch so schlecht?**	ist mighn doych zoa shlehkht
Can I get you a drink?	**Möchten Sie etwas trinken?**	**murkhtern** zee **ehtvahss** trinkern
Are you waiting for someone?	**Warten Sie auf jemanden?**	**vahrtern** zee owf **yaymahndern**
Are you free this evening?	**Sind Sie heute abend frei?**	zint zee **hoyter** aabernt frigh

Would you like to go out with me tonight?	Möchten Sie heute abend mit mir ausgehen?	murkhtern zee hoyter aabernt mit meer owsgayern
Would you like to go dancing?	Möchten Sie gern tanzen gehen?	murkhtern zee gehrn tahntsern gayern
I know a good discotheque.	Ich kenne eine gute Diskothek.	ikh kehner ighner gooter diskottayk
Shall we go to the cinema (movies)?	Wollen wir ins Kino gehen?	vollern veer ins keeno gayern
Would you like to go for a drive?	Wollen wir ein bißchen durch die Gegend fahren?	vollern veer ighn bisskhern doorkh dee gaygernt faarern
Where shall we meet?	Wo treffen wir uns?	voa trehfern veer uns
I'll pick you up at your hotel.	Ich hole Sie in Ihrem Hotel ab.	ikh hoaler zee in eererm hottehl ahp
I'll call for you at 8.	Ich hole Sie um 8 Uhr ab.	ikh hoaler zee um 8 oor ahp
May I take you home?	Darf ich Sie nach Hause bringen?	dahrf ikh zee naakh howzer bringern
Can I see you again tomorrow?	Kann ich Sie morgen wiedersehen?	kahn ikh zee morgern veederrzayern
What's your telephone number?	Wie ist Ihre Telefonnummer?	vee ist eerer taylayfoannummerr

... and you might answer:

I'd love to, thank you.	Danke, sehr gern.	dahnker zayr gehrn
Thank you, but I'm busy.	Vielen Dank, aber ich habe keine Zeit.	feelern dahnk aaberr ikh haaber kighner tsight
No, I'm not interested, thank you.	Nein, das interessiert mich nicht.	nighn dahss intehrehsseert mikh nikht
Leave me alone, please.	Lassen Sie mich bitte in Ruhe!	lahssern zee mikh bitter in rooer
Thank you. It's been a wonderful evening.	Danke, es war ein wunderbarer Abend.	dahnker ehss vaar ighn voonderrbaarerr aabernt
I've enjoyed myself.	Ich habe mich gut unterhalten.	ikh haaber mikh goot unterrhahltern

Shopping guide

This shopping guide is designed to help you find what you want with ease, accuracy and speed. It features:

1. a list of all major shops, stores and services (p. 98)
2. some general expressions required when shopping to allow you to be specific and selective (p. 100)
3. full details of the shops and services most likely to concern you. Here you'll find advice, alphabetical lists of items and conversion charts listed under the headings below.

LAUNDRY, see page 29/HAIRDRESSER'S, see page 30

Einkaufsführer

Shops, stores and services   *Geschäfte, Läden usw.*

Shops in Germany, Austria and Switzerland usually open around 8 or 9 a.m. and close at 6 or 6.30 p.m. Some close for an hour or two at noon—but never department stores. On Saturdays shops in Germany and Austria remain open until noon or 2 p.m. (the first Saturday of the month German shops are open until 6 p.m.). In Switzerland most shops remain open until 4 or 5 p.m. on Saturdays, usually taking Monday morning off.

Where's the nearest ...?	**Wo ist der/die/das nächste ...?**	voa ist derr/dee/dahss naikhster
antique shop	**das Antiquitäten-geschäft**	dahss ahntikvittaytern-gershehft
art gallery	**die Kunstgalerie**	dee kunstgahlehree
baker's	**die Bäckerei**	dee behkerrigh
bank	**die Bank**	dee bahnk
barber's	**der Friseur**	derr frizurr
beauty salon	**der Kosmetiksalon**	derr kosmaytikzahlong
bookshop	**die Buchhandlung**	dee bukhhahndlung
butcher's	**die Fleischerei/ Metzgerei**	dee flighsherrigh/ mehtsgerrigh
cake shop	**die Konditorei**	dee kondittorrigh
camera shop	**das Fotogeschäft**	dahss foatogershehft
chemist's	**die Apotheke**	dee ahpottayker
dairy	**die Milchhandlung**	dee milkhhahndlung
delicatessen	**das Delikatessen-geschäft**	dahss dehlikkahtehssern-gershehft
dentist	**der Zahnarzt**	derr tsaanahrtst
department store	**das Warenhaus**	dahss vaarernhowss
doctor	**der Arzt**	derr ahrtst
dress shop	**das Modengeschäft**	dahss moaderngershehft
drugstore	**die Apotheke**	dee ahpottayker
dry cleaner's	**die chemische Reinigung**	dee khaymisher righnig-gung
electrician	**der Elektriker**	derr aylehktrikkerr
fishmonger's	**die Fischhandlung**	dee fishhahndlung
flea market	**der Flohmarkt**	derr floamahrkt
florist's	**das Blumengeschäft**	dahss bloomerngershehft
furrier's	**das Pelzgeschäft**	dahss pehltsgershehft
greengrocer's	**die Gemüsehandlung**	dee germewzerhahndlung
grocery	**das Lebensmittel-geschäft**	dahss laybernsmitterl-gershehft

hairdresser's (ladies/men)	**der Damenfriseur/ Herrenfriseur**	derr **daa**mernfrizurr/ **heh**rernfrizurr
hardware store	**die Eisenwaren- handlung**	dee **ighzern**vaarern- hahndlung
health food shop	**das Reformhaus**	dahss reh**form**howss
hospital	**das Krankenhaus**	dahss **krahn**kernhowss
ironmonger's	**die Eisenwaren- handlung**	dee **ighzern**vaarern- hahndlung
jeweller's	**der Juwelier**	derr yuvveh**leer**
launderette	**der Waschsalon**	derr **vahsh**zahlong
laundry	**die Wäscherei**	dee vehsher**righ**
library	**die Bibliothek**	dee biblio**tayk**
market	**der Markt**	derr mahrkt
newsagent's	**der Zeitungshändler**	derr **tsigh**tungshehndlerr
newsstand	**der Zeitungsstand**	derr **tsigh**tungsshtahnt
optician	**der Optiker**	derr **op**tikkerr
pastry shop	**die Konditorei**	dee kondit**torrigh**
photographer	**der Fotograf**	derr foato**graaf**
police station	**die Polizeiwache**	dee **pol**litsighvahkher
post office	**das Postamt**	dahss **post**ahmt
second-hand shop	**der Gebrauchtwaren- laden**	derr ger**browkht**vaarern- laadern
shoemaker's (repairs)	**der Schuhmacher**	derr **shoo**mahkherr
shoe shop	**das Schuhgeschäft**	dahss **shoo**gershehft
shopping centre	**das Einkaufszentrum**	dahss **ighn**kowfstsehntrum
souvenir shop	**der Andenkenladen**	derr **ahn**dehnkernlaadern
sporting goods shop	**das Sportgeschäft**	dahss **shport**gershehft
stationer's	**das Schreibwaren- geschäft**	dahss **shrighp**vaarern- gershehft
supermarket	**der Supermarkt**	derr **zoo**perrmahrkt
tailor's	**der Schneider**	derr **shnigh**derr
telegraph office	**das Telegrafenamt**	dahss taylay**graa**fernahmt
tobacconist's	**der Tabakladen**	derr **tah**bahklaadern
toy shop	**das Spielwaren- geschäft**	dahss **shpeel**vaarern- gerhehft
travel agency	**das Reisebüro**	dahss **righ**zerbewroa
vegetable store	**die Gemüsehandlung**	dee ger**mew**zerhahndlung
veterinarian	**der Tierarzt**	derr **teer**ahrtst
watchmaker's	**der Uhrmacher**	derr **oor**mahkherr
wine merchant's	**die Weinhandlung**	dee **vighn**hahndlung

EINGANG	ENTRANCE
AUSGANG	EXIT
NOTAUSGANG	EMERGENCY EXIT

General expressions   *Allgemeine Redewendungen*

Where?   *Wo?*

Where's there a good ...?	**Wo gibt es einen guten/eine gute/ein gutes ...?**	voa gipt ehss ighnern gootern/ighner gooter/ighn gooterss
Where can I find ...?	**Wo finde ich ...?**	voa finder ikh
Where's the main shopping area?	**Wo ist das Geschäftsviertel?**	voa ist dahss gershehftsfeerterl
Is it far from here?	**Ist es weit von hier?**	ist ehss vight fon heer
How do I get there?	**Wie komme ich dorthin?**	vee kommer ikh dorthin

Service   *Bedienung*

Can you help me?	**Können Sie mir helfen?**	kurnern zee meer hehlfern
I'm just looking.	**Ich sehe mich nur um.**	ikh zayer mikh noor um
I want ...	**Ich möchte ...**	ikh murkhter
Can you show me some ...?	**Können Sie mir einige ... zeigen?**	kurnern zee meer ighnigger ... tsighgern
Do you sell ...?	**Verkaufen Sie ...?**	fehrkowfern zee
I'd like to buy ...	**Ich möchte ... kaufen.**	ikh murkhter ... kowfern
Do you have any ...?	**Haben Sie ...?**	haabern zee
Where's the ... department?	**Wo ist die ... -Abteilung?**	voa ist dee ... ahptighlung
Where is the lift (elevator)/escalator?	**Wo ist der Fahrstuhl/die Rolltreppe?**	voa ist derr faarshtool/dee roltrehper

That one   *Das da*

Can you show me ...?	**Können Sie mir ... zeigen?**	kurnern zee meer ... tsighgern
that/those	**das da/die dort**	dahss daa/dee dort
the one in the window/in the display case	**das im Schaufenster/in der Vitrine**	dahss im showfehnsterr/in derr vitreener

Defining the article   *Beschreibung des Artikels*

It must be ...	**Es muß ... sein.**	ehss muss ... zighn
big	**groß**	groass
cheap	**billig**	billikh
dark	**dunkel**	dunkerl
good	**gut**	goot
heavy	**schwer**	shvayr
large	**groß**	groass
light (weight)	**leicht**	lighkht
light (colour)	**hell**	hehl
oval	**oval**	oavaal
rectangular	**rechteckig**	rehkhtehkikh
round	**rund**	runt
small	**klein**	klighn
square	**viereckig**	feerehkikh
sturdy	**robust**	robbust
I don't want anything too expensive.	**Ich möchte nichts allzu Teures.**	ikh murkhter nikhts ahlltsu toyrerss

Preference   *Ich hätte lieber ...*

Can you show me some more?	**Können Sie mir noch andere zeigen?**	kurnern zee meer nokh ahnderrer tsighgern
Haven't you anything ...?	**Haben Sie nichts ...?**	haabern zee nikhts
cheaper/better	**Billigeres/Besseres**	billiggerrerss/behsserrerss
larger/smaller	**Größeres/Kleineres**	grursserrerss/klighnerrerss

How much?   *Wieviel?*

How much is this?	**Wieviel kostet das?**	veefeel kostert dahss
I don't understand.	**Ich verstehe nicht.**	ikh fehrshtayer nikht
Please write it down.	**Schreiben Sie es bitte auf.**	shrighbern zee ehss bitter owf
I don't want to spend more than ... marks.	**Ich möchte nicht mehr als ... Mark ausgeben.**	ikh murkhter nikht mayr ahlss ... mahrk owsgaybern

---

AUSVERKAUF   SALE

COLOURS, see page 113

Decision *Entscheidung*

It's not quite what I want.	**Es ist nicht ganz das, was ich möchte.**	ehss ist nikht gahnts dahss vahss ikh **murkh**ter
No, I don't like it.	**Nein, das gefällt mir nicht.**	nighn dahss ger**fehlt** meer nikht
I'll take it.	**Ich nehme es.**	ikh **nay**mer ehss

Ordering *Bestellen*

Can you order it for me?	**Können Sie es mir bestellen?**	**kur**nern zee ehss meer ber**shteh**lern
How long will it take?	**Wie lange dauert es?**	vee **lahn**ger **dow**errt ehss

Delivery *Lieferung*

I'll take it with me.	**Ich nehme es mit.**	ikh **nay**mer ehss mit
Deliver it to the ... Hotel.	**Liefern Sie es bitte ins Hotel ...**	**lee**fern zee ehss **bit**ter ins hot**tehl**
Please send it to this address.	**Senden Sie es bitte an diese Anschrift.**	**zehn**dern zee ehss **bit**ter ahn **dee**zer **ahn**shrift
Will I have any difficulty with the customs?	**Werde ich Schwierigkeiten mit dem Zoll haben?**	**vayr**der ikh **shvee**rikh-**kigh**tern mit daym tsol **haa**bern

Paying *Bezahlen*

Where do I pay?	**Wo ist die Kasse?**	voa ist dee **kahs**ser
How much is it?	**Wieviel kostet es?**	vee**feel kos**tert ehss
Can I pay with this credit card?	**Kann ich mit dieser Kreditkarte bezahlen?**	kahn ikh mit **dee**zerr kray**dit**kahrter ber**tsaa**lern
Do you accept ...?	**Nehmen Sie ...?**	**nay**mern zee
dollars	**Dollar**	**dol**lahr
pounds	**Pfund**	pfunt
traveller's cheques	**Reiseschecks**	**righ**zershehks
Do I have to pay the VAT (sales tax)?	**Muß ich die Mehrwertsteuer bezahlen?**	muss ikh dee **mayr**vayrt-shtoyerr ber**tsaa**lern
Haven't you made a mistake in the bill?	**Haben Sie sich nicht verrechnet?**	**haa**bern zee zikh nikht fehr**rehkh**nert

Anything else?   *Sonst noch etwas?*

No, thanks, that's all.	**Nein danke, das ist alles.**	nighn **dahn**ker dahss ist **ahl**erss
Yes. I want ...	**Ja, ich möchte ...**	yaa ikh **murkh**ter
Show me ...	**Zeigen Sie mir ...**	**tsigh**gern zee meer
May I have a bag, please?	**Kann ich bitte eine Tragetasche haben?**	kahn ikh **bitt**er **igh**ner **traa**gertahsher **haab**ern

Dissatisfied   *Unzufrieden*

Can you please exchange this?	**Können Sie das bitte umtauschen?**	**kurn**ern zee dahss **bitt**er **um**towshern
I want to return this.	**Ich möchte das zurückgeben.**	ikh **murkh**ter dahss tsoo**rewk**gaybern
I'd like a refund. Here's the receipt.	**Ich möchte das Geld zurückerstattet haben. Hier ist die Quittung.**	ikh **murkh**ter dahss gehlt tsoo**rewk**ehrshtahtert **haab**ern. heer ist dee **kvitt**ung

---

Kann ich Ihnen helfen?	Can I help you?
Was wünschen Sie?	What would you like?
Welche ... möchten Sie?	What ... would you like?
Farbe/Form Qualität/Menge	colour/shape quality/quantity
Es tut mir leid, das haben wir nicht.	I'm sorry, we haven't any.
Das haben wir nicht vorrätig.	We're out of stock.
Sollen wir es für Sie bestellen?	Shall we order it for you?
Nehmen Sie es mit oder sollen wir es Ihnen senden?	Will you take it with you or shall we send it?
Sonst noch etwas?	Anything else?
Das macht ... Mark, bitte.	That's ... marks, please.
Die Kasse ist dort drüben.	The cash desk is over there.

Bookshop *Buchhandlung*

In Germany, bookshops and stationers' are usually separate shops, though the latter will often sell paperbacks. Newspapers and magazines are sold at newsstands.

Where's the nearest ...?	Wo ist der/die/das nächste ...?	voa ist derr/dee/dahss naikhster
bookshop	die Buchhandlung	dee bukhhahndlung
stationer's	das Schreibwaren- geschäft	dahss shrighpvaarern- gershehft
newsstand	der Zeitungsstand	derr tsightungsshtahnt
Where can I buy an English-language newspaper?	Wo kann ich eine englischer Zeitung kaufen?	voa kahn ikh ighner ehnglisher tsightung kowfern
Where's the guide- book section?	Wo stehen die Reiseführer?	voa shtayern dee righzerfewrerr
Where do you keep the English books?	Wo stehen die englischen Bücher?	voa shtayern dee ehnglishern bewkherr
Have you any of ... 's books in English?	Haben Sie ein Buch von ... in Englisch?	haabern zee ighn bookh fon ... in ehnglish
Do you have second- hand books?	Haben Sie auch anti- quarische Bücher?	haaben zee owkh ahnti- kvaarisher bewkherr
I want a/an/ some ...	Ich möchte ...	ikh murkhter
address book	ein Adressen- büchlein	ighn ahdrehssern- bewkhlighn
ball-point pen	einen Kugelschreiber	ighnern koogerlshrighberr
book	ein Buch	ighn bukh
calendar	einen Kalender	ighnern kahlehnderr
carbon paper	Durchschlagpapier	doorkhshlaagpahpeer
cellophane tape	Klebstreifen	klaypshtrighfern
crayons	Buntstifte	buntshtifter
dictionary	ein Wörterbuch	ighn vurrterrbookh
German-English	deutsch-englisch	doych-ehnglish
pocket dictionary	ein Taschen- wörterbuch	ighn tahshernvurrterr- bookh
drawing paper	Zeichenpapier	tsighkhernpahpeer
drawing pins	Reißwecken	righstsvehkern
envelopes	Briefumschläge	breefumshlaiger
eraser	einen Radiergummi	ighnern rahdeergummi
exercise book	ein Schreibheft	ighn shrighphehft

felt-tip pen	einen Filzstift	ighnern filtsshtift
fountain pen	einen Füllfeder-halter	ighnern fewlfayderrhahlterr
glue	Leim	lighm
grammar book	eine Grammatik	ighner grahmahtik
guidebook	einen Reiseführer	ighnern righzerfewrerr
ink	Tinte	tinter
black/red/blue	schwarz/rot/blau	shvahrts/roat/blow
(adhesive) labels	(selbstklebende) Etikette	(zehlpstklaybernder) ehtikkehter
magazine	eine Illustrierte	ighner illustreerter
map	eine Landkarte	ighner lahntkahrter
map of the town	einen Stadtplan	ighnern shtahtplaan
road map of ...	eine Straßenkarte von ...	ighner shtraassernkahrter fon
mechanical pencil	einen Drehbleistift	ighnern drayblighshtift
newspaper	eine Zeitung	ighner tsightung
American	amerikanische	ahmehrikkaanisher
English	englische	ehnglisher
notebook	ein Notizheft	ighn nottitshehft
note paper	Briefpapier	breefpahpeer
paintbox	einen Malkasten	ighnern maalkahstern
paper	Papier	pahpeer
paperback	ein Taschenbuch	ighn tahshernbookh
paperclips	Büroklammern	bewroaklahmmern
paper napkins	Papierservietten	pahpeerzehrviehtern
paste	Klebstoff	klaypshtof
pen	eine Feder	ighner fayderr
pencil	einen Bleistift	ighnern blighshtift
pencil sharpener	einen Bleistift-spitzer	ighnern blighshtiftshpitserr
playing cards	Spielkarten	shpeelkahrtern
pocket calculator	einen Taschenrechner	ighnern tahshernrehknnerr
postcard	eine Postkarte	ighner postkahrter
propelling pencil	einen Drehbleistift	ighnern drayblighshtift
refill (for a pen)	eine Ersatzpatrone	ighner ehrzahtspahtroaner
rubber	einen Radiergummi	ighnern rahdeergummi
ruler	ein Lineal	ighn linnayaal
staples	Heftklammern	hehftklahmmern
string	Bindfaden/Schnur	bintfaadern/shnoor
thumbtacks	Reißzwecken	righstsvehkern
tissue paper	Seidenpapier	zighdernpahpeer
typewriter ribbon	ein Farbband	ighn fahrpbahnt
typing paper	Schreibmaschinen-papier	shrighpmahsheenern-pahpeer
writing pad	einen Schreibblock	ighnern shrighpblok

Camping equipment   *Campingausrüstung*

I'd like a/an/ some ...	Ich hätte gern ...	ikh hetter gehrn
bottle-opener	einen Flaschenöffner	ighnern flahshernurfnerr
bucket	einen Eimer	ighnern ighmerr
butane gas	Butangas	buttaangaass
campbed	ein Feldbett	ighn fehltbeht
can opener	einen Büchsenöffner	ighnern bewksernurfnerr
candles	Kerzen	kehrtsern
chair	einen Stuhl	ighnern shtool
folding chair	Klappstuhl	klahpshtool
charcoal	Holzkohle	holtskoaler
clothes pegs	Wäscheklammern	vehsherklahmrrn
compass	einen Kompaß	ighnern kompahss
cool box	eine Kühltasche	ighner kewltahsher
corkscrew	einen Korkenzieher	ighnern korkerntseeherr
crockery	Geschirr	gershir
cutlery	Besteck	bershtehk
deckchair	einen Liegestuhl	ighnern leegershtool
dishwashing detergent	Spülmittel	shpewlmitterl
first-aid kit	einen Verbandkasten	ighnern fehrbahntkahstern
fishing tackle	Angelzeug	ahngerltsoyg
flashlight	eine Taschenlampe	ighner tahshernlahmper
food box	einen Proviant-behälter	ighnern provviahnt-berhehlterr
frying-pan	eine Bratpfanne	ighner braatpfahner
groundsheet	einen Zeltboden	ighnern tsehltboadern
hammer	einen Hammer	ighnern hahmerr
hammock	eine Hängematte	ighner hehngermahter
haversack	eine Provianttasche	ighner provviahnttahsher
ice pack	einen Kühlbeutel	ighnern kewlboyterl
kerosene	Petroleum	paytroalayum
lamp	eine Lampe	ighner lahmper
lantern	eine Laterne	ighner lahtehrner
matches	Streichhölzer	shtrighkhhurltserr
(air)mattress	eine (Luft)matratze	ighner (luft)mahtrahtser
methylated spirits	Brennspiritus	brehnshpeerittuss
mosquito net	ein Mückennetz	ighn mewkernnehts
pail	einen Eimer	ighnern ighmerr
paper napkins	Papierservietten	pahpeerzehrviehtern
paraffin	Petroleum	paytroalayum
penknife	ein Taschenmesser	ighn tahshernmehsserr
picnic basket	einen Picknickkorb	ighnern piknikkorp
plastic bag	einen Plastikbeutel	ighnern plahstikboyterl

CAMPING, see page 32

rope	**ein Seil**	ighn zighl
rucksack	**einen Rucksack**	ighnern rukzahk
saucepan	**einen Kochtopf**	ighnern kokhtopf
scissors	**eine Schere**	ighner shayrer
screwdriver	**einen Schrauben-**	ighnern shrowbern-
	zieher	tseeherr
sleeping bag	**einen Schlafsack**	ighnern shlaafzahk
stew pot	**einen Schmortopf**	ighnern shmoartopf
table	**einen Tisch**	ighnern tish
folding table	**Klapptisch**	klahptish
tent	**ein Zelt**	ighn tsehlt
tent pegs	**Heringe**	hayringer
tent pole	**eine Zeltstange**	ighner tsehltshtahnger
tinfoil	**Aluminiumfolie**	ahlumeeniumfoalier
tin opener	**einen Büchsenöffner**	ighnern bewksernurfnerr
tongs	**eine Zange**	ighner tsahnger
torch	**eine Taschenlampe**	ighner tahshernlahmper
vacuum flask	**eine Thermosflasche**	ighner tehrmosflahsher
washing powder	**Waschpulver**	vahshpulferr
washing-up liquid	**Spülmittel**	shpewlmitterl
water carrier	**einen Wasserkanister**	ighnern vahsserkahnisterr
water flask	**eine Feldflasche**	ighner fehltflahsher
wood alcohol	**Brennspiritus**	brehnshpeerittuss

Crockery *Geschirr*

cups	**Tassen**	tahssern
mugs	**Becher**	behkherr
plates	**Teller**	tehlerr
saucers	**Untertassen**	unterrtahssern
tumblers	**Wassergläser**	vahsserrglaizerr

Cutlery *Besteck*

forks	**Gabeln**	gaaberln
knives	**Messer**	mehsserr
dessert knives	**Dessertmesser**	dehssayrmehsserr
spoons	**Löffel**	lurferl
teaspoons	**Teelöffel**	taylurferl
made of plastic	**aus Plastik**	owss plahstik
made of stainless	**aus rostfreiem**	owss rostfrigherm
steel	**Stahl**	shtaal

Chemist's (drugstore) *Apotheke*

In German, a chemist's is called *Apotheke* (ahpott**ay**ker). They don't sell cameras, books and the like. At night and on Sundays all chemists' display the address of the nearest one open. If you're looking for toiletries, household articles or film, try a *Drogerie* (droge**hree**). You'll also find non-prescription medicine available in a *Drogerie*.

This section has been divided into two parts:

1. Pharmaceutical—medicine, first-aid, etc.
2. Toiletry—toilet articles, cosmetics

General *Allgemeines*

Where's the nearest (all-night) chemist's?	**Wo ist die nächste Apotheke (mit Nachtdienst)?**	voa ist dee **naikh**ster ahpott**ay**ker (mit **nahkht**deenst)
What time does the chemist's open/close?	**Um wieviel Uhr öffnet/schließt die Apotheke?**	um **vee**feel oor **urf**nert/shleest dee ahpott**ay**ker

1—Pharmaceutical *Arzneien*

I want something for ...	**Ich möchte etwas gegen ...**	ikh **murkh**ter **eht**vahss **gay**gern
a cold	**eine Erkältung**	**igh**ner ehr**keh**ltung
a cough	**Husten**	**hoo**stern
a hangover	**einen Kater**	**igh**nern **kaa**terr
hay fever	**Heuschnupfen**	**hoy**shnupfern
insect bites	**Insektenstiche**	in**zehk**ternshtikher
sunburn	**Sonnenbrand**	**zonn**ernbrahnt
travel sickness	**Reisekrankheit**	**righ**zerkrahnk-hight
an upset stomach	**Magenverstimmung**	**maag**ernfehrshtimmung
Can you make up this prescription for me?	**Können Sie mir dieses Rezept machen?**	**kurn**ern zee meer **dee**zerss reht**sehpt mahkh**ern
Can I get it without a prescription?	**Kann ich das ohne Rezept bekommen?**	kahn ikh dahss **oa**ner reht**sehpt** ber**komm**ern
Shall I wait?	**Soll ich warten?**	zol ikh **vahr**tern

DOCTOR, see page 137

Do you have homoeopathic remedies?	Haben Sie homöopathische Mittel?	haabern zee hommuroppahtisher mitterl
Can I have a/an/some ...?	Kann ich ... haben?	kahn ikh ... haabern
analgesic	ein Schmerzmittel	ighn shmehrtsmitterl
antiseptic cream	eine Wundsalbe	ighner vuntzahlber
aspirin	Aspirin	ahspireen
bandage	einen Verband	ighnern fehrbahnt
elastic bandage	eine elastische Binde	ighner ehlahstisher binder
Band-Aids	Heftpflaster	hehftpflahsterr
contraceptives	ein Verhütungsmittel	ighn fehrhewtungsmitterl
corn plasters	Hühneraugenpflaster	hewnerrowgernpflahsterr
cotton wool (absorbent cotton)	Watte	vahter
cough drops	Hustenpastillen	hoosternpahstillern
disinfectant	ein Desinfektionsmittel	ighn dehsinfehktsioansmitterl
ear drops	Ohrentropfen	oarerntropfern
Elastoplast	Heftpflaster	hehftpflahsterr
eye drops	Augentropfen	owgerntropfern
gauze	Verbandmull	fehrbahntmul
insect repellent/spray	einen Insektenschutz/ein Insektizid	ighnern inzehkternshuts/ighn inzehktitseet
iodine	Jod	yoat
laxative	ein Abführmittel	ighn ahpfewrmitterl
mouthwash	Mundwasser	muntvahsserr
nose drops	Nasentropfen	naazerntropfern
painkiller	ein Schmerzmittel	ighn shmehrtsmitterl
sanitary towels (napkins)	Damenbinden	daamernbindern
sleeping pills	Schlaftabletten	shlaaftahblehtern
suppositories	Zäpfchen	tsehpfkhern
tampons	Tampons	tahmpongs
thermometer	ein Thermometer	ighn tehrmommayterr
throat lozenges	Halspastillen	hahlspahstillern
tranquillizers	Beruhigungsmittel	berrooiggungsmitterl
vitamin pills	Vitamintabletten	vittahmeentahblehtern

| GIFT | POISON |
| NICHT EINNEHMEN | FOR EXTERNAL USE ONLY |

2—Toiletry *Toilettenartikel*

I'd like a/an/some ...	Ich hätte gern ...	ikh hehter gehrn
acne cream	eine Aknesalbe	ighner ahknerzahlber
after-shave lotion	ein Rasierwasser	ighn rahzeervahssserr
astringent	ein Adstringens	ighn ahdstringehns
bath salts	Badesalz	baaderzahlts
bubble bath	ein Schaumbad	ighn showmbaat
cologne	ein Kölnischwasser	ighn kurlnishvahssserr
cream	eine Creme	ighner kraym
cleansing cream	Reinigungscreme	righnniggungskraym
for greasy/ normal/dry skin	für fettige/normale/ trockene Haut	fewr fehtigger/normahler/ trokkehner howt
foundation cream	Grundierungs- creme	grundeerungskraym
moisturizing cream	Feuchtigkeitscreme	foykhtikhkightskraym
night cream	Nachtcreme	nahkhtkraym
cuticle remover	Nagelhautentferner	naagerlhowtehntfehrnerr
deodorant	ein Deodorant	ighn dehoddoarahnt
depilatory cream	Haarentfernungs- mittel	haarehntfehrnungsmitterl
emery board	eine Sandpapierfeile	ighner zahntpahpeerfighler
eye liner	einen Lidstift	ighnern leedshtift
eye pencil	einen Augenbrauen- stift	ighnern owgernbrowern- shtift
eye shadow	einen Lidschatten	ighnern leedshahtern
face powder	Gesichtspuder	gerzikhtspooderr
foot cream	Fußcreme	fooskraym
foot powder	Fußpuder	foospooderr
hand cream	Handcreme	hahntkraym
interdental cleaners	medizinische Zahn- stocher	mayditseenisher tsaan- shtokherr
lipsalve	eine Lippenpomade	ighner lippernpommaader
lipstick	einen Lippenstift	ighnern lippernshtift
make-up remover pads	Abschminkwatte	ahpshminkvahter
mascara	Wimperntusche	vimperrntusher
nail brush	eine Nagelbürste	ighner naagerlbewrster
nail clippers	eine Nagelzange	ighner naagerltsahnger
nail file	eine Nagelfeile	ighner naagerlfighler
nail polish	Nagellack	naagerllahk
nail polish remover	Nagellackentferner	naagerllahkehntfehrnerr
nail scissors	eine Nagelschere	ighner naagerlshayrer
perfume	ein Parfüm	ighn pahrfewm
powder	Puder	pooderr
razor	einen Rasierapparat	ighnern rahzeerahpahraat
razor blades	Rasierklingen	rahzeerklingern

rouge	**Rouge**	roozh
safety pins	**Sicherheitsnadeln**	zikherrhightsnaaderln
shaving brush	**einen Rasierpinsel**	ighnern rahzeerpinzerl
shaving cream	**Rasiercreme**	rahzeerkraym
soap	**eine Seife**	ighner zighfer
sponge	**einen Schwamm**	ighnern shvahm
sun-tan cream	**Sonnencreme**	zonnernkraym
sun-tan oil	**Sonnenöl**	zonnernurl
talcum powder	**Körperpuder**	kurrperrpooderr
tissues	**Papiertücher**	pahpeertewkherr
toilet paper	**Toilettenpapier**	toahlehternpahpeer
toilet water	**ein Toilettenwasser**	ighn toahlehternvahsserr
toothbrush	**eine Zahnbürste**	ighner tsaanbewrster
toothpaste	**Zahnpasta**	tsaanpahstah
towel	**ein Handtuch**	ighn hahnttukh
tweezers	**eine Pinzette**	ighner pintsehter

For your hair *Für Ihr Haar*

bobby pins	**Haarklemmen**	haarklehmern
colour shampoo	**ein Tönungsshampoo**	ighn turnungsshahmpoo
comb	**einen Kamm**	ighnern kahm
curlers	**Lockenwickler**	lokkernviklerr
dry shampoo	**ein Trockenshampoo**	ighn trokkernshahmpoo
hairbrush	**eine Haarbürste**	ighner haarbewrster
hair dye	**ein Haarfärbemittel**	ighn haarfehrbermitterl
hairgrips	**Haarklemmen**	haarklehmern
hair lotion	**Haarwasser**	haarvahsserr
hairpins	**Haarnadeln**	haarnaaderln
hair slide	**eine Haarspange**	ighner haarshpahnger
hair spray	**einen Haarspray**	ighnern haarshpray
setting lotion	**einen Haarfestiger**	ighnern haarfehstiggerr
shampoo	**ein Haarwaschmittel**	ighn haarvahshmitterl
for dry/greasy	**für trockenes/**	fewr trokkernerss/
(oily) hair	**fettiges Haar**	fehtiggerss haar
tint	**ein Tönungsmittel**	ighn turnungsmitterl
wig	**eine Perücke**	ighner pehrewker

For the baby *Für den Säugling*

baby food	**Säuglingsnahrung**	zoyglingsnaarung
dummy (pacifier)	**einen Schnuller**	ighnern shnullerr
feeding bottle	**eine Saugflasche**	ighner zowgflahsher
nappies (diapers)	**Windeln**	vinderln

Clothing *Bekleidung*

If you want to buy something specific, prepare yourself in advance. Look at the list of clothing on page 116. Get some idea of the colour, material and size you want. They're all listed on the next few pages.

General *Allgemeines*

I'd like ...	**Ich möchte ...**	ikh **murkhter**
I want ... for a 10-year-old boy/girl.	**Ich möchte ... für einen Jungen/ ein Mädchen von 10 Jahren.**	ikh **murkhter** ... fewr **ighnern yungern**/ ighn **maitkhern** fon 10 **yaarern**
I want something like this.	**Ich möchte etwas in dieser Art.**	ikh **murkhter ehtvahss** in **deezerr** aart
I like the one in the window.	**Das im Schaufenster gefällt mir.**	dahss im **showfehnsterr** ger**fehlt** meer
How much is that per metre?	**Wieviel kostet der Meter?**	**veefeel kostert** derr **mayterr**

1 centimetre (cm.)	= 0.39 in.	1 inch	= 2.54 cm.
1 metre (m.)	= 39.37 in.	1 foot	= 30.5 cm.
10 metres	= 32.81 ft.	1 yard	= 0.91 m.

Colour *Farbe*

I want something in ...	**Ich möchte etwas in ...**	ikh **murkhter ehtvahss** in
I want a darker/ lighter shade.	**Ich möchte es etwas dunkler/heller.**	ikh **murkhter** ehss **ehtvahss dunklerr/hellerr**
I want something to match this.	**Ich möchte etwas hierzu Passendes.**	ikh **murkhter ehtvahss heertsoo pahssernderss**
I don't like the colour.	**Die Farbe gefällt mir nicht.**	dee **fahrber** ger**fehlt** meer nikht
Is it colour fast?	**Ist es farbecht?**	ist ehss **fahrpehkht**

NUMBERS, see page 147

beige	**beige**	bayzh
black	**schwarz**	shvahrts
blue	**blau**	blow
brown	**braun**	brown
fawn	**hellbraun**	hehlbrown
golden	**golden**	goldern
green	**grün**	grewn
grey	**grau**	grow
mauve	**lila**	leelah
orange	**orange**	orrahngzher
pink	**rosa**	roazah
purple	**violett**	violleht
red	**rot**	roat
scarlet	**scharlachrot**	shahrlahkhroat
silver	**silbern**	zilberrn
turquoise	**türkisfarben**	tewrkeesfahrbern
white	**weiß**	vighss
yellow	**gelb**	gehlp
light ...	**hell ...**	hehl
dark ...	**dunkel ...**	dunkerl

| uni | gestreift | gepunktet | kariert | gemustert |
| (unni) | (gershtrighft) | (gerpunktert) | (kahreert) | (germusterrt) |

Fabric *Stoff*

Do you have anything in ...?	**Haben Sie etwas in ...?**	haabern zee ehtvahss in
Is that ...?	**Ist das ...?**	ist dahss
handmade	**Handarbeit**	hahntahrbight
imported	**importiert**	importeert
made here	**inländisches Fabrikat**	inlehndisherss fahbrikkaat
I want something thinner.	**Ich möchte etwas Dünneres.**	ikh murkhter ehtvahss dewnerrerss
Do you have any better quality?	**Haben Sie eine bessere Qualität?**	haabern zee ighner behssserrer kvahlittait

cambric	**Batist**	bahtist
camel-hair	**Kamelhaar**	kahmaylhaar
corduroy	**Kordsamt**	kortzahmt
cotton	**Baumwolle**	bowmvoller
crepe	**Krepp**	krehp
denim	**Drillich**	drillikh
felt	**Filz**	filts
flannel	**Flanell**	flahnehl
gabardine	**Gabardine**	gahbardin
lace	**Spitze**	shpitser
leather	**Leder**	layderr
linen	**Leinen**	lighnern
poplin	**Popeline**	popperleen
rayon	**Kunstseide**	kunstzighder
satin	**Satin**	zahtehng
silk	**Seide**	zighder
suede	**Wildleder**	viltlayderr
towelling (terrycloth)	**Frottee**	frottay
velvet	**Samt**	zahmt
velveteen	**Manchester**	mahnshehsterr
wool	**Wolle**	voller
worsted	**Kammgarn**	kahmgahrn

Is it ...?	**Ist es ...?**	ist ehss
pure cotton	**reine Baumwolle**	righner bowmvoller
synthetic	**synthetisch**	zewntaytish
wash and wear	**bügelfrei**	bewgerlfrigh
crease (wrinkle) resistant	**knitterfrei**	knitterrfrigh
Is it hand washable/ machine washable?	**Kann man es mit der Hand/in der Maschine waschen?**	kahn mahn ehss mit derr hahnt/in derr mahsheener vahshern
Will it shrink?	**Läuft es beim Waschen ein?**	loyft ehss bighm vahshern ighn

Size *Größe*

I take size 38.	**Ich habe Größe 38.**	ikh haaber grursser 38
Could you measure me?	**Können Sie mir Maß nehmen?**	kurnern zee meer maass naymern
I don't know the German sizes.	**Ich kenne die deutschen Größen nicht.**	ikh kehner dee doychern grurssern nikht

Sizes can vary somewhat from one manufacturer to another, so be sure to try on shoes and clothing before you buy.

Women *Damen*

Dresses/Suits					
American	8	10	12	14	16	18
British	10	12	14	16	18	20
Continental	36	38	40	42	44	46

Stockings						Shoes			
American	8	8½	9	9½	10	10½	6	7	8	9
British							4½	5½	6½	7½
Continental	0	1	2	3	4	5	37	38	40	41

Men *Herren*

Suits/Overcoats						Shirts			
American British	36	38	40	42	44	46	15	16	17	18
Continental	46	48	50	52	54	56	38	41	43	45

Shoes								
American British	5	6	7	8	8½	9	9½	10	11
Continental	38	39	41	42	43	43	44	44	45

A good fit? *Paßt es?*

Can I try it on?	**Kann ich es anprobieren?**	kahn ikh ehss ahnprobbeerern
Where's the fitting room?	**Wo ist die Umkleidekabine?**	voa ist dee umklighderkahbeener
Is there a mirror?	**Gibt es einen Spiegel?**	gipt ehss ighnern shpeegerl
It fits very well.	**Es paßt sehr gut.**	ehss pahst zayr goot
It doesn't fit.	**Es paßt nicht.**	ehss pahst nikht

NUMBERS, see page 147

It's too . . .	Es ist zu . . .	ehss ist tsu
short/long	kurz/lang	koorts/lahng
tight/loose	eng/weit	ehng/vight
How long will it take to alter?	Wie lange brauchen Sie, um es zu ändern?	vee lahnger browkhern zee um ehss tsoo ehnderrn

Clothes and accessories   *Kleidungsstücke und Zubehör*

I would like a/an/some . . .	Ich hätte gern . . .	ikh hehter gehrn
bathing cap	eine Badekappe	ighner baaderkahper
bathing suit	einen Badeanzug	ighnern baaderahntsook
bathrobe	einen Bademantel	ighnern baadermahnterl
blouse	eine Bluse	ighner bloozer
bow tie	eine Fliege	ighner fleeger
bra	einen Büstenhalter	ighnern bewsternhahlterr
braces	Hosenträger	hoazerntraigerr
briefs	eine Unterhose	ighner unterrhoazer
cap	eine Mütze	ighner mewtser
cardigan	eine Wolljacke	ighner volyahker
coat	einen Mantel	ighnern mahnterl
dress	ein Kleid	ighn klight
dressing gown	einen Morgenrock	ighnern morgernrok
evening dress (woman's)	ein Abendkleid	ighn aaberntklight
frock	ein Kleid	ighn klight
fur coat	einen Pelzmantel	ighnern pehltsmahnterl
girdle	einen Hüfthalter	ighnern hewfthahlterr
gloves	Handschuhe	hahntshooer
handbag	eine Handtasche	ighner hahnttahsher
handkerchief	ein Taschentuch	ighn tahsherntookh
hat	einen Hut	ighnern hoot
jacket	ein Jackett/eine Jacke	ighn zhahkeht/ighner yahker
jeans	Jeans	"jeans"
jersey	eine Strickjacke	ighner shtrikyahker
jumper (Br.)	einen Pullover	ighnern pulloaverr
leather trousers	eine Lederhose	ighner layderrhoazer
nightdress	ein Nachthemd	ighn nahkhthehmt
pair of . . .	ein Paar . . .	ighn paar
panties	einen Schlüpfer	ighnern shlewpferr
pants (Am.)	eine Hose	ighner hoazer
panty girdle	ein Strumpfhalterhöschen	ighn shtrumpfhahlterrhurskhern
panty hose	eine Strumpfhose	ighner shtrumpfhoazer

pullover	einen Pullover	ighnern pulloaverr
roll-neck (turtle-neck)	mit Rollkragen	mit rolkraagern
round-neck	mit rundem Ausschnitt	mit runderm owsshnit
V-neck	mit V-Ausschnitt	mit fowowsshnit
with long/short sleeves	mit langen/kurzen Ärmeln	mit lahngern/koortsern ehrmerln
without sleeves	ärmellos	ehrmerlloass
pyjamas	einen Schlafanzug	ighnern shlaafahntsoog
raincoat	einen Regenmantel	ighnern raygernmahnterl
scarf	ein Halstuch	ighn hahlstookh
shirt	ein Hemd	ighn hehmt
shorts	Shorts	"shorts"
skirt	einen Rock	ighnern rok
slip	einen Unterrock	ighnern unterrrok
socks	Socken	zokkern
stockings	Strümpfe	shtrewmpfer
suit (man's)	einen Anzug	ighnern ahntsoog
suit (woman's)	ein Kostüm	ighn kostewm
suspenders (Am.)	Hosenträger	hoazerntraigerr
sweater	einen Pullover	ighnern pulloaverr
sweatshirt	ein Sweatshirt	ighn "sweatshirt"
swimming trunks	eine Badehose	ighner baaderhoazer
swimsuit	einen Badeanzug	ighnern baaderahntsoog
T-shirt	ein T-Shirt	ighn "T-shirt"
tie	eine Krawatte	ighner krahvahter
tights	eine Strumpfhose	ighner shtrumpfhoazer
tracksuit	einen Trainingsanzug	ighnern trainingsahntsoog
trousers	eine Hose	ighner hoazer
umbrella	einen Regenschirm	ighnern raygernshirm
underpants	eine Unterhose/ einen Slip	ighner unterrhoazer/ ighnern "slip"
undershirt	ein Unterhemd	ighn unterrhehmt
vest (Am.)	eine Weste	ighner vehster
vest (Br.)	ein Unterhemd	ighn unterrhehmt
waistcoat	eine Weste	ighner vehster

belt	der Gürtel	derr gewrterl
buckle	die Schnalle	dee shnahler
button	der Knopf	derr knopf
pocket	die Tasche	dee tahsher
press stud (snap fastener)	der Druckknopf	derr drukknopf
zip (zipper)	der Reißverschluß	derr righsfehrshluss

Shoes *Schuhe*

I'd like a pair of ...	Ich möchte ein Paar ...	ikh **murkh**ter ighn paar
boots	**Stiefel**	**shtee**ferl
moccasins	**Mokassins**	mok**kahss**ins
plimsolls (sneakers)	**Turnschuhe**	**toorn**shooer
rain boots	**Gummistiefel**	**gummishtee**ferl
sandals	**Sandalen**	**zahn**daalern
shoes	**Schuhe**	**shooer**
flat	**flache**	**flah**kher
with a heel	**mit hohen**	mit **hoa**ern
	Absätzen	**ahp**zehtsern
with leather soles	**mit Ledersohlen**	mit **lay**derzoalern
with rubber soles	**mit Gummisohlen**	mit **gummi**zoalern
slippers	**Hausschuhe**	**howss**shooer
These are too ...	Diese sind zu ...	**dee**zer zint tsu
narrow/wide	**eng/weit**	ehng/vight
large/small	**groß/klein**	groass/klighn
Do you have a larger/ smaller size?	Haben Sie eine größere/kleinere Nummer?	**haa**bern zee **igh**ner **grurss**errer/**kligh**nerrer **nummerr**
Do you have the same in black?	Haben Sie die gleichen in Schwarz?	**haa**bern zee dee **gligh**khern in shvahrts
cloth/leather	**Stoff/Leder**	shtof/**lay**derr
rubber/suede	**Gummi/Wildleder**	**gummi**/**vilt**layderr
Is it genuine leather?	Ist es echtes Leder?	ist ehss **ehkh**ters **lay**derr
I need some shoe polish/shoelaces.	Ich brauche Schuhcreme/ Schnürsenkel.	ikh **brow**kher **shook**raym/ **shnewr**zehnkerl

Shoes worn out? Here's the key to getting them fixed again:

Can you repair these shoes?	Können Sie diese Schuhe reparieren?	**kurn**ern zee **dee**zer **shoo**er rehpah**ree**rern
Can you stitch this?	Können Sie das nähen?	**kurn**ern zee dahss **nai**ern
I want new soles and heels.	Ich möchte neue Sohlen und Absätze.	ikh **murkh**ter **noy**er **zoa**lern unt **ahp**zehtser
When will they be ready?	Wann sind sie fertig?	vahn zint zee **fehr**tikh

COLOURS, see page 113

Electrical appliances *Elektrische Geräte*

220 volt, 50-cycle A.C. is almost universal in Germany as well as in Austria and Switzerland.

What's the voltage?	**Welche Spannung haben Sie hier?**	vehlkher shpahnung haabern zee heer
Do you have a battery for this?	**Haben Sie eine Batterie hierfür?**	haabern zee ighner bahterree heerfewr
This is broken. Can you repair it?	**Das ist kaputt. Können Sie es reparieren?**	dahss ist kahput. kurnern zee ehss rehpahreerern
Can you show me how it works?	**Können Sie mir zeigen, wie es funktioniert?**	kurnern zee meer tsighgern vee ehss funktsionneert
I'd like a video cassette.	**Ich möchte eine Videokassette.**	ikh murkhter ighner veedehokkahssehter
I'd like a/an/ some ...	**Ich möchte ...**	ikh murkhter
adaptor	**einen Zwischen-stecker**	ighnern tsvishern-shtehkerr
amplifier	**einen Verstärker**	ighnern fehrshtairkerr
bulb	**eine Glühbirne**	ighner glewbeerner
cassette recorder	**einen Kassetten-recorder**	ighnern kahssehtern-rehkorderr
clock-radio	**einen Radiowecker**	ighnern raadiovehkerr
compact disc player	**einen CD-Spieler**	ighnern tsaydayshpeelerr
extension lead (cord)	**eine Verlängerungs-schnur**	ighner fehrlehngerrungs-shnoor
hair dryer	**einen Haartrockner**	ighnern haartroknerr
headphones	**einen Kopfhörer**	ighnern kopfhurrerr
(travelling) iron	**ein (Reise)bügeleisen**	ighn (righzer)bewgerlighzern
lamp	**eine Lampe**	ighner lahmper
plug	**einen Stecker**	ighnern shtehkerr
portable ...	**Koffer-** ...	kofferr
radio	**ein Radio**	ighn raadio
car radio	**Autoradio**	owtorraadio
record player	**einen Plattenspieler**	ighnern plahternshpeelerr
shaver	**einen Rasierapparat**	ighnern rahzeerahpahraat
speakers	**Lautsprecher**	lowtshprehkerr
(colour) television	**einen (Farb)fernseher**	ighnern (fahrp)fehrnzayerr
transformer	**einen Transformator**	ighnern trahnsformaator
video-recorder	**einen Videorecorder**	ighnern veedehorrehkorderr

Grocery *Lebensmittelgeschäft*

I'd like some bread, please.	**Ich möchte ein Brot, bitte.**	ikh murkhter ighn broat bitter
What sort of cheese do you have?	**Welche Käsesorten haben Sie?**	vehlkher kaizerzortern haabern zee
A piece of ...	**Ein Stück von ...**	ighn shtewk fon
this one	**diesem**	deezerm
the one on the shelf	**dem auf dem Regal**	daym owf daym rehgaal
I'll have one of those, please.	**Ich möchte eins von denen, bitte.**	ikh murkhter ighnss fon daynern bitter
May I help myself?	**Kann ich mich selbst bedienen?**	kahn ikh mikh zehlpst berdeenern
I'd like ...	**Ich möchte ...**	ikh murkhter
a kilo of apples	**ein Kilo Äpfel**	ighn keelo ehpferl
half a kilo of tomatoes	**ein halbes Kilo Tomaten**	ighn hahlbers keelo tommaatern
100 grams of butter	**100 Gramm Butter**	100 grahm butterr
a litre of milk	**einen Liter Milch**	ighnern leeterr milkh
half a dozen eggs	**ein halbes Dutzend Eier**	ighn hahlbers dutsernd igherr
4 slices of ham	**4 Scheiben Schinken**	4 shighbern shinkern
a box of chocolate	**eine Schachtel Schokolade**	ighner shahkhterl shokkollaader
a jar of jam	**ein Glas Marmelade**	ighn glaass mahrmerlaader
a tin (can) of peaches	**eine Büchse Pfirsiche**	ighner bewkser pfeerzikher
a tube of mustard	**eine Tube Senf**	ighner toober zehnf
a packet of tea	**eine Packung Tee**	ighner pahkung tay

Weights and measures

1 kilogram or kilo (kg.) = 1000 grams (g.)

100 g. = 3.5 oz.	½ kg. = 1.1 lb.
200 g. = 7.0 oz.	1 kg. = 2.2 lb.

1 oz. = 28.35 g.
1 lb. = 453.60 g.

---

1 litre (l.) = 0.88 imp. quarts = 1.06 U.S. quarts

1 imp. quart = 1.14 l.	1 U.S. quart = 0.95 l.
1 imp. gallon = 4.55 l.	1 U.S. gallon = 3.8 l.

FOOD, see also page 64

Jeweller's—Watchmaker's *Juwelier – Uhrmacher*

I want a small present for ...	Ich möchte ein kleines Geschenk für ...	ikh murkhter ighn klighnerss gershehnk fewr
Could I please see that?	Könnte ich das bitte sehen?	kurnter ikh dahss bitter zayern
Do you have anything in gold?	Haben Sie etwas in Gold?	haabern zee ehtvahss in golt
How many carats is this?	Wieviel Karat hat es?	veefeel kahraat haht ehss
Is this real silver?	Ist das Echtsilber?	ist dahss ekhtzilberr
Can you repair this watch?	Können Sie diese Uhr reparieren?	kurnern zee deezer oor rehpahreerern
I'd like a/an/some ...	Ich möchte ...	ikh murkhter
alarm clock	einen Wecker	ighnern vehkerr
bangle	einen Armreif	ighnern ahrmrighf
battery	eine Batterie	ighner bahterree
bracelet	ein Armband	ighn ahrmbahnt
chain bracelet	Gliederarmband	gleederrahrmbahnt
charm bracelet	Amulettarmband	ahmullehtahrmbahnt
brooch	eine Brosche	ighner brosher
chain	eine Kette	ighner kehter
charm	ein Amulett	ighn ahmulleht
cigarette case	ein Zigarettenetui	ighn tsiggahrehternehtvee
cigarette lighter	ein Feuerzeug	ighn foyerrtsoyg
clip	einen Klipp	ighnern klip
clock	eine Uhr	ighner oor
cross	ein Kreuz	ighn kroyts
cuckoo clock	eine Kuckucksuhr	ighner kukkuksoor
cuff links	Manschettenknöpfe	mahnshehternknurpfer
cutlery	Tafelbesteck	taaferlbershtehk
earrings	Ohrringe	oarringer
gem	einen Edelstein	ighnern ayderlshtighn
jewel box	ein Schmuckkästchen	ighn shmukkehstkhern
music box	eine Spieldose	ighner shpeeldoazer
necklace	eine Halskette	ighner hahlskehter
pendant	einen Anhänger	ighnern ahnhehngerr
pin	eine Anstecknadel	ighner ahnshtehknaaderl
pocket watch	eine Taschenuhr	ighner tahshernoor
powder compact	eine Puderdose	ighner pooderrdoazer

ring	einen Ring	ighnern ring
engagement ring	Verlobungsring	fehrloabungsring
signet ring	Siegelring	zeegerlring
wedding ring	Ehering	ayerring
rosary	einen Rosenkranz	ighnern roazernkrahnts
silverware	Tafelsilber	taaferlzilberr
tie clip	einen Krawatten-klipp	ighnern krahvahternklip
tie pin	eine Krawatten-nadel	ighner krahvahternnaaderl
watch	eine Uhr	ighner oor
automatic	automatische	owtomaatisher
digital	Digital-	diggitaal
quartz	Quarz-	kvahrts
with a second hand	mit Sekundenzeiger	mit zehkunderntsighgerr
waterproof	wasserdicht	wahsserrdikht
watchstrap	ein Uhrarmband	ighn oorahrmbahnt
wristwatch	eine Armbanduhr	ighner ahrmbahntoor

amber	Bernstein	behrnshtighn
amethyst	Amethyst	ahmehtist
chromium	Chrom	kroam
copper	Kupfer	kupferr
coral	Koralle	korrahler
crystal	Kristall	kristahl
cut glass	geschliffenes Glas	gershliffernerss glahss
diamond	Diamant	diahmahnt
emerald	Smaragd	smahrahgt
enamel	Email	ehmahi
gold	Gold	golt
gold-plated	vergoldet	fehrgoldert
ivory	Elfenbein	ehlfernbighn
jade	Jade	yaader
onyx	Onyx	oaniks
pearl	Perle	pehrler
pewter	Zinn	tsin
platinum	Platin	plaateen
ruby	Rubin	rubeen
sapphire	Saphir	zahfeer
silver	Silber	zilberr
silver-plated	versilbert	fehrzilbert
stainless steel	rostfreier Stahl	rostfrigherr shtaal
topaz	Topas	toppaass
turquoise	Türkis	tewrkeess

Optician *Optiker*

I've broken my glasses.	**Meine Brille ist zerbrochen.**	mighner briller ist tsehrbrokhern
Can you repair them for me?	**Können Sie sie reparieren?**	kurnern zee zee rehpahreerern
When will they be ready?	**Wann ist sie fertig?**	vahn ist zee fehrtikh
Can you change the lenses?	**Können Sie die Gläser auswechseln?**	kurnern zee dee glaizerr owsvehkserln
I want tinted lenses.	**Ich möchte getönte Gläser.**	ikh murkhter gerturnter glaizerr
The frame is broken.	**Das Gestell ist zerbrochen.**	dahss gershtehl ist tsehrbrokhern
I'd like a spectacle case.	**Ich möchte ein Brillenetui.**	ikh murkhter ighn brillernehtvee
I'd like to have my eyesight checked.	**Ich möchte meine Augen kontrollieren lassen.**	ikh murkhter mighner owgern kontrolleerern lahssern
I'm short-sighted/ long-sighted.	**Ich bin kurzsichtig/ weitsichtig.**	ikh bin kurtszikhtikh/ vightzikhtikh
I want some contact lenses.	**Ich möchte Kontaktlinsen.**	ikh murkhter kontahktlinzern
I've lost one of my contact lenses.	**Ich habe eine Kontaktlinse verloren.**	ikh haaber ighner kontahktlinzer fehrloarern
Could you give me another one?	**Können Sie mir eine Ersatzlinse geben?**	kurnern zee meer ighner errzahtslinzer gaybern
I have hard/soft lenses.	**Ich habe harte/ weiche Linsen.**	ikh haaber hahrter/ vighkher linzern
Have you any contact-lens liquid?	**Haben Sie eine Flüssigkeit für Kontaktlinsen?**	haabern zee ighner flewssikhkight fewr kontahktlinzern
I'd like to buy a pair of sunglasses.	**Ich hätte gern eine Sonnenbrille.**	ikh hehter gehrn ighner zonnernbriller
May I look in a mirror?	**Kann ich mich im Spiegel sehen?**	kahn ikh mikh im shpeegerl zayern
I'd like to buy a pair of binoculars.	**Ich hätte gern ein Fernglas.**	ikh hehter gehrn ighn fehrnglaass

Photography *Fotogeschäft*

I want a(n) ... camera.	**Ich möchte einen ... Fotoapparat.**	ikh **murkh**ter **igh**nern ... **foato**ahpahraat
automatic	**automatischen**	owtom**maa**tishern
inexpensive	**billigen**	**bil**liggern
simple	**einfachen**	**ighn**fahkhern
Show me some cine (movie) cameras, please.	**Zeigen Sie mir bitte einige Filmkameras.**	**tsigh**gern zee meer **bit**ter **igh**nigger **film**kahmehraass
Show me that one in the window.	**Zeigen Sie mir die im Schaufenster.**	**tsigh**gern zee meer dee im **show**fehnsterr
I'd like to have some passport photos taken.	**Ich möchte Paßbilder machen lassen.**	ikh **murkh**ter **pahss**bilderr **mahkh**ern **lahss**ern

Film *Filme*

I'd like a film for this camera.	**Ich hätte gern einen Film für diese Kamera.**	ikh **heht**er gehrn **igh**nern film fewr **dee**zer **kah**mehraa
black and white	**Schwarzweißfilm**	shvahrts**vighs**film
colour	**Farbfilm**	**fahrp**film
colour negative	**Farbnegativfilm**	fahrp**neh**gahteeffilm
colour slide	**Film für Farbdias**	film fewr **fahrp**deeahss
cartridge	**eine Kassette**	**igh**ner kahs**seht**er
roll film	**ein Rollfilm**	ighn **rol**film
24/36 exposures	**vierundzwanzig/ sechsunddreißig Aufnahmen**	feeruntts**vahn**tsikh/ **zehks**untdrigh**ssikh** **owf**naamern
this size	**dieses Format**	**dee**zers for**maat**
this ASA/DIN number	**diese ASA/DIN-Zahl**	**dee**zer **aa**zaa/deen tsaal
artificial light type	**Kunstlichtfilm**	**kunst**likhtfilm
daylight type	**Tageslichtfilm**	**taa**gerslikhtfilm
fast (high speed)	**hochempfindlich**	**hoak**hehmpfintlikh
fine grain	**Feinkorn**	**fighn**korn

Processing *Entwickeln*

How much do you charge for developing?	**Was kostet das Entwickeln?**	vahss **kost**ert dahss ehnt**vik**kerln

NUMBERS, see page 147

I want ... prints of each negative.	Ich möchte ... Abzüge von jedem Negativ.	ikh murkhter ... ahptsewger fon yayderm nehgahteef
with a mat finish	matt	maht
with a glossy finish	Hochglanz	hokhglahnts
Will you please enlarge this?	Können Sie das bitte vergrößern?	kurnern zee dahss bitter fehrgrursserrn
When will the photos be ready?	Wann sind die Fotos fertig?	vahn zint dee foatoss fehrtikh

Accessories and repairs *Zubehör und Reparaturen*

I want a/an/some ...	Ich möchte ...	ikh murkhter ...
battery	eine Batterie	ighner bahterree
cable release	einen Drahtauslöser	ighnern draatowslurzer
camera case	eine Fototasche	ighner foatotahsher
(electronic) flash	einen (Elektronen) blitz	ighnern (aylehktroanern) blits
filter	einen Filter	ighnern filterr
for black and white	für schwarzweiß	fewr shvahrtsvighss
for colour	für Farbe	fewr fahrber
lens	ein Objektiv	ighn obyehkteef
telephoto lens	ein Teleobjektiv	ighn taylerobyehkteef
wide-angle lens	ein Weitwinkelobjektiv	ighn vightvinkerlobyehkteef
lens cap	einen Objektivdeckel	ighnern obyehkteefdehkerl
Can you repair this camera?	Können Sie diesen Fotoapparat reparieren?	kurnern zee deezern foatoahpahraat rehpahreerern
The film is jammed.	Der Film klemmt.	derr film klehmt
There's something wrong with the ...	Mit ... stimmt etwas nicht.	mit ... shtimt ehtvahss nikht
exposure counter	dem Bildzählwerk	daym bilttsailvehrk
film winder	dem Filmtransport	daym filmtrahnsport
flash attachment	dem Blitzgerät	daym blitsgerrait
lens	dem Objektiv	daym obyehkteef
light meter	dem Belichtungsmesser	daym berlikhtungsmehsser
rangefinder	dem Entfernungsmesser	daym ehntfehrnungsmehsser
shutter	dem Verschluß	daym fehrshluss

Tobacconist's *Tabakladen*

Cigarettes are sold in specialized tobacco shops, at kiosks and from vending machines. In Switzerland you can also buy cigarettes in restaurants, supermarkets, etc.

A packet of cigarettes, please.	**Eine Schachtel Zigaretten, bitte.**	ighner shahkhterl tsiggahrehtern bitter
Do you have any American/English cigarettes?	**Haben Sie amerikanische/ englische Zigaretten?**	haabern zee ahmehrikkaanisher/ ehnglisher tsiggahrehtern
I'd like a carton.	**Ich möchte eine Stange.**	ikh murkhter ighner shtahnger
Give me a/some ..., please.	**Geben Sie mir bitte ...**	gaybern zee meer bitter
candy	**Bonbons**	bongbongs
chewing gum	**Kaugummi**	kowgummi
chewing tobacco	**Kautabak**	kowtahbahk
chocolate	**Schokolade**	shokkollaader
cigarette case	**ein Zigarettenetui**	ighn tsiggahrehternehtvee
cigarette holder	**eine Zigaretten- spitze**	ighner tsiggahrehtern- shpitser
cigarettes	**Zigaretten**	tsiggahrehtern
filter-tipped	**mit Filter**	mit filterr
without filter	**ohne Filter**	oaner filterr
light/dark tobacco	**heller/dunkler Tabak**	hehlerr/dunklerr tahbahk
mild/strong	**milder/starker**	milderr/shtahrkerr
menthol	**Menthol-**	mehntoal
king-size	**extra lang**	ehkstraa lahng
cigars	**Zigarren**	tsiggahrern
lighter	**ein Feuerzeug**	ighn foyerrtsoyg
lighter fluid/gas	**Benzin/Gas fürs Feuerzeug**	behntseen/gaass fewrs foyerrtsoyg
matches	**Streichhölzer**	shtrighkhhurltserr
pipe	**eine Pfeife**	ighner pfighfer
pipe cleaners	**Pfeifenreiniger**	pfighfernrighniggerr
pipe tobacco	**Pfeifentabak**	pfighferntahbahk
pipe tool	**ein Pfeifenbesteck**	ighn pfighfernbershtehk
postcard	**eine Postkarte**	ighner postkahrter
snuff	**Schnupftabak**	shnupftahbahk
stamps	**Briefmarken**	breefmahrkern
sweets	**Bonbons**	bongbongs
wick	**einen Docht**	ighnern dokht

Miscellaneous   *Verschiedenes*

Souvenirs   *Andenken*

Here are some suggestions for articles which you might like
to bring back as a souvenir or a gift from Germany.

Bavarian peasant dress	**das Dirndl(kleid)**	dahss **deerndl**(klight)
beer stein	**der Bierkrug**	derr **beerkroog**
glassware	**die Glaswaren**	dee **glahs**vaarern
leather goods	**die Lederwaren**	dee **lay**derrvaarern
music box	**die Spieldose**	dee **shpeel**doazer
porcelain	**das Porzellan**	dahss portseh**laan**
waterproof woollen overcoat	**der Lodenmantel**	derr **loa**dernmahnterl
wood carving	**die Holzschnitzarbeit**	dee **holts**shnitsahrbight

The high quality of Austrian and Swiss winter sports equipment is well known. But petit-point embroidery and porcelain in Austria and linens and organdies in Switzerland are
also good buys. Consider leather goods and *Lederhosen*
(knee-length leather trousers) in Austria, and don't miss the
fabulous array of watches and luscious chocolate in Switzerland.

chocolate	**die Schokolade**	dee shokko**laa**der
cuckoo clock	**die Kuckucksuhr**	dee **kukk**uksoor
embroidery	**die Stickerei**	dee shtikker**righ**
linen	**das Leinenzeug**	dahss **lighn**erntsoyg
ski equipment	**die Skiausrüstung**	dee **shee**owsrewstung
Swiss army knife	**das Schweizer Armeemesser**	dahss **shvights**err ahrmaymehsserr
Tyrolean hat	**der Tirolerhut**	derr teeroalerr**hoot**
Tyrolean pipe	**die Tiroler Pfeife**	dee teeroalerr **pfigh**fer
watch	**die Uhr**	dee oor

Records—Cassettes   *Schallplatten – Kassetten*

Do you have any records by ...?	**Haben Sie Schallplatten von ...?**	haabern zee **shahl**plahtern fon
Can I listen to this record?	**Kann ich diese Platte hören?**	kahn ikh **dee**zer **plah**ter hurrern

L.P. (33 rpm)	die Langspielplatte (33 UpM)	dee lahngshpeelplahter (drighuntdrighssik oo pay ehm)
E.P. (45 rpm)	45 UpM	fewnfuntfeertsik oo pay ehm
single	die Single	dee "single"

Have you any songs by ...?	Haben Sie Lieder von ...?	haabern zee leederr fon
I'd like a ...	Ich hätte gern ...	ikh hehter gehrn
cassette	eine Kassette	ighner kahssehter
video cassette	eine Videokassette	ighner veedehokkahssehter
compact disc	eine Compact Disc	ighner "compact disc"
chamber music	die Kammermusik	dee kahmerrmuzeek
classical music	die klassische Musik	dee klahssisher muzeek
folk music	die Volksmusik	dee folksmuzeek
instrumental music	die Instrumental-musik	dee instrumehntaalmuzeek
jazz	der Jazz	derr dzhaiss
light music	die Unterhaltungs-musik	dee unterrhahltungsmuzeek
orchestral music	die Orchestermusik	dee orkehsterrmuzeek
pop music	die Popmusik	dee popmuzeek

Toys *Spielwaren*

I'd like a toy/game ...	Ich möchte ein Spielzeug/Spiel ...	ikh murkhter ighn shpeeltsoyg/shpeel
for a boy	für einen Jungen	fewr ighnern yungern
for a 5-year-old girl	für ein 5-jähriges Mädchen	fewr ighn 5yairiggerss maitkhern
ball	einen Ball	ighnern bahl
bucket and spade (pail and shovel)	Eimer und Schaufel	ighmerr unt showferl
building blocks	einen Baukasten	ighnern bowkahstern
card game	ein Kartenspiel	ighn kahrternshpeel
chess set	ein Schachspiel	ighn shahkhshpeel
doll	eine Puppe	ighner pupper
electronic game	ein elektronisches Spiel	ighn aylektroanishers shpeel
roller skates	Rollschuhe	rolshooer

NUMBERS, see page 147

Your money: banks—currency

Banking hours in Germany are usually from 8.30 a.m. to 1 p.m. and from 2.30 to 4 p.m., Monday to Friday (Thursday until 5.30 p.m.). Hours are slightly different in Austria and Switzerland. Small currency-exchange offices, indicated by the words *Geldwechsel* or *Wechselstube* are sometimes open outside regular banking hours.

The *Deutsche Mark* (abbreviated to *DM* and called *D-Mark* —**day** mahrk) is the unit of currency in Germany. It's divided into 100 *Pfennig* (**pfeh**nikh), abbreviated *Pf*.

Coins: 1, 2 and 5 marks; 1, 2, 5, 10 and 50 pfennigs.
Banknotes: 5, 10, 20, 50, 100, 500 and 1,000 marks.

In Austria, the basic unit is the *Schilling* (**shil**ling), abbreviated *S*. It's divided into 100 *Groschen* (**gro**shern), abbreviated *g*.

Coins: 1, 5, 10 and 20 schillings; 10 and 50 groschen.
Banknotes: 20, 50, 100, 500 and 1,000 schillings.

The *Franken* (**frahn**kern), usually abbreviated *Fr.*, is the Swiss unit of currency. There are 100 *Rappen* (**rah**pern), abbreviated *Rp.*, to a franc.

Coins: 1, 2 and 5 francs; 5, 10, 20 and 50 Rappen.
Banknotes: 10, 20, 50, 100, 500 and 1,000 francs.

Credit cards may be used in an increasing number of hotels, restaurants, shops, etc. Signs are posted indicating which cards are accepted.

Traveller's cheques are accepted by hotels, travel agents and many shops, although the exchange rate is invariably better at a bank. Eurocheques are also accepted.

Where's the nearest bank?	**Wo ist die nächste Bank?**	voa ist dee **naikh**ster bahnk
Where is the currency exchange office?	**Wo ist die Wechsel-stube?**	voa ist dee **vehk**serl-shtoober

At the bank *In der Bank*

I want to change some dollars/pounds.	Ich möchte Dollar/Pfund wechseln.	ikh murkhter dollahr/pfunt vehkserln
I want to cash a traveller's cheque.	Ich möchte einen Reisescheck einlösen.	ikh murkhter ighnern righzershehk ighnlurzern
What's the exchange rate?	Wie ist der Wechselkurs?	vee ist der vehkserlkoorss
How much commission do you charge?	Welche Gebühr erheben Sie?	vehlkher gerbewr ehrhaybern zee
Can you telex my bank in London?	Können Sie meiner Bank in London ein Telex schicken?	kurnern zee mighnerr bahnk in london ighn taylehks shikkern
I have a/an/some ...	Ich habe ...	ikh haaber
bank card	eine Kontokarte	ighner kontokkahrter
credit card	eine Kreditkarte	ighner krayditkahrter
Eurocheques	Eurocheques	oyroshehks
introduction from ...	einen Empfehlungsbrief von ...	ighnern ehmpfaylungsbreef fon
letter of credit	einen Kreditbrief	ighnern krayditbreef
I'm expecting some money from New York. Has it arrived yet?	Ich erwarte Geld aus New York. Ist es schon angekommen?	ikh ehrvahrter gehlt owss "New York". ist ehss shoan ahngerkommern
Please give me ... notes (bills) and some small change.	Geben Sie mir bitte ... Scheine und etwas Kleingeld.	gaybern zee meer bitter ... shighner unt ehtvahss klighngehlt
Give me ... large notes and the rest in small notes.	Geben Sie mir ... große Scheine und den Rest in kleinen Scheinen.	gaybern zee meer ... groasser shighner unt dayn rehst in klighnern shighnern

Depositing — Withdrawing *Einzahlen – Abheben*

I want to ...	Ich möchte ...	ikh murkhter
open an account	ein Konto eröffnen	ighn konto ehrurfnern
withdraw ...	... abheben	... ahphaybern
Where should I sign?	Wo muß ich unterschreiben?	voa muss ikh unterrshrighbern

NUMBERS, see page 147

I want to deposit this in my account.	**Ich möchte das auf mein Konto einzahlen.**	ikh murkhter dahss owf mighn konto ighntsaalern

Business terms *Geschäftsausdrücke*

My name is ...	**Ich heiße ...**	ikh highsser
Here's my card.	**Hier ist meine Karte.**	heer ist mighner kahrter
I have an appointment with Mr./ Mrs. ...	**Ich bin mit Herrn/ Frau ... verabredet.**	ikh bin mit hehrn/frow ... fehrahpraydert
Can you give me an estimate of the cost?	**Können Sie mir einen Kostenvoranschlag machen?**	kurnern zee meer ighnern kosternfoarahnshlaak mahkhern
What's the rate of inflation?	**Wie hoch ist die Inflationsrate?**	vee hoakh ist dee inflahtsioansraater
Can you provide me with an interpreter/ a secretary?	**Können Sie mir einen Dolmetscher/eine Sekretärin besorgen?**	kurnern zee meer ighnern dolmehtssherr/ighner zaykraytairin berzoargern
Where can I make photocopies?	**Wo kann ich Fotokopien machen?**	voa kahn ikh foatokopeeern mahkhern

amount	**der Betrag**	derr bertraag
balance	**die Bilanz**	dee billahnts
capital	**das Kapital**	dahss kahpittaal
cheque book	**das Scheckbuch**	dahss shehkbookh
contract	**der Vertrag**	derr fehrtraag
expenses	**die Unkosten**	dee oonkostern
interest	**die Zinsen**	dee tsinzern
investment	**die Kapitalanlage**	dee kahpittaalahnlaager
invoice	**die Rechnung**	dee rehkhnung
loss	**der Verlust**	derr fehrlust
mortgage	**die Hypothek**	dee hippotayk
payment	**die Zahlung**	dee tsaalung
percentage	**der Prozentsatz**	derr protsehntzahts
profit	**der Gewinn**	derr gervin
purchase	**der Kauf**	derr kowf
sale	**der Verkauf**	derr fehrkowf
share	**die Aktie**	dee ahktsier
transfer	**die Überweisung**	dee ewberrvighzung
value	**der Wert**	derr vayrt

At the post office

The offices of Germany's *Bundespost* are open from 8 a.m. to 6 p.m. They close at noon on Saturdays. Swiss post offices are open from 7.30 a.m. to midday and from 1.30 to 6.30 p.m. (8 to 11 a.m. on Saturdays). In Austria, post offices are open from 8 a.m. to midday and from 2 to 5 p.m. (8 to 10 or noon on Saturdays). Letter boxes (mailboxes) are painted yellow in Germany and Switzerland and yellow or blue in Austria. In principal cities, some post offices are open outside the normal hours. Remember that for telephoning and cables you should go to the post office—there are no separate telephone or cable offices.

Where's the nearest post office?	**Wo ist das nächste Postamt?**	voa ist dahss **naikh**ster **post**ahmt
What time does the post office open/close?	**Wann öffnet/schließt das Postamt?**	vahn **urf**nert/**shleest** dahss **post**ahmt
A stamp for this letter/postcard, please.	**Eine Briefmarke für diesen Brief/diese Postkarte, bitte.**	**igh**ner **breef**maarker fewr **dee**zern breef/**dee**zer **post**kaarter **bit**ter
A ...-pfennig stamp, please.	**Eine Briefmarke zu ... Pfennig, bitte.**	**igh**ner **breef**maarker tsoo ... **pfen**nikh **bit**ter
What's the postage for a letter to London?	**Was kostet ein Brief nach London?**	vahss **kos**tert ighn breef naakh **lon**don
What's the postage for a postcard to Los Angeles?	**Was kostet eine Postkarte nach Los Angeles?**	vahss **kos**tert **igh**ner **post**kaarter naakh los **ehnd**zehrlerss
Where's the letter box (mailbox)?	**Wo ist der Briefkasten?**	voa ist derr **breef**kahstern
I want to send this by ...	**Ich möchte dies ... senden.**	ikh **murkh**ter deess ... **zehn**dern
airmail	**per Luftpost**	pehr **luft**post
express (special delivery)	**per Expreß**	pehr ehks**prehss**
registered mail	**per Einschreiben**	pehr **ighn**shrighbern

I want to send this parcel.	Ich möchte dieses Paket schicken.	ikh **murkh**ter **dee**zers **pah**kayt **shikk**ern
At which counter can I cash an international money order?	An welchem Schalter kann ich eine internationale Postanweisung einlösen?	ahn **vehl**kherm **shahl**terr kahn ikh **igh**ner interrnahtsio**aaa**ler post**ahn**vighzung **ighn**lurzern
Where's the poste restante (general delivery)?	Wo ist der Schalter für postlagernde Sendungen?	voa ist derr **shahl**terr fewr **post**laagerrnder **zehn**dungern
Is there any mail for me? My name is ...	Ist Post für mich da? Ich heiße ...	ist post fewr mikh daa? ikh **high**sser

BRIEFMARKEN	STAMPS
PAKETE	PARCELS
POSTANWEISUNGEN	MONEY ORDERS

Telegrams *Telegramme*

For telegrams you should go to the post office. Main branches also offer a fax and telex service.

I want to send a telegram/telex/fax	Ich möchte ein Telegramm/Telex/ Telefax aufgeben.	ikh **mirkh**ter ighn taylay**grahm**/**tay**lehks/ **tay**layfahks **owf**gaybern
May I please have a form?	Kann ich bitte ein Formular haben?	kahn ikh **bitt**er ighn form**ul**aar **haa**bern
How much is it per word?	Was kostet es pro Wort?	vahss **kost**ert ehss proa vort

Telephoning *Telefonieren*

The telephone networks of Germany, Austria and Switzerland are almost entirely automated. Coin- and card-operated booths are to be found on the street, with instructions posted inside, often in English. Telephone cards can be purchased from post offices.

International calls can be made from almost all public telephones in Germany and in Switzerland. In Austria, only some are equipped for long-distance calls. If you need assistance in placing the call, go to the post office or ask at your hotel.

Phone numbers are given in pairs. Note that, in telephoning, *zwei* becomes *zwo* (tsvoa).

Where's the telephone?	**Wo ist das Telefon?**	voa ist dahss taylay**foan**
Where's the nearest telephone booth?	**Wo ist die nächste Telefonzelle?**	voa ist dee **naikh**ster taylay**foan**tsehler
May I use your phone?	**Darf ich Ihr Telefon benutzen?**	dahrf ikh eer taylay**foan** bernutsern
Do you have a telephone directory for Bonn?	**Haben Sie ein Telefonbuch von Bonn?**	**haa**bern zee ighn taylay**foan**bukh fon bon
What's the dialling (area) code for ...?	**Wie ist die Vorwählnummer von ...?**	vee ist dee **foar**vailnummerr fon
How do I get the international operator?	**Welche Nummer hat die (internationale) Vermittlung?**	**vehl**kher **nummerr** haht dee (interrnahtsion**naaler**) **fehr**mitlung

Operator   *Vermittlung*

Good morning, I want Hamburg 12 34 56.	**Guten Morgen. Ich möchte Hamburg 12 34 56.**	**goo**tern **mor**gern. ikh **murkh**ter **hahm**boorg 12 34 56
Can you help me get this number?	**Können Sie mir helfen, diese Nummer zu bekommen?**	**kur**nern zee meer **hehl**fern **dee**zer **nummerr** tsoo ber**kom**mern
I want to place a personal (person-to-person) call.	**Ich möchte ein Gespräch mit Voranmeldung.**	ikh **murkh**ter ighn **ger**shpraikh mit **foar**ahnmehldung
I want to reverse the charges (call collect).	**Ich möchte ein R-Gespräch anmelden.**	ikh **murkh**ter ighn **ehr**-gershpraikh **ahn**mehldern

NUMBERS, see page 147

Telefon

Speaking *Am Apparat*

Hello. This is ... speaking.	**Hallo. Hier spricht ...**	hahloa. heer shprikht
I want to speak to ...	**Ich möchte ... sprechen.**	ikh murkhter ... shprehkhern
I want extension ...	**Ich möchte Nebenanschluß ...**	ikh murkhter naybern-ahnshluss
Speak louder/more slowly, please.	**Sprechen Sie bitte etwas lauter/langsamer.**	shprehkhern zee bitter ehtvahss lowterr/lahng-zaamerr

Bad luck *Pech gehabt*

Would you please try again later?	**Würden Sie es bitte später noch einmal versuchen?**	vewrdern zee ehss bitter shpaiterr nokh ighnmaal fehrzookhern
Operator, you gave me the wrong number.	**Fräulein, Sie haben mich falsch verbunden.**	froylighn zee haabern mikh fahlsh fehrbundern
We were cut off.	**Wir sind unterbrochen worden.**	veer zint unterrbrokhern vordern

Telephone alphabet *Buchstabiertabelle*

A	**Anton**	ahntoan	O	**Otto**	otto
Ä	**Ärger**	ehrgerr	Ö	**Ökonom**	urkonnoam
B	**Berta**	behrtah	P	**Paula**	powlah
C	**Caesar**	tsaizahr	Q	**Quelle**	kvehler
CH	**Charlotte**	shahrlotter	R	**Richard**	rikhahrt
D	**Dora**	doarah	S	**Samuel**	zaamuehl
E	**Emil**	aymeel	SCH	**Schule**	shooler
F	**Friedrich**	freedrikh	T	**Theodor**	tayoddoar
G	**Gustav**	gustahf	U	**Ulrich**	ulrikh
H	**Heinrich**	highnrikh	Ü	**Übel**	ewberl
I	**Ida**	eedah	V	**Viktor**	viktor
J	**Julius**	yooliuss	W	**Wilhelm**	vilhehlm
K	**Kaufmann**	kowfmahn	X	**Xanthippe**	ksahntipper
L	**Ludwig**	loodvikh	Y	**Ypsilon**	ewpseelon
M	**Martha**	mahrtah	Z	**Zacharias**	tsahkhahreeahss
N	**Nordpol**	nortpoal			

Not there *Nicht da*

When will he/she be back?	**Wann ist er/sie zurück?**	vahn ist ehr/zee tsoorewk
Will you tell him/her I called?	**Würden Sie ihm/ihr sagen, daß ich angerufen habe?**	vewrdern zee eem/eer zaagern dahss ikh ahngerroofern haaber?
My name's ...	**Mein Name ist ...**	mighn naamer ist
Would you ask him/her to call me?	**Würden Sie ihn/sie bitten, mich anzurufen?**	vewrdern zee een/zee bittern mikh ahntsooroofern
Would you please take a message?	**Würden Sie bitte etwas ausrichten?**	vewrdern zee bitter ehtvahss owsrikhtern

Charges *Gebühren*

What was the cost of that call?	**Was hat das Gespräch gekostet?**	vahss haht dahss gershpraikh gerkostert
I want to pay for the call.	**Ich möchte das Gespräch bezahlen.**	ikh murkhter dahss gershpraikh bertsaalern

---

👈	👉
Ein Anruf für Sie.	There's a telephone call for you.
Welche Nummer haben Sie gewählt?	What number are you calling?
Die Linie ist besetzt.	The line's engaged.
Es meldet sich niemand.	There's no answer.
Sie sind falsch verbunden.	You've got the wrong number.
Das Telefon funktioniert nicht.	The phone is out of order.
Einen Augenblick, bitte.	Just a moment.
Bitte bleiben Sie am Apparat.	Hold on, please.
Er/Sie ist im Augenblick nicht da.	He's/She's out at the moment.

Doctor

To be at ease, make sure your health insurance policy covers any illness or accident while on holiday. If not, ask your insurance representative, automobile association or travel agent for details of special health insurance.

General *Allgemeines*

Can you get me a doctor?	**Können Sie einen Arzt holen?**	kurnern zee ighnern ahrtst hoalern
Is there a doctor here?	**Gibt es hier einen Arzt?**	gipt ehss heer ighnern ahrtst
I need a doctor quickly.	**Ich brauche schnell einen Arzt.**	ikh browkher shnehl ighnern ahrtst
Where's there a doctor who speaks English?	**Wo gibt es einen Arzt, der Englisch spricht?**	voa gipt ehss ighnern ahrtst derr ehnglish shprikht
Where's the surgery (doctor's office)?	**Wo ist die Arztpraxis?**	voa ist dee ahrtstprahksiss
What are the surgery (office) hours?	**Wann sind die Sprechstunden?**	vahn zint dee shprekhshtundern
Could the doctor come to see me here?	**Könnte der Arzt mich hier behandeln?**	kurnter derr ahrtst mikh heer berhahnderln
What time can the doctor come?	**Wann kann der Arzt kommen?**	vahn kahn derr ahrtst kommern
Can you recommend a/an ...?	**Können Sie mir ... angeben?**	kurnern zee meer ... ahngaybern
general practitioner	**einen praktischen Arzt**	ighnern prahktishern ahrtst
children's doctor	**einen Kinderarzt**	ighnern kinderrahrtst
eye specialist	**einen Augenarzt**	ighnern owgernahrtst
gynaecologist	**einen Frauenarzt**	ighnern frowernahrtst
Can I have an appointment ...?	**Kann ich ... einen Termin haben?**	kahn ikh ... ighnern tehrmeen haabern
tomorrow	**morgen**	morgern
as soon as possible	**so bald wie möglich**	zo bahlt vee murglikh

CHEMIST'S, see page 108

Parts of the body *Körperteile*

appendix	der Blinddarm	derr blintdahrm
arm	der Arm	derr ahrm
artery	die Arterie	dee ahrtayrier
back	der Rücken	derr rewkern
bladder	die Blase	dee blaazer
bone	der Knochen	derr knokhern
bowel	der Darm	derr dahrm
breast	die Brust	dee brust
chest	der Brustkorb	derr brustkorp
ear	das Ohr	dahss oar
eye	das Auge	dahss owger
face	das Gesicht	dahss gerzikht
finger	der Finger	derr fingerr
foot	der Fuß	derr fooss
gland	die Drüse	dee drewzer
hand	die Hand	dee hahnt
head	der Kopf	derr kopf
heart	das Herz	dahss hehrts
jaw	der Kiefer	derr keeferr
joint	das Gelenk	dahss gerlehnk
kidney	die Niere	dee neerer
knee	das Knie	dahss knee
leg	das Bein	dahss bighn
lip	die Lippe	dee lipper
liver	die Leber	dee layberr
lung	die Lunge	dee lunger
mouth	der Mund	derr munt
muscle	der Muskel	derr muskerl
neck	der Hals	derr hahls
nerve	der Nerv	derr nehrf
nervous system	das Nervensystem	dahss nehrfernzewstaym
nose	die Nase	dee naazer
rib	die Rippe	dee ripper
shoulder	die Schulter	dee shulterr
skin	die Haut	dee howt
spine	die Wirbelsäule	dee veerberlzoyler
stomach	der Magen	derr maagern
tendon	die Sehne	dee zayner
thigh	der Schenkel	derr shehnkerl
throat	der Hals	derr hahls
thumb	der Daumen	derr dowmern
toe	die Zehe	dee tsayer
tongue	die Zunge	dee tsunger
tonsils	die Mandeln	dee mahnderln
vein	die Vene	dee vayner

Accident—Injury   *Unfall – Verletzung*

There has been an accident.	**Es ist ein Unfall passiert.**	ehss ist ighn **un**fahl pah**sseert**
My child has had a fall.	**Mein Kind ist hingefallen.**	mighn kint ist **hin**gerfahlern
He/She has hurt his/her head.	**Er/Sie ist am Kopf verletzt.**	ehr/zee ist ahm kopf fehr**lehtst**
He's/She's unconscious.	**Er/Sie ist bewußtlos.**	ehr/zee ist ber**vust**loass
He's/She's bleeding (heavily).	**Er/Sie blutet (stark).**	ehr/zee **bloo**tert (shtahrk)
He's/She's (seriously) injured.	**Er/Sie ist (schwer) verletzt.**	ehr/zee ist (shvayr) fehr**lehtst**
His/Her arm is broken.	**Sein/Ihr Arm ist gebrochen.**	zighn/eer ahrm ist ger**brok**hern
His/Her ankle is swollen.	**Sein/Ihr Knöchel ist geschwollen.**	zighn/eer **knurk**herl ist ger**shvoll**ern
I've been stung.	**Ich bin gestochen worden.**	ikh bin ger**shtok**hern **voar**dern
I've got something in my eye.	**Ich habe etwas im Auge.**	ikh **haa**ber **eht**vahss im **ow**ger
I've got a/an ...	**Ich habe ...**	ikh **haa**ber
blister	eine Blase	**igh**ner **blaa**zer
boil	einen Furunkel	**igh**nern foo**run**kerl
bruise	eine Quetschung	**igh**ner **kveht**shung
burn	eine Brandwunde	**igh**ner **brahnt**vunder
cut	eine Schnittwunde	**igh**ner **shnit**vunder
graze	eine Abschürfung	**igh**ner **ahp**shewrfung
insect bite	einen Insektenstich	**igh**nern in**zehk**ternshtikh
lump	eine Beule	**igh**ner **boy**ler
rash	einen Ausschlag	**igh**nern **owss**shlaag
sting	einen Stich	**igh**nern shtikh
strained muscle	eine Muskelzerrung	**igh**nern **musk**erltsehrrung
swelling	eine Schwellung	**igh**ner **shveh**lung
wound	eine Wunde	**igh**ner **vun**der
Could you have a look at it?	**Sehen Sie es bitte mal an.**	**zay**ern zee ehss **bit**ter maal ahn
I can't move my ... It hurts.	**Ich kann den/die/das ... nicht bewegen. Es tut weh.**	ikh kahn dayn/dee/dahss ... nikht ber**vay**gern. ehss toot vay

Wo haben Sie Schmerzen?	Where does it hurt?
Was für Schmerzen haben Sie?	What kind of pain is it?
dumpfe/stechende pulsierende/anhaltende unregelmäßig auftretende	dull/sharp throbbing/constant on and off
Es ist ...	It's ...
gebrochen/verstaucht verrenkt/gerissen	broken/sprained dislocated/torn
Sie müssen geröntgt werden.	I want you to have an X-ray taken.
Sie bekommen einen Gipsverband.	You'll get a plaster.
Es ist infiziert.	It is infected.
Sind Sie gegen Wundstarrkrampf geimpft?	Have you been vaccinated against tetanus?
Ich gebe Ihnen ein Antiseptikum/Schmerzmittel.	I'll give you an antiseptic/a painkiller.
In ... Tagen möchte ich Sie wiedersehen.	I'd like you to come back in ... days.

Illness *Krankheit*

I'm not feeling well.	**Ich fühle mich nicht wohl.**	ikh **few**ler mikh nikht voal
I'm ill.	**Ich bin krank.**	ikh bin krahnk
I feel dizzy/sick.	**Mir ist schwindlig/übel.**	meer ist **shvind**likh/**ew**berl
I've got a fever.	**Ich habe Fieber.**	ikh **haa**ber **fee**berr
My temperature is 38 degrees.	**Ich habe 38° Fieber.**	ikh **haa**ber 38 graat **fee**berr
I've been vomiting.	**Ich habe mich übergeben.**	ikh **haa**ber mikh ewberr**gay**bern
I'm constipated.	**Ich habe Verstopfung.**	ikh **haa**ber fehr**shto**pfung
I've got diarrhoea.	**Ich habe Durchfall.**	ikh **haa**ber **doorkh**fahl
My ... hurts.	**Mein ... tut weh.**	mighn ... toot vay

I've got (a/an) ...	Ich habe ...	ikh **haaber**
asthma	**Asthma**	**ahst**mah
backache	**Rückenschmerzen**	**rew**kernshmehrtsern
cold	**eine Erkältung**	**igh**ner ehr**keh**ltung
cough	**Husten**	**hoos**tern
cramps	**Krämpfe**	**krehm**pfer
earache	**Ohrenschmerzen**	**oa**rernshmehrtsern
headache	**Kopfschmerzen**	**kopf**shmehrtsern
indigestion	**eine Verdauungs-** **störung**	**igh**ner fehr**dow**ungs- shturrung
nosebleed	**Nasenbluten**	**naa**zernblootern
palpitations	**Herzklopfen**	**hehrts**klopfern
rheumatism	**Rheumatismus**	roy**mah**tismuss
sore throat	**Halsschmerzen**	**hahls**shmehrtsern
stiff neck	**einen steifen Nacken**	**igh**nern **shtigh**fern **nah**kern
stomach ache	**Magenschmerzen**	**maa**gernshmehrtsern
sunstroke	**einen Sonnenstich**	**igh**nern **zon**nernshtikh
I have difficulties breathing.	**Ich habe Atem-** **beschwerden.**	ikh **haaber aa**term- bershvayrdern
I have a pain in my chest.	**Ich habe Schmerzen** **in der Brust.**	ikh **haaber shmehrts**ern in derr brust
I had a heart attack ... years ago.	**Ich hatte vor ...** **Jahren einen Herz-** **anfall.**	ikh **hahter** for ... **yaa**rern **igh**nern **hehrts**- ahnfahl
My blood pressure is too high/too low.	**Mein Blutdruck ist** **zu hoch/zu niedrig.**	mighn **bloot**druk ist tsu hoakh/tsu **need**rikh
I'm allergic to ...	**Ich bin gegen ...** **allergisch.**	ikh bin **gay**gern ... ah**lehr**gish
I'm a diabetic.	**Ich bin Diabetiker.**	ikh bin diah**bay**tikkerr

At the gynaecologist's   *Beim Frauenarzt*

I have period pains.	**Ich habe Menstrua-** **tionsbeschwerden.**	ikh **haaber** mehnstruah- tsioansbershvayrdern
I have a vaginal infection.	**Ich habe eine** **Scheidenentzündung.**	ikh **haaber igh**ner **shigh**dernehntsewndung
I'm on the pill.	**Ich nehme die Pille.**	ikh **naymer** dee **pill**er
I haven't had my period for 2 months.	**Ich habe seit zwei** **Monaten meine** **Periode nicht mehr** **gehabt.**	ikh **haaber** zight tsvigh **moan**ahtern **migh**ner **pehr**ioader nikht mayr ger**hahpt**
I'm pregnant.	**Ich bin schwanger.**	ikh bin **shvahn**gerr

Wie lange fühlen Sie sich schon so?	How long have you been feeling like this?
Haben Sie das zum ersten Mal?	Is it the first time you've had this?
Ich werde Ihre Temperatur/Ihren Blutdruck messen.	I'll take your temperature/blood pressure.
Streifen Sie bitte den Ärmel hoch.	Roll up your sleeve, please.
Bitte machen Sie den Oberkörper frei.	Please undress down to the waist.
Legen Sie sich bitte hierhin.	Please lie down over here.
Machen Sie den Mund auf.	Open your mouth.
Tief atmen, bitte.	Breathe deeply.
Husten Sie bitte.	Cough, please.
Wo haben Sie Schmerzen?	Where do you feel the pain?
Sie haben ...	You've got (a/an) ...
Blasenentzündung	cystitis
Blinddarmentzündung	appendicitis
...entzündung	inflammation of ...
Gelbsucht	jaundice
eine Geschlechtskrankheit	venereal disease
Grippe	flu
Lebensmittelvergiftung	food poisoning
Lungenentzündung	pneumonia
Magenschleimhautentzündung	gastritis
Masern	measles
Ich gebe Ihnen eine Spritze.	I'll give you an injection.
Ich brauche eine Blutprobe/Stuhlprobe/Urinprobe.	I want a specimen of your blood/stools/urine.
Sie müssen ... Tage im Bett bleiben.	You must stay in bed for ... days.
Sie sollten einen Spezialisten aufsuchen.	I want you to see a specialist.
Sie müssen zu einer Generaluntersuchung ins Krankenhaus.	I want you to go to the hospital for a general check-up.

Prescription – Treatment *Rezept – Behandlung*

This is my usual medicine.	**Gewöhnlich nehme ich dieses Medikament.**	gervurnlikh **nay**mer ikh **dee**zerss maydikah**mehnt**
Can you give me a prescription for this?	**Können Sie mir dafür ein Rezept geben?**	**kur**nern zee meer dah**fewr** ighn reh**tsehpt gay**bern
Can you prescribe some sleeping pills/an antidepressant?	**Können Sie mir Schlaftabletten/ein Mittel gegen Depressionen verschreiben?**	**kur**nern zee meer **shlaaf**tahblehtern/ighn **mitt**erl **gay**gern daypreh-**ssio**anern fehr**shrigh**bern
I'm allergic to anti-biotics/penicillin.	**Ich bin allergisch gegen Antibiotika/Penizillin.**	ikh bin ah**lehr**gish **gay**gern ahntib**bio**atikkah/pehnit**sillin**
I don't want any-thing too strong.	**Ich möchte kein zu starkes Mittel.**	ikh **murkh**ter kighn tsu **shtahr**kers **mitt**erl
How many times a day should I take it?	**Wie oft täglich soll ich es nehmen?**	vee oft **taig**likh zol ikh ehss **nay**mern
Must I swallow them whole?	**Muß ich sie ganz schlucken?**	muss ikh zee gahnts **shluk**kern

---

Wie werden Sie behandelt?	What treatment are you having?
Welches Medikament nehmen Sie?	What medicine are you taking?
Als Spritze oder Tabletten?	By injection or orally?
Nehmen Sie von dieser Medizin ... Teelöffel ...	Take ... teaspoons of this medicine ...
Nehmen Sie eine Tablette mit einem Glas Wasser ...	Take one pill with a glass of water ...
alle ... Stunden	every ... hours
... mal täglich	... times a day
vor/nach jeder Mahlzeit	before/after each meal
morgens/abends	in the morning/at night
wenn Sie Schmerzen haben	if there is any pain
während ... Tagen	for ... days

CHEMIST'S, see page 108

Fee *Honorar*

How much do I owe you?	**Wieviel bin ich Ihnen schuldig?**	**vee**feel bin ikh **ee**nern **shul**dikh
May I have a receipt for my health insurance?	**Kann ich bitte eine Quittung für meine Krankenkasse haben?**	kahn ikh **bit**ter **igh**ner **kvit**tung fewr **migh**ner **krahn**kern**kah**sser **haa**bern
Can I have a medical certificate?	**Können Sie mir ein ärztliches Zeugnis ausstellen?**	**kur**nern zee meer ighn **ehrts**likhers **tsoyg**niss **owss**shteh**lern
Would you fill in this health insurance form, please?	**Würden Sie bitte dieses Krankenkassen-Formular ausfüllen?**	**vew**rdern zee **bit**ter **dee**zers **krahn**kern**kah**ssern-formull**aar** **owss**fewlern

Hospital *Krankenhaus*

Please notify my family.	**Benachrichtigen Sie bitte meine Familie.**	bern**ahkh**rikhtiggern zee **bit**ter **migh**ner fah**mee**lier
What are the visiting hours?	**Wann ist Besuchszeit?**	vahn ist ber**zookhs**tsight
When can I get up?	**Wann darf ich aufstehen?**	vahn dahrf ikh **owf**shtayern
When will the doctor come?	**Wann kommt der Arzt?**	vahn komt derr ahrtst
I'm in pain.	**Ich habe Schmerzen.**	ikh **haa**ber **shmehr**tsern
I can't eat/sleep.	**Ich kann nicht essen/ schlafen.**	ikh kahn nikht **eh**ssern/ **shlaa**fern
Where is the bell?	**Wo ist die Klingel?**	voa ist dee **klin**gerl

nurse	**die Krankenschwester**	dee **krahn**kern**shveh**sterr
patient	**der Patient/die Patientin**	derr pahts**iehnt**/dee pahts**iehn**tin
anaesthesia	**die Narkose**	dee nahr**koa**zer
blood transfusion	**die Bluttransfusion**	dee **bloott**rahns**fu**zioan
injection	**die Spritze**	dee **shprit**ser
operation	**die Operation**	dee oppehrahts**ioan**
bed	**das Bett**	dahss beht
bedpan	**die Bettpfanne**	dee **beht**pfahner
thermometer	**das Thermometer**	dahss tehrmom**may**terr

Dentist *Zahnarzt*

Can you recommend a good dentist?	**Können Sie mir einen guten Zahnarzt empfehlen?**	kurnern zee meer ighnern gootern tsaanahrtst ehmpfaylern
Can I make an (urgent) appointment to see Dr ...?	**Kann ich einen (dringenden) Termin bei Herrn/Frau Dr. ... haben?**	kahn ikh ighnern (dringerndern) tehrmeen bigh hehrn/frow doktor ... haabern
Can't you possibly make it earlier than that?	**Geht es wirklich nicht eher?**	gayt ehss virklikh nikht ayer
I have toothache.	**Ich habe Zahnschmerzen.**	ikh haaber tsaanshmehrtsern
Is it an abscess/ infection?	**Ist es ein Abszeß/ eine Infektion?**	ist ehss ighn ahpstsehss/ ighner infehktsioan
This tooth hurts.	**Dieser Zahn schmerzt.**	deezerr tsaan shmehrtst
at the top at the bottom in the front at the back	**oben unten vorne hinten**	oabern untern forner hintern
Can you fix it temporarily?	**Können Sie ihn provisorisch behandeln?**	kurnern zee een provvizoarish berhahnderln
I don't want it extracted.	**Ich möchte ihn nicht ziehen lassen.**	ikh murkhter een nikht tseeern lahssern
Could you give me an anaesthetic?	**Können Sie mir eine Spritze geben?**	kurnern zee meer ighner shpritser gaybern
I've lost a filling.	**Ich habe eine Plombe verloren.**	ikh haaber ighner plomber fehrloarern
The gum ...	**Das Zahnfleisch ...**	dahss tsahnflighsh
is very sore is bleeding	**ist wund blutet**	ist vunt blootert
I've broken this denture.	**Mein Gebiß ist zerbrochen.**	mighn gerbiss ist tsehrbrokhern
Can you repair this denture?	**Können Sie das Gebiß reparieren?**	kurnern zee dahss gerbiss rehpahreerern
When will it be ready?	**Wann ist es fertig?**	vahn ist ehss fehrtikh

Reference section

Where do you come from?   *Woher kommen Sie?*

I'm from ...	**Ich komme aus ...**	ikh **kommer** ows
Africa	**Afrika**	ahfrikkah
Asia	**Asien**	aaziern
Australia	**Australien**	owstraaliern
Europe	**Europa**	oyroapah
North America	**Nordamerika**	nortahmayrikkah
South America	**Südamerika**	zewdahmayrikkah
Austria	**Österreich**	ursterrighkh
Belgium	**Belgien**	behlgiern
Canada	**Kanada**	kahnahdah
China	**China**	kheenah
Croatia	**Kroatien**	kroahtsiern
Denmark	**Dänemark**	dainermahrk
England	**England**	ehnglahnt
Finland	**Finnland**	finlahnt
France	**Frankreich**	frahnkrighkh
Germany	**Deutschland**	doychlahnt
Great Britain	**Großbritannien**	groasbrittahniern
Greece	**Griechenland**	greekhernlahnt
Hungary	**Ungarn**	oongahrn
Ireland	**Irland**	eerlahnt
Israel	**Israel**	izrahayl
Italy	**Italien**	itaaliern
Japan	**Japan**	yaapahn
Liechtenstein	**Liechtenstein**	likhternshtighn
Luxembourg	**Luxemburg**	luksermboorg
Netherlands	**den Niederlanden**	dayn neederlahndern
Norway	**Norwegen**	norvaygern
Poland	**Polen**	poalern
Portugal	**Portugal**	portuggah'
Russia	**Rußland**	russlahnt
Scotland	**Schottland**	shotlahnt
Slovakia	**Slowakei**	slovvahkigh
South Africa	**Südafrika**	zewdahfrikkah
Spain	**Spanien**	shpaaniern
Sweden	**Schweden**	shvaydern
Switzerland	**der Schweiz**	derr shvights
United States	**den Vereinigten Staaten**	dayn fehrighnigtern shtaatern
Wales	**Wales**	''Wales''

Numbers *Zahlen*

0	**null**	nul
1	**eins**	ighns
2	**zwei**	tsvigh
3	**drei**	drigh
4	**vier**	feer
5	**fünf**	fewnf
6	**sechs**	zehks
7	**sieben**	zeebern
8	**acht**	ahkht
9	**neun**	noyn
10	**zehn**	tsayn
11	**elf**	ehlf
12	**zwölf**	tsvurlf
13	**dreizehn**	drightsayn
14	**vierzehn**	feertsayn
15	**fünfzehn**	fewnftsayn
16	**sechzehn**	zehkhtsayn
17	**siebzehn**	zeeptsayn
18	**achtzehn**	ahkhtsayn
19	**neunzehn**	noyntsayn
20	**zwanzig**	tsvahntsikh
21	**einundzwanzig**	ighnunttsvahntsikh
22	**zweiundzwanzig**	tsvighunttsvahntsikh
23	**dreiundzwanzig**	drighunttsvahntsikh
24	**vierundzwanzig**	feerunttsvahntsikh
25	**fünfundzwanzig**	fewnfunttsvahntsikh
26	**sechsundzwandzig**	zehksunttsvahntsikh
27	**siebenundzwanzig**	zeebernunttsvahntsikh
28	**achtundzwanzig**	ahkhtunttsvahntsikh
29	**neunundzwanzig**	noynunttsvahntsikh
30	**dreißig**	drighssikh
31	**einunddreißig**	ighnuntdrighssikh
32	**zweiunddreißig**	tsvighuntdrighssikh
33	**dreiunddreißig**	drighuntdrighssikh
40	**vierzig**	feertsikh
50	**fünfzig**	fewnftsikh
60	**sechzig**	zehkhtsikh
70	**siebzig**	zeeptsikh
80	**achtzig**	ahkhtsikh
90	**neunzig**	noyntsikh
100	**(ein)hundert**	(ighn)hunderrt
101	**hunderteins**	hunderrtighnss
102	**hundertzwei**	hunderrttsvigh
110	**hundertzehn**	hunderrttsayn
120	**hundertzwanzig**	hunderrttsvahntsikh

200	**zweihundert**	**tsvigh**hunderrt
300	**dreihundert**	**drigh**hunderrt
400	**vierhundert**	**feer**hunderrt
500	**fünfhundert**	**fewnf**hunderrt
600	**sechshundert**	**zehks**hunderrt
700	**siebenhundert**	**zee**bernhunderrt
800	**achthundert**	**ahkht**hunderrt
900	**neunhundert**	**noyn**hunderrt
1000	**(ein)tausend**	**(ighn)towzernt**
1100	**tausendeinhundert**	towzernt**ighn**hunderrt
1200	**tausendzweihundert**	towzernt**tsvigh**hunderrt
2000	**zweitausend**	**tsvigh**towzernt
10,000	**zehntausend**	**tsayn**towzernt
50,000	**fünfzigtausend**	**fewnftsikh**towzernt
100,000	**hunderttausend**	**hunderrt**towzernt
1,000,000	**eine Million**	**ighner millioan**
1,000,000,000	**eine Milliarde**	**ighner milliahrder**

first	**erste**	**ehrster**
second	**zweite**	**tsvigh**ter
third	**dritte**	**dritter**
fourth	**vierte**	**feerter**
fifth	**fünfte**	**fewnfter**
sixth	**sechste**	**zehkster**
seventh	**siebte**	**zeebter**
eighth	**achte**	**ahkhter**
ninth	**neunte**	**noynter**
tenth	**zehnte**	**tsaynter**

once	**einmal**	**ighn**maal
twice	**zweimal**	**tsvigh**maal
three times	**dreimal**	**drigh**maal

a half	**eine Hälfte**	**ighner hehlfter**
half a …	**ein halber …**	ighn **hahl**berr
half of …	**die Hälfte von …**	dee **hehlfter** fon
half (adj.)	**halb**	hahlp
a quarter	**ein Viertel**	ighn **feerterl**
one third	**ein Drittel**	ighn **dritterl**
a pair of	**ein Paar**	ighn paar
a dozen	**ein Dutzend**	ighn **dutsernd**
3.4%	**3,4 Prozent**	drigh **kommah** feer pro**tsehnt**
1981	**neunzehnhundert-einundachtzig**	noyntsaynhunderrt-**ighn**untahkhtsikh
1992	**neunzehnhundert-zweiundneunzig**	noyntsaynhunderrt-**tsvigh**undnoyntsikh
2003	**zweitausenddrei**	tsvightowzernt**drigh**

Year and age   *Jahre und Alter*

year	**das Jahr**	dahss yaar
leap year	**das Schaltjahr**	dahss **shahl**tyaar
decade	**das Jahrzehnt**	dahss **yaar**tsaynt
century	**das Jahrhundert**	dahss **yaar**hundert
this year	**dieses Jahr**	**dee**zers yaar
last year	**letztes Jahr**	**leht**sters yaar
next year	**nächstes Jahr**	**naikh**sters yaar
each year	**jedes Jahr**	**yay**ders yaar
2 years ago	**vor 2 Jahren**	foar tsvigh **yaar**ern
in one year	**in einem Jahr**	in **igh**nerm yaar
in the eighties	**in den achtziger Jahren**	in dayn **ahkht**siggerr **yaar**ern
from the 19th century	**vom 19. Jahrhundert**	fom **noynt**sayntern **yaar**hundertt
in the 20th century	**im 20. Jahrhundert**	im **tsvahnt**sikhstern **yaar**hundertt
old/young	**alt/jung**	ahlt/yung
old/new	**alt/neu**	ahlt/noy
How old are you?	**Wie alt sind Sie?**	vee ahlt zint zee
I'm 30 years old.	**Ich bin 30 Jahre alt.**	ikh bin **drigh**ssik **yaar**er ahlt
He/She was born in 1960.	**Er/Sie ist 1960 geboren.**	ehr/zee ist noyntsaynhun- **derrtzehkht**sik gerboarern
What is his/her age?	**Wie alt ist er/sie?**	vee ahlt ist ehr/zee
Children under 16 are not admitted.	**Kindern unter 16 Jahren ist der Zutritt verboten.**	**kinderrn** unter **zehkht**sayn **yaar**ern ist derr **tsu**tritt fehr**boa**tern

Seasons   *Jahreszeiten*

spring	**der Frühling**	derr **frew**ling
summer	**der Sommer**	derr **zom**merr
autumn	**der Herbst**	derr hehrpst
winter	**der Winter**	derr **vin**terr
in spring	**im Frühling**	im **frew**ling
during the summer	**während des Sommers**	**vai**rernt dehss **zom**merrs
high season	**die Hauptsaison**	dee **howpt**zehzong
low season (before/ after season)	**die Vorsaison/ die Nachsaison**	dee **foar**zehzong/ dee **nahkh**zehzong

Months *Monate*

January	**Januar**	yahnuaar
February	**Februar**	faybruaar
March	**März**	mehrts
April	**April**	ahpril
May	**Mai**	migh
June	**Juni**	yooni
July	**Juli**	yooli
August	**August**	owgust
September	**September**	sehptehmberr
October	**Oktober**	oktoaberr
November	**November**	novvehmberr
December	**Dezember**	daytsehmberr

after June	**nach Juni**	nahkh yooni
before July	**vor Juli**	foar yooli
during the month of August	**während des Monats August**	vairernt dehss moanahts owgust
in September	**im September**	im zehptehmberr
until October	**bis Oktober**	biss oktoaberr
not until November	**nicht vor November**	nikht foar novehmberr
since December	**seit Dezember**	zight dehtsehmberr
last month	**im letzten Monat**	im lehtstern moanaht
next month	**im nächsten Monat**	im naikhstern moanaht
the month before	**der vorhergehende Monat**	derr foarhayrgayernder moanaht
the month after	**der folgende Monat**	derr folgernder moanaht
the beginning of January	**Anfang Januar**	ahnfahnk yahnuaar
the middle of February	**Mitte Februar**	miterr faybruaar
the end of March	**Ende März**	ehnder mehrts

Days and date *Tage – Datum*

What day is it today?	**Welchen Tag haben wir heute?**	vehlkhern taag haabern veer hoyter
Sunday	**Sonntag**	zontaag
Monday	**Montag**	moantaag
Tuesday	**Dienstag**	deenstaag
Wednesday	**Mittwoch**	mitvokh
Thursday	**Donnerstag**	donnerrstaag
Friday	**Freitag**	frightaag
Saturday	**Samstag/Sonnabend**	zahmstaag/zonnaabernt

What's the date today?	**Den wievielten haben wir heute?**	dayn veefeeltern haabern veer hoyter
It's ...	**Es ist ...**	ehss ist
July 1	**der 1. Juli**	derr ehrster yooli
March 10	**der 10. März**	derr tsaynter mehrts
When's your birthday?	**Wann haben Sie Geburtstag?**	vahn haabern zee gerburtstaag
August 2nd.	**Am 2. August.**	ahm tsvighter owgust
in the morning	**am Morgen**	ahm morgern
during the day	**tagsüber**	taagsewberr
in the afternoon	**am Nachmittag**	ahm nahkhmittaag
in the evening	**am Abend**	ahm aabernt
at night	**nachts**	nahkhts
the day before yesterday	**vorgestern**	foargehsterrn
yesterday	**gestern**	gehsterrn
today	**heute**	hoyter
tomorrow	**morgen**	morgern
the day after tomorrow	**übermorgen**	ewberrmorgern
the day before	**der vorhergehende Tag**	derr foarhayrgayernder taag
the next day	**der Tag danach**	derr taag dahnaakh
two days ago	**vor zwei Tagen**	foar tsvigh taagern
in three days' time	**in drei Tagen**	in drigh taagern
last week	**letzte Woche**	lehtster vokher
next week	**nächste Woche**	naikhster vokher
for a fortnight (two weeks)	**zwei Wochen lang**	tsvigh vokhern lahng
day off	**der freie Tag**	derr frigher taag
holiday	**der Feiertag**	derr figherrtaag
holidays (vacation)	**die Ferien/der Urlaub**	dee fayriern/derr oorlowp
week	**die Woche**	dee vokher
weekend	**das Wochenende**	dahss vokhernehnder
working day	**der Werktag**	derr vehrktaag

Greetings and wishes   *Grüße und Wünsche*

Merry Christmas!	**Fröhliche Weihnachten!**	frurlikher vighnahkhtern
Happy New Year!	**Glückliches Neues Jahr!**	glewklikhers noyers yaar

Happy Easter!	**Frohe Ostern!**	froaer oasterrn
Happy birthday!	**Alles Gute zum Geburtstag!**	ahlerss gooter tsum gerburtstaag
Best wishes!	**Alles Gute!**	ahlers gooter
Congratulations!	**Herzlichen Glück-wunsch!**	hehrtslikhern glewkvunsh
Good luck/All the best!	**Viel Glück!**	feel glewk
Have a good trip!	**Gute Reise!**	gooter righzer
Have a good holiday!	**Schöne Ferien!**	shurner fayriern
Best regards from ...	**Herzliche Grüße von ...**	hehrtslikher grewsser fon
My regards to ...	**Beste Grüße an ...**	behster grewsser ahn

Public holidays *Feiertage*

Only national holidays in Germany (D), Austria (A) or Switzerland (CH) are cited below.

Jan. 1	**Neujahr**	New Year's Day	D A CH
Jan. 2			CH*
Jan. 6	**Dreikönigstag**	Epiphany	A
May 1	**Tag der Arbeit**	Labour Day	D A
Aug. 1	**Nationalfeiertag**	National Day	CH*
Aug. 15	**Mariä Himmel-fahrt**	Assumption Day	A
Oct. 3	**Tag der Deutschen Einheit**	National Unity Day	D
Oct. 26	**Nationalfeiertag**	National Day	A
Nov. 1	**Allerheiligen**	All Saints' Day	A
Dec. 8	**Mariä Empfängnis**	Immaculate Conception	A
Dec. 25	**1. Weihnachtstag**	Christmas Day	D A CH
Dec. 26	**2. Weihnachtstag**	St. Stephen's Day	D A CH*
Movable dates:	**Karfreitag**	Good Friday	D CH*
	Ostermontag	Easter Monday	D A CH*
	Christi Himmelfahrt	Ascension	D A CH
	Pfingstmontag	Whit Monday	D A CH*
	Fronleichnam	Corpus Christi	A

*Most cantons

What time is it? *Wie spät ist es?*

Excuse me. Can you tell me the time?	**Verzeihung. Können Sie mir bitte sagen, wie spät es ist?**	fehrtsighung. kurnern zee meer bitter zaagern vee shpait ehss ist
It's ...	**Es ist ...**	ehss ist
five past one	**fünf nach eins***	fewnf nakh ighns
ten past two	**zehn nach zwei**	tsayn nakh tsvigh
a quarter past three	**viertel nach drei**	feerterl nahkh drigh
twenty past four	**zwanzig nach vier**	tsvahntsikh nahkh feer
twenty-five past five	**fünf vor halb sechs**	fewnf foar hahlp zehks
half past six	**halb sieben**	hahlp zeebern
twenty-five to seven	**fünf nach halb sieben**	fewnf nakh hahlp zeebern
twenty to eight	**zwanzig vor acht**	tsvahntsikh foar ahkht
a quarter to nine	**viertel vor neun**	feerterl foar noyn
ten to ten	**zehn vor zehn**	tsayn foar tsayn
five to eleven	**fünf vor elf**	fewnf foar ehlf
twelve o'clock (noon/midnight)	**zwölf Uhr (Mittag/Mitternacht)**	tsvurlf oor (mittaag/mitterrnahkht)
in the morning	**morgens**	morgerns
in the afternoon	**nachmittags**	nahkhmittaags
in the evening	**abends**	aabernds
The train leaves at ...	**Der Zug fährt um ...**	derr tsoog fairt um
13.04 (1.04 p.m.)	**dreizehn Uhr vier**	drightsayn oor feer
0.40 (0.40 a.m.)	**null Uhr vierzig**	nul oor feertsikh
in five minutes	**in fünf Minuten**	in fewnf minnootern
in a quarter of an hour	**in einer Viertelstunde**	in ighnerr feerterlshtunder
half an hour ago	**vor einer halben Stunde**	foar ighnerr hahlbern shtunder
about two hours	**ungefähr zwei Stunden**	ungerfair tsvigh shtundern
more than 10 minutes	**über 10 Minuten**	ewberr tsayn minnootern
less than 30 seconds	**weniger als 30 Sekunden**	vayniggerr ahlss drighssikh zehkundern
The clock is fast/slow.	**Die Uhr geht vor/nach.**	dee oor gayt foar/nahkh

---

* In ordinary conversation, time is expressed as shown here. However, official time uses a 24-hour clock which means that after noon hours are counted from 13 to 24.

Common abbreviations *Gebräuchliche Abkürzungen*

Abf.	Abfahrt	departure
ACS	Automobil-Club der Schweiz	Automobile Association of Switzerland
ADAC	Allgemeiner Deutscher Automobil-Club	General Automobile Association of Germany
a.M.	am Main	on the river Main
Ank.	Ankunft	arrival
a.Rh.	am Rhein	on the river Rhine
AvD	Automobil-Club von Deutschland	Automobile Club of Germany
Bhf	Bahnhof	railway station
Bez.	Bezirk	district
bzw.	beziehungsweise	respectively
DB	Deutsche Bundesbahn	Federal German Railway
d.h.	das heißt	i.e. (that is)
DIN	Deutsche Industrie-Norm	German Industrial Standard
Frl.	Fräulein	Miss
G.	Gasse	lane
Hbf.	Hauptbahnhof	main railway station
Hr.	Herr	Mr.
LKW	Lastkraftwagen	lorry/truck
MEZ	Mitteleuropäische Zeit	Central European Time
Mio.	Million	million
Mrd.	Milliarde	1000 millions (billion)
n.Chr.	nach Christus	A.D.
ÖAMTC	Österreichischer Automobil-Motorrad- und Touring-Club	Austrian Automobile, Motorcycle and Touring Association
ÖBB	Österreichische Bundesbahnen	Austrian Federal Railways
PKW	Personenkraftwagen	motor car
Pl.	Platz	square
PS	Pferdestärke	horsepower
PTT	Post, Telephon, Telegraph	Post, Telephone and Telegraph Office
SBB	Schweizerische Bundesbahnen	Swiss Federal Railways
St.	Stock	floor
Str.	Straße	street
TCS	Touring-Club der Schweiz	Swiss Touring Club
usw.	und so weiter	etc.
v.Chr.	vor Christus	B.C.
z.B.	zum Beispiel	e.g. (for example)
z.Z.	zur Zeit	at present

Signs and notices *Aufschriften und Hinweise*

Achtung	Caution
Aufzug	Lift (elevator)
Ausgang	Exit
Auskunft	Information
Außer Betrieb	Out of order
Ausverkauf	Sale
Ausverkauft	Sold out
Belegt	Full/No vacancies
Besetzt	Occupied
Bitte klingeln	Please ring
Bitte nicht stören	Do not disturb
Damen	Ladies
Drücken	Push
Eingang	Entrance
Eintreten ohne zu klopfen	Enter without knocking
Eintritt frei	No admission charge
Frei	Vacant
Frisch gestrichen	Wet paint
Für Unbefugte verboten	No trespassing
Gefahr	Danger
Geschlossen	Closed
Heiß	Hot
Herren	Men
Kalt	Cold
Kasse	Cash desk
Kein Zutritt	No entrance
Lebensgefahr	Danger of death
Lift	Lift (elevator)
Nicht berühren	Do not touch
Notausgang	Emergency exit
Notruf	Emergency
Nur für Anlieger	Residents only
Privatweg	Private road
Radweg	Cycle path
Rauchen verboten	No smoking
Reserviert	Reserved
Unbefugtes Betreten verboten	No trespassing
... verboten	... forbidden/prohibited
Vorsicht	Caution
Vorsicht, bissiger Hund	Beware of the dog
Ziehen	Pull
Zimmer frei	Vacancies
Zu verkaufen	For sale
Zu vermieten	To let (for hire)

Emergency *Notfall*

Call the police	**Rufen Sie die Polizei**	roofern zee dee pollitsigh
DANGER	**GEFAHR**	gerfaar
FIRE	**FEUER**	foyerr
Gas	**Gas**	gaass
Get a doctor	**Holen Sie einen Arzt**	hoalern zee ighnern ahrtst
Go away	**Gehen Sie weg**	gayern zee vehk
HELP	**HILFE**	hilfer
Get help	**Holen Sie Hilfe**	hoalern zee hilfer
I'm ill	**Ich bin krank**	ikh bin krahnk
I'm lost	**Ich habe mich verirrt**	ikh haaber mikh fehreert
LOOK OUT	**VORSICHT**	foarzikht
POLICE	**POLIZEI**	pollitsigh
Quick	**Schnell**	shnehl
STOP	**HALT**	hahlt
Stop that man/ woman	**Haltet den Mann/ die Frau**	hahltert dayn mahn/ dee frow
STOP THIEF	**HALTET DEN DIEB**	hahltert dayn deep

Emergency telephone numbers *Notrufnummern*

	Austria	Germany	Switzerland
Fire	122	112	118
Ambulance	144	112	
Police	133	110	117

Lost property—Theft *Fundsachen – Diebstahl*

Where's the ...?	**Wo ist ...?**	voa ist
lost-property (lost and found) office	**das Fundbüro**	dahss funtbewroa
police station	**die Polizeiwache**	dee pollitsighvahkher
I want to report a theft.	**Ich möchte einen Diebstahl anzeigen.**	ikh murkhter ighnern deepshtaal ahntsighgern
My ... has been stolen.	**Mein(e) ... ist mir gestohlen worden.**	mighn(er) ... ist meer gershtoalern voardern
I've lost my wallet.	**Ich habe meine Brieftasche verloren.**	ikh haaber mighner breeftahsher fehrloarern

CAR ACCIDENTS, see page 78

Conversion tables

Centimetres and inches

To change centimetres into inches, multiply by .39.

To change inches into centimetres, multiply by 2.54.

	in.	feet	yards
1 mm.	0.039	0.003	0.001
1 cm.	0.39	0.03	0.01
1 dm.	3.94	0.32	0.10
1 m.	39.40	3.28	1.09

	mm.	cm.	m.
1 in.	25.4	2.54	0.025
1 ft.	304.8	30.48	0.305
1 yd.	914.4	91.44	0.914

(32 metres = 35 yards)

Temperature

To convert centigrade into degrees Fahrenheit, multiply centigrade by 1.8 and add 32.

To convert degrees Fahrenheit into centigrade, subtract 32 from Fahrenheit and divide by 1.8.

REFERENCE SECTION

Kilometres into miles

1 kilometre (km.) = 0.62 miles

km.	10	20	30	40	50	60	70	80	90	100	110	120	130
miles	6	12	19	25	31	37	44	50	56	62	68	75	81

Miles into kilometres

1 mile = 1.609 kilometres (km.)

miles	10	20	30	40	50	60	70	80	90	100
km.	16	32	48	64	80	97	113	129	145	161

Fluid measures

1 litre (l.) = 0.88 imp. quart or 1.06 U.S. quart

1 imp. quart = 1.14 l.	1 U.S. quart = 0.95 l.
1 imp. gallon = 4.55 l.	1 U.S. gallon = 3.8 l.

litres	5	10	15	20	25	30	35	40	45	50
imp. gal.	1.1	2.2	3.3	4.4	5.5	6.6	7.7	8.8	9.9	11.0
U.S. gal.	1.3	2.6	3.9	5.2	6.5	7.8	9.1	10.4	11.7	13.0

Weights and measures

1 kilogram or kilo (kg.) = 1000 grams (g.)

100 g. = 3.5 oz.	½ kg. = 1.1 lb.
200 g. = 7.0 oz.	1 kg. = 2.2 lb.

1 oz. = 28.35 g.
1 lb. = 453.60 g.

Allerlei Wissenswertes

CLOTHING SIZES, see page 115/YARDS AND INCHES, see page 112

Basic Grammar

Here is a brief outline of some essential features of German grammar.

Articles

All nouns in German are either masculine, feminine or neuter, and they are classified by the article which precedes them.

1. Definite article (the):

			Plural:
masc.	*der* **Mann**	the man	*die* **Männer**
fem.	*die* **Frau**	the woman	*die* **Frauen**
neut.	*das* **Kind**	the child	*die* **Kinder**

2. Indefinite article (a/an):

masc.	*ein* **Zug**	a train
fem.	*eine* **Reise**	a trip
neut.	*ein* **Flugzeug**	a plane

Nouns and adjectives

1. All nouns are written with a capital letter. The rules for constructing the plural are very complex.

2. **Declension:** According to their use in the sentence, German articles, nouns and modifying adjectives undergo related changes. The tables below show the declension of all three parts of speech.

	masc. sing.	masc. plur.
subject	der reiche Mann	die reichen Männer
direct object	den reichen Mann	die reichen Männer
possessive	des reichen Mannes	der reichen Männer
indirect object	dem reichen Mann	den reichen Männern

	fem. sing.	fem. plur.
subject	die schöne Frau	die schönen Frauen
direct object	die schöne Frau	die schönen Frauen
possessive	der schönen Frau	der schönen Frauen
indirect object	der schönen Frau	den schönen Frauen

	neuter sing.	neuter plur.
subject	das kleine Kind	die kleinen Kinder
direct object	das kleine Kind	die kleinen Kinder
possessive	des kleinen Kindes	der kleinen Kinder
indirect object	dem kleinen Kind	den kleinen Kindern

The indefinite article is declined in a slightly different way, as is the modifying adjective.

	masc.	fem.
subject	ein reicher Mann	eine schöne Frau
direct object	einen reichen Mann	eine schöne Frau
possessive	eines reichen Mannes	einer schönen Frau
indirect object	einem reichen Mann	einer schönen Frau

	neuter	plur.
subject	ein kleines Kind	keine* großen Leute
direct object	ein kleines Kind	keine großen Leute
possessive	eines kleinen Kindes	keiner großen Leute
indirect object	einem kleinen Kind	keinen großen Leuten

If declined without an article the adjectives take the endings of the definite article, except in the possessive, which you'll hardly use: **guter Wein** (good wine), **kalte Milch** (cold milk), **warmes Wasser** (hot water).

3. **Demonstrative adjectives:** In spoken German "that" is usually expressed by the definite article, but contrary to the

---

* **ein** has no plural, but the negative **kein** (declined in singular like **ein**) does.

article, it is stressed. "This" **dieser, diese, dieses** and plural **diese** is declined like the definite article.

das Buch (that book)   **dieser Platz** (this seat)

4. **Possessive adjectives:** These agree in number and gender with the noun they modify, i.e., with the thing possessed and not the possessor. In singular they are declined like the indefinite article, and in plural like the definite. Note that **Ihr** meaning "your" in the polite form is capitalized.

	masc. or neut.	fem. or plur.
my	**mein**	**meine**
your	**dein**	**deine**
his/its	**sein**	**seine**
her	**ihr**	**ihre**
our	**unser**	**unsere**
your	**euer**	**eure**
their	**ihr**	**ihre**
your (pol.)	**Ihr**	**Ihre**

5. **Comparatives and superlatives:** These are formed by adding **-er (-r)** and **-est (-st)** respectively, very often together with an umlaut.

alt (old)   **kurz** (short)
älter (older)   **kürzer** (shorter)
ältest (oldest)   **kürzest** (shortest)

Adverbs

Many adjectives are used in their undeclined form as adverbs.

schnell   quick, quickly
gut   good, well

There are a few irregularities:

glücklich – glücklicherweise   happy — happily
anders   differently
besonders   especially
gleichfalls   as well, (the) same

Viel indicates quantity and **sehr** intensity:

Er arbeitet viel.	He works a lot.
Er ist sehr müde.	He's very tired.

Personal pronouns

	subject	direct object	indirect object
I	ich	mich	mir
you	du	dich	dir
he	er	ihn	ihm
she	sie	sie	ihr
it	es	es	ihm
we	wir	uns	uns
you	ihr	euch	euch
they	sie	sie	ihnen
you	Sie	Sie	Ihnen

Note: There are two forms for "you" in German: **du** and **Sie; du** (plur.: **ihr**) is used when talking to relatives, close friends and children (and between young people); **Sie** (both sing. and plur.) in all other cases. **Sie** is written with a capital **S**. The verb has the same form as that of the 3rd person plural.

Verbs

Here we are concerned only with the infinitive, the present tense, and the imperative.

Learn these two important **auxiliary verbs:**

sein (to be)	**haben** (to have)
ich bin (I am)	**ich habe** (I have)
du bist (you are)	**du hast** (you have)
er, sie, es ist (he, she, it is)	**er, sie, es hat** (he, she, it has)
wir sind (we are)	**wir haben** (we have)
ihr seid (you are)	**ihr habt** (you have)
sie sind (they are)	**sie haben** (they have)
Sie sind (you are)	**Sie haben** (you have)

The infinitive of practically all verbs ends in **-en.** Here are the endings for the present tense:

ich liebe	I love
du liebst	you love
er, sie, es liebt	he, she, it loves
wir lieben	we love
ihr liebt	you love
sie, Sie lieben	they, you love

Here are four useful irregular verbs in the present tense:

	können (to be able)	**gehen** (to go)	**sehen** (to see)	**tun** (to do)
ich	kann	gehe	sehe	tue
du	kannst	gehst	siehst	tust
er/sie/es	kann	geht	sieht	tut
wir	können	gehen	sehen	tun
ihr	könnt	geht	seht	tut
sie/Sie	können	gehen	sehen	tun

For both regular and irregular verbs, the **imperative** is formed by reversing the order of the verb and the personal pronoun.

Gehen wir!	Let's go!
Gehen Sie!	Go!

Negatives

Negatives are formed with **nicht.**

Er ist nicht hier.	He is not here.

Questions

These are formed by inverting the subject and the verb (putting the verb first, the subject second).

Sprechen Sie English?	Do you speak English?

Dictionary
and alphabetical index

English–German

| *f* feminine | *m* masculine | *nt* neuter | *pl* plural |

anywhere irgendwo
apartment *(flat)* Wohnung f 22
aperitif Aperitif m 59
appendicitis Blinddarmentzündung f 142
appendix Blinddarm m 138
appetizer Vorspeise f 41
apple Apfel m 53, 64, 120
apple juice Apfelsaft m 61
appliance Gerät nt 119
appointment Verabredung f 131; Termin m 137, 145
apricot Aprikose f 53
April April m 150
archaeology Archäologie f 83
architect Architekt m 83
area code Vorwählnummer f 134
arm Arm m 138, 139
arrangement *(set price)* Pauschale f 20
arrival Ankunft f 16, 65, 68
arrive, to ankommen 68, 130
art Kunst f 83
artery Arterie f 138
art gallery Kunstgalerie f 81, 98
artichoke Artischocke f 41
artificial künstlich 124
artist Künstler(in) m/f 83
ashtray Aschenbecher m 27, 36
Asia Asien *(nt)* 146
ask, to fragen 36, 76; bitten 136
asparagus Spargel m 41, 50
aspirin Aspirin nt 109
asthma Asthma nt 141
at an, bei 14
at least mindestens 26
at once sofort 31
aubergine Aubergine f 49
August August m 150
aunt Tante f 93
Australia Australien *(nt)* 146
Austria Österreich *(nt)* 146
Austrian österreichisch 18
automatic automatisch 122, 124; mit Automatik 20
autumn Herbst m 149
avalanche Lawine f 79
awful scheußlich 84, 94

B

baby Baby nt 24; Säugling m 111
baby food Säuglingsnahrung f 111
babysitter Babysitter m 27
back Rücken m 138

backache Rückenschmerzen m/pl 141
bacon Speck m 38, 46
bad schlecht 14, 95
bag Tasche f 17, 18; Tragetasche f 103
baggage Gepäck nt 17, 18, 26, 31, 71
baggage cart Kofferkuli m 18, 71
baggage check Gepäckaufbewahrung f 67, 71
baggage locker Schließfach nt 18, 67, 71
baked gebacken 44, 47
baker's Bäckerei f 98
balance *(account)* Bilanz f 131
balcony Balkon m 23
ball *(inflated)* Ball m 128
ballet Ballett m 88
ball-point pen Kugelschreiber m 104
banana Banane f 53, 64
bandage Verband m 109
Band-Aid Heftpflaster nt 109
bangle Armreif m 121
bank *(finance)* Bank f 98, 129, 130
bank card Kontokarte f 130
banknote Schein m 130
bar *(chocolate)* Tafel f 64
barber's Friseur m 30, 98
bass *(fish)* Barsch m 44
bath *(hotel)* Bad nt 23, 24, 27
bathing cap Badekappe f 116
bathing suit Badeanzug m 116
bathrobe Bademantel m 116
bathroom Bad nt 27
bath towel Badetuch nt 27
battery Batterie f 75, 78, 119, 121, 125
bay leaf Lorbeer m 50
be, to sein 10, 162
beach Strand m 90
bean Bohne f 49
beard Bart m 31
beautiful schön 13, 84
beauty salon Kosmetiksalon m 30, 98
be back, to zurück sein 21, 136
bed Bett nt 24, 142, 144
bed and breakfast Übernachtung mit Frühstück f 24
bedpan Bettpfanne f 144
beef Rindfleisch nt 45
beer Bier nt 56, 64
beer stein Bierkrug m 127
beet(root) rote Beete f 50
before vor 14
begin, to beginnen 80, 87, 88

beginner Anfänger(in) m/f 91
beginning Anfang m 150
behind hinter 15, 77
beige beige 113
Belgium Belgien (nt) 146
bell (electric) Klingel f 144
bellboy Page m 26
below unten 15
belt Gürtel m 117
berth Schlafplatz m 69, 70, 71
best beste 152
better besser 13, 25, 101, 113
between zwischen 15
beverage Getränk nt 61
bicycle Fahrrad nt 74
big groß 13, 25
bilberry Blaubeere f, Heidelbeere f 54
bill Rechnung f 31, 63
billion (Am.) Milliarde f 148
binoculars Fernglas nt 123
bird Vogel m 85
birth Geburt f 25
birthday Geburtstag m 151, 152
biscuit (Br.) Keks m 64
bitter bitter 62
black schwarz 38, 105, 113
blackberry Brombeere f 53
blackcurrant schwarze Johannisbeere f 53
bladder Blase f 138
blade Klinge f 110
blanket Decke f 27
bleach Aufhellung f 30
bleed, to bluten 139, 145
blind (window) Rollo nt 29
blister Blase f 139
block, to verstopfen 28
blood Blut nt 142
blood pressure Blutdruck m 141, 142
blood transfusion Bluttransfusion f 144
blouse Bluse f 116
blow-dry Fönen nt 30
blue blau 113
blueberry Blaubeere f, Heidelbeere f 53
boar (wild) Wildschwein nt 48
boarding house Pension f 19, 22
boat Schiff m, Boot nt 74
bobby pin Haarklemme f 111
body Körper m 138
boil Furunkel m 139
boiled gekocht 47, 51
bone Knochen m 138

book Buch nt 11, 104
book, to reservieren (lassen) 69
booking office Reservierungsschal-
ter m 19; Platzreservierung f 67
booklet (of tickets) Fahrscheinheft
nt 72
bookshop Buchhandlung f 98, 104
boot Stiefel m 118
born geboren 149
botanical gardens Botanischer Garten m 81
botany Botanik f 83
bottle Flasche f 17, 56, 59
bottle-opener Flaschenöffner m 106
bowel Darm m 138
bow tie Fliege f 116
box Schachtel f 120
boxing Boxen nt 89
boy Junge m 112, 128
boyfriend Freund m 93
bra Büstenhalter m 116
bracelet Armband f 121
braces (suspenders) Hosenträger
m/pl 116
braised geschmort 47
brake Bremse f 78
brake fluid Bremsflüssigkeit f 75
brandy Weinbrand m, Kognak m 59
bread Brot m 36, 38, 64, 120
breaded paniert 44
break, to zerbrechen 123, 145;
(sich) brechen 139
breakdown van Abschleppwagen m
78
breakfast Frühstück nt 24, 34, 38
breast Brust f 138
breathe, to atmen 141, 142
bridge Brücke f 85
briefs Unterhose f 116
bring, to bringen 12, 71
bring down, to herunterbringen 31
British Brite (Britin) m/f 93
broiled vom Rost 40; gegrillt 47
broken kaputt 29, 119; gebrochen 140
brooch Brosche f 121
brother Bruder m 93
brown braun 113
bruise Quetschung f 139
brush Bürste f 111
Brussels sprouts Rosenkohl m 50
bubble bath Schaumbad nt 110
bucket Eimer m 106, 128
buckle Schnalle f 117
build, to (er)bauen 83

building Gebäude nt 81, 82, 83
building blocks/bricks Baukasten m 128
bulb (Glüh)birne f 28, 75, 119
burn Brandwunde f 139
bus Bus m 18, 19, 65, 72, 73, 80
business Geschäft nt 131
business trip Geschäftsreise f 93
bus stop Bushaltestelle f 72, 73
busy beschäftigt 96
but aber 15
butane gas Butangas nt 32, 106
butcher's Fleischerei f, Metzgerei f 98
butter Butter f 36, 38, 64
button Knopf m 29, 117
buy, to kaufen 82, 100

C

cabbage Kohl m 50
cabin (ship) Kabine f 74
cable Telegramm nt 133
cable car Seilbahn f 74
café Café nt 33
cake Kuchen m 37, 54, 64
cake shop Konditorei f 33, 98
calculator Rechner m 105
calendar Kalender m 104
call (phone) (Telefon)gespräch nt 135, 136; Anruf m 136
call, to (give name) heißen 10; (summon) rufen 78, 79, 156; (phone) anrufen 136; (wake) wecken 71
call at, to (boat) anlegen 74
calm ruhig 90
camel-hair Kamelhaar nt 114
camera Fotoapparat m 124, 125
camera case Fototasche f 125
camera shop Fotogeschäft nt 98
camp, to zelten 32
campbed Feldbett nt 106
camping Camping nt 32
camping equipment Camping-ausrüstung f 106
camp site Campingplatz m 32
can (of peaches) Büchse f 120
can (to be able) können 11, 12, 163
Canada Kanada (nt) 146
Canadian Kanadier(in) m/f 93
cancel, to annullieren 65
candle Kerze f 106
candy Bonbon nt 126
can opener Büchsenöffner m 106

cap Mütze f 116
caper Kaper f 51
capital (finance) Kapital nt 131
car Auto nt, Wagen m 19, 20, 26, 32, 75, 76, 78
carat Karat nt 121
caravan Wohnwagen m 32
caraway Kümmel m 51
carbon paper Durchschlagpapier nt 104
carbonated mit Kohlensäure 61
carburetor Vergaser m 78
card Karte f 93, 131
card game Kartenspiel nt 128
cardigan Wolljacke f 116
car hire Autoverleih m 19, 20
car number Kraftfahrzeugnummer f 25
car park Parkplatz m 77
car racing Autorennen nt 89
car radio Autoradio nt 119
car rental Autoverleih m 19, 20
carrot Karotte f 50
carry, to tragen 21
carton (of cigarettes) Stange (Zigaretten) f 17, 126
cartridge (camera) Kassette f 124
case (cigarettes, glasses) Etui nt 121, 123
cash, to einlösen 130, 133
cash desk Kasse f 103, 155
cassette Kassette f 119, 127, 128
castle Schloß nt, Burg f 85
catalogue Katalog m 82
cathedral Kathedrale f, Dom m 81
Catholic katholisch 84
cauliflower Blumenkohl m 49
caution Vorsicht f 79, 155; Achtung f 155
cave Höhle f 81
celery Sellerie m 50
cellophane tape Klebstreifen m 104
cemetery Friedhof m 81
centimetre Zentimeter m 112
centre Zentrum m 19, 21, 76
century Jahrhundert nt 149
ceramics Keramik f 83
cereal Getreideflocken f/pl 38
certificate Zeugnis nt 144
chain (jewellery) Kette f 121
chair Stuhl m 106
chamber music Kammermusik f 128
champagne (German) Sekt m 59
change (money) Kleingeld nt 77, 130

change, to wechseln 18, 123, 130; *(train)* umsteigen 65, 68, 73; *(reservation)* umbuchen 65
chapel Kapelle f 81
charcoal Holzkohle f 106
charge Gebühr f 32, 136; Rechnung f 28
charge, to berechnen 24; *(commission)* erheben 130
cheap billig 14, 24, 25, 101
check Scheck m 130; *(restaurant)* Rechnung f 63
check, to kontrollieren 75, 123; prüfen 75; *(luggage)* aufgeben 71
check book Scheckbuch nt 131
check in, to *(airport)* einchecken 65
check out, to abreisen 31
checkup *(medical)* Untersuchung f 142
cheers! Prost! 60
cheese Käse m 37, 38, 52, 64
chef Küchenchef m 40
chemist's Apotheke f 98, 108
cheque Scheck m 130
cheque book Scheckbuch nt 131
cherry Kirsche f 53
chess Schach nt 93
chess set Schachspiel nt 128
chest Brust(korb) m 138, 141
chewing gum Kaugummi m 126
chicken Huhn nt 48
chicory Endivie f; *(Am.)* Chicorée f 49
child Kind nt 24, 62, 82, 93, 139, 149, 159
children's doctor Kinderarzt m 137
China China *(nt)* 146
chips Pommes frites f/pl 49; *(Am.)* Kartoffelchips m/pl 64
chives Schnittlauch m 51
chocolate Schokolade f 38, 61, 64, 120, 126, 127
choice Wahl f 40
chop Kotelett nt 46
Christmas Weihnachten nt 151
church Kirche f 81, 84
cider Apfelwein m 59
cigar Zigarre f 126
cigarette Zigarette f 17, 95, 126
cigarette lighter Feuerzeug nt 121
cine camera Filmkamera f 124
cinema Kino nt 86, 96
cinnamon Zimt m 51
circle *(theatre)* Rang m 87
city Stadt f 81, 92

clam Muschel f 44
classical klassisch 128
clean sauber 62
clean, to reinigen 29, 76
cleansing cream Reinigungscreme f 110
cloakroom Garderobe f 87
clock Uhr f 119, 121, 153
clock-radio Radiowecker m 119
close *(near)* nahe 78, 98
close, to schließen 10, 82, 108, 132, 155
closed geschlossen 155
cloth Stoff m 118
clothes Kleider nt/pl 29, 116
clothes peg Wäscheklammer f 106
clothing Bekleidung f 112
cloud Wolke f 94
clove Nelke f 50
coach *(bus)* Bus m 72
coat Mantel m 116
coconut Kokosnuß f 54
cod Kabeljau m, Dorsch m 44
coffee Kaffee m 38, 61, 64
cognac Kognak m 59
coin Münze f 83
cold kalt 13, 24, 38, 62, 155
cold *(illness)* Erkältung f 108, 141
cold cuts Aufschnitt m 64
collect call R-Gespräch nt 134
cologne Kölnischwasser nt 110
colour Farbe f 103, 112, 124, 125
colour chart Farbtabelle f 30
colour fast farbecht 112
colour film Farbfilm m 124
colour negative Farbnegativ nt 124
colour shampoo Tönungsshampoo nt 111
colour slide Farbdia nt 124
colour television *(set)* Farbfernseher m 119
comb Kamm m 111
come, to kommen 36, 59, 92, 95, 137, 144, 146
comedy Komödie f 86
commission Gebühr f 86
common *(frequent)* gebräuchlich 154
compact disc Compact Disc f 127
compartment Abteil nt 70
compass Kompaß m 106
complaint Reklamation f 62
concert Konzert nt 88
concert hall Konzerthalle f 81, 88
conductor *(orchestra)* Dirigent m 88

confirm, to bestätigen 65
confirmation Bestätigung f 23
congratulation Glückwunsch m 152
connection (train) Anschluß m 65, 68
constipation Verstopfung f 140
contact lens Kontaktlinse f 123
contain, to enthalten 37
contraceptive Verhütungsmittel nt 109
contract Vertrag m 131
control Kontrolle f 16
convent Kloster nt 81
convention hall Kongreßhalle f 81
conversion Umrechnung f 157
cookie Keks m 64
cool box Kühltasche f 106
copper Kupfer nt 122
corduroy Kordsamt m 114
cork Korken m 62
corkscrew Korkenzieher m 106
corn (Am.) Mais m 50; (foot) Hühnerauge nt 109
corner Ecke f 21, 36, 77
corn plaster Hühneraugenpflaster nt 109
cost Kosten pl 131
cost, to kosten 10, 20, 80, 133
cotton Baumwolle f 114
cotton wool Watte f 109
cough Husten m 108, 141
cough, to husten 142
cough drops Hustenpastillen f/pl 109
counter Schalter m 133
country Land nt 93
countryside Landschaft f, Land nt 85
court house Gericht(sgebäude) nt 81
cousin Cousin(e) m/f 93
cramp Krampf m 141
cranberry Preiselbeere f 53
crayfish (river) Krebs m 41, 44
crayon Buntstift m 104
cream Sahne f 54, 61; (toiletry) Creme f 110
credit Kredit m 130
credit card Kreditkarte f 20, 31, 63, 102, 130
cress Kresse f 51
crisps Kartoffelchips m/pl 64
crockery Geschirr nt 106, 107
croissant Hörnchen nt 38
cross Kreuz nt 121
cross-country skiing Langlauf m 91
crossing (by sea) Überfahrt f 74
crossroads Kreuzung f 77

cruise Kreuzfahrt f 74
crystal Kristall m 122
cuckoo clock Kuckucksuhr f 121, 127
cucumber Gurke f 50
cuff link Manschettenknopf m 121
cuisine Küche f 35
cup Tasse f 36, 61, 107
curler Lockenwickler m 111
currency Währung f 129
currency exchange office Wechselstube f 18, 67, 129
current Strömung f 90
curtain Vorhang m 28
customs Zoll m 16, 102
cut (wound) Schnittwunde f 139
cut, to schneiden 30
cut off, to (phone) unterbrechen 135
cut glass geschliffenes Glas nt 122
cutlery Besteck nt 106, 107; Tafelbesteck nt 121
cutlet Kotelett nt 45
cycling Radfahren nt 89
cystitis Blasenentzündung f 142

D

dairy Milchhandlung f 98
dance, to tanzen 88, 96
danger Gefahr f 155, 156
dangerous gefährlich 90
dark dunkel 24, 56, 101, 112, 113
date (day) Datum nt 25, 150; (appointment) Verabredung f 95; (fruit) Dattel f 53
daughter Tochter f 93
day Tag m 16, 20, 26, 32, 80, 150, 151
daylight Tageslicht nt 124
day off freier Tag m 151
decade Jahrzehnt nt 149
decaffeinated koffeinfrei 38, 61
December Dezember m 150
decision Entscheidung f 24, 102
deck (ship) Deck nt 74
deck-chair Liegestuhl m 91, 106
declare, to (customs) verzollen 17
deep tief 142
delay Verspätung f 69
delicatessen Delikatessengeschäft nt 98
deliver, to liefern 102
delivery Lieferung f 102
Denmark Dänemark (nt) 146

eighteen achtzehn 147
eighth achte 148
eighty achtzig 147
elastic elastisch 109
elastic bandage elastische Binde f 109
Elastoplast Heftpflaster nt 109
electric(al) elektrisch 119
electrician Elektriker m 98
electricity (facilities) Stromanschluß m 32
electronic elektronisch 125, 128
elevator Fahrstuhl m 27, 100; Aufzug m 155
eleven elf 147
embarkation point Anlegeplatz m 74
embroidery Stickerei f 127
emerald Smaragd m 122
emergency Notfall m 156; (phone) Notruf m 155, 156
emergency exit Notausgang m 27, 99, 155
emery board Sandpapierfeile f 110
empty leer 13
enamel Email nt 122
end Ende nt 69, 150
endive Chicorée f; (Am.) Endivie f 49
engaged (phone) besetzt 136
engagement ring Verlobungsring m 122
engine (car) Motor m 78
England England (nt) 146
English englisch 104, 126
English englisch nt 11, 16, 84, 137
English Engländer(in) m/f 93
enjoyable angenehm 31
enjoy oneself, to sich gut unterhalten 96
enlarge, to vergrößern 125
enough genug 14
enquiry Auskunft f 68
entrance Eingang m 67, 99; Zutritt m 155
entrance fee Eintritt m 82
envelope Briefumschlag m 27, 104
equipment Ausrüstung f 91, 106
eraser Radiergummi m 105
escalator Rolltreppe f 100
especially besonders 161
estimate (cost) Kostenvoranschlag m 131
Europe Europa (nt) 146
evening Abend m 9, 87, 95, 96, 151, 153

evening dress Abendgarderobe f 88; (woman) Abendkleid nt 116
everything alles 31
exchange, to umtauschen 103
exchange rate Wechselkurs m 18, 130
excursion Ausflug m 80
excuse me Entschuldigung 26, 78; Verzeihung 70, 153
exercise book Schreibheft nt 104
exhaust pipe Auspuff m 78
exhibition Ausstellung f 81
exit Ausgang m 67, 99, 155; (motorway) Ausfahrt f 79
expect, to erwarten 130
expenses Unkosten pl 131
expensive teuer 13, 19, 24, 101
exposure (photography) Aufnahme f 124
express per Expreß 132
expression Ausdruck m 9; Redewendung f 100
expressway Autobahn f 76
extension (phone) Nebenanschluß m 135
extension cord/lead Verlängerungsschnur f 119
extra zusätzlich 24
extract, to (tooth) ziehen 145
eye Auge nt 123, 138, 139
eye drops Augentropfen m/pl 109
eye liner Lidstift m 110
eye pencil Augenbrauenstift m 110
eye shadow Lidschatten m 110
eye specialist Augenarzt m 137

F

fabric Stoff m 113
face Gesicht nt 138
face-pack Gesichtsmaske f 30
face powder Gesichtspuder m 110
factory Fabrik f 81
fair Messe f 81
fall (autumn) Herbst m 149
family Familie f 93, 144
fan Ventilator m 28
fan belt Keilriemen m 75
far weit 14, 21, 100
fare Fahrpreis m 21, 68, 73
farm Bauernhof m 85
fat Fett nt 37
father Vater m 93
faucet Wasserhahn m 28
February Februar m 150

fee *(doctor)* Honorar nt 144
feeding bottle Saugflasche f 111
feel, to *(physical state)* sich fühlen 140, 142
felt Filz m 114
felt-tip pen Filzstift m 105
fennel Fenchel m 50
ferry Fähre f 74
fever Fieber nt 140
few wenige 14; *(a)* einige 14
field Feld nt 85
fifteen fünfzehn 147
fifth fünfte 148
fifty fünfzig 147
fig Feige f 53
file *(tool)* Feile f 110
fill in, to ausfüllen 26, 144
filling *(tooth)* Plombe f 145
filling station Tankstelle f 75
film Film m 86, 124, 125
film winder Filmtransport m 125
filter Filter m 125, 126
filter-tipped mit Filter 126
find, to finden 10, 11, 84, 100
fine *(OK)* gut 24
fine arts bildende Künste f/pl 83
fine grain *(film)* Feinkorn 124
finger Finger m 138
fire Feuer nt 156
first erste 68, 72, 148
first-aid kit Verbandkasten m 106
first class erste Klasse f 69
first name Vorname m 25
fish Fisch m 43
fish, to angeln 90
fishing permit Angelschein m 90
fishing tackle Angelzeug nt 106
fishmonger's Fischhandlung f 98
fit, to passen 115
fitting room Umkleidekabine f 115
five fünf 147
fix, to flicken 75, 145
fizzy *(mineral water)* mit Kohlensäure 61
flannel Flanell m 114
flash *(photography)* Blitzlicht nt 125
flash attachment Blitzgerät nt 125
flashlight Taschenlampe f 106
flat flach 118
flat *(apartment)* Wohnung f 22
flat tyre Reifenpanne f 75; Platter m 78
flea market Flohmarkt m 81
flight Flug m 65

flight number Flugnummer f 65
floor Etage f 27; Stock m 154
florist's Blumengeschäft nt 98
flounder Flunder f 44
flour Mehl nt 37
flower Blume f 85
flu Grippe f 142
fluid Flüssigkeit f 75
fog Nebel m 94
folding chair Klappstuhl m 106
folding table Klapptisch m 107
folk music Volksmusik f 128
food Essen nt 37, 62; Nahrung f 111
food box Proviantbehälter m 106
food poisoning Lebensmittelvergiftung f 142
foot Fuß m 138
football Fußball m 89
foot cream Fußcreme f 110
footpath Fußweg m 85
foot powder Fußpuder m 110
for für 14; während 143
forbid, to verbieten 155
forest Wald m 85
fork Gabel f 36, 62, 107
form *(document)* Formular nt 133; Schein m 25, 26
fortnight zwei Wochen f/pl 151
fortress Festung f 81
forty vierzig 147
forwarding address Nachsendeadresse f 31
fountain Brunnen m, Springbrunnen m 81
fountain pen Füllfederhalter m 105
four vier 147
fourteen vierzehn 147
fourth vierte 148
fowl Geflügel nt 48
frame *(glasses)* Gestell nt 123
France Frankreich *(nt)* 146
free frei 13, 70, 82, 95, 155
french fries Pommes frites f/pl 49
fresh frisch 53, 62
Friday Freitag m 150
fried gebraten 44, 47
fried egg Spiegelei nt 38
friend Freund(in) m/f 93, 95
fringe Ponyfransen f/pl 30
frock Kleid nt 116
frog Frosch m 41
from von 14
front vorne, Vorder- 75
frost Frost m 94

fruit Obst nt 37, 53
fruit cocktail Obstsalat m 53, 54
fruit juice Fruchtsaft m 37, 61
frying-pan Bratpfanne f 106
full voll 13; belegt 155
full board Vollpension f 24
full insurance Vollkaskoversicherung f 20
fur coat Pelzmantel m 116
furniture Möbel nt/pl 83
furrier's Pelzgeschäft nt 98

G

gallery Galerie f 81
game Spiel nt 128; (food) Wild nt 40
garage (parking) Garage f 26; (repairs) Reparaturwerkstatt f 78
garden Garten m 85
gardens Grünanlage f 81
garlic Knoblauch m 51
gas Gas nt 156
gasoline Benzin nt 75, 78
gastritis Magenschleimhautentzündung f 142
gauze Verbandmull m 109
gem Edelstein m 121
general allgemein 26, 100
general delivery postlagernd 133
general practitioner praktischer Arzt m 137
gentleman Herr m 155
genuine echt 118
geology Geologie f 83
German deutsch 114
German Deutsch nt 11, 95
Germany Deutschland (nt) 146
get, to (find) finden 19, 21; (obtain) bekommen 10, 32, 90, 108, 134; (taxi) bestellen 31; (fetch) holen 137, 156
get back, to zurück sein 80
get off, to aussteigen 73
get to, to kommen nach/zu 19, 100; ankommen in 70
get up, to aufstehen 144
gherkin Essiggurke f 50, 64
gift (present) Geschenk nt 17
ginger Ingwer m 51
girdle Hüfthalter m 116
girl Mädchen nt 112, 128
girlfriend Freundin f 93, 95
give, to geben 12, 13, 123, 126
give way (traffic) Vorfahrt gewähren 79

glad (to know you) sehr erfreut 92
gland Drüse f 138
glass Glas nt 36, 56, 59, 60, 62, 143
glasses Brille f 123
glassware Glaswaren f/pl 127
gloomy düster 84
glove Handschuh m 116
glue Leim m 105
go, to gehen 96, 163
go away, to weggehen 156
go out, to ausgehen 96
gold Gold nt 121, 122
golden golden 113
gold-plated vergoldet 122
golf Golf nt 89
golf course Golfplatz m 89
good gut 13, 101
good-bye auf Wiedersehen 9
Good Friday Karfreitag m 152
goods Waren f/pl 16
goose Gans f 48
gooseberry Stachelbeere f 53
gram Gramm nt 120
grammar book Grammatik f 105
grape (Wein)traube f 53, 64
grape juice Traubensaft m 61
grapefruit Grapefruit f, Pampelmuse f 53
grapefruit juice Grapefruitsaft m 38
gravy Soße f 48
gray grau 113
graze Abschürfung f 139
greasy fettig 30, 110, 111
great (excellent) prima 95
Great Britain Großbritannien (nt) 146
Greece Griechenland (nt) 146
green grün 113
green bean grüne Bohne f 49
greengrocer's Gemüsehandlung f 98
green salad grüner Salat m 50
greeting Begrüßung f 9; Gruß m 151
grey grau 113
grilled gegrillt 44, 47; vom Rost 40
grocery Lebensmittelgeschäft nt 98, 120
groundsheet Zeltboden m 106
group Gruppe f 82
guide Fremdenführer(in) m/f 80
guidebook (Reise)führer m 82, 104, 105
gum (teeth) Zahnfleisch nt 145
gynaecologist Frauenarzt m 137, 141

H

habit Gewohnheit f 34
haddock Schellfisch m 44
hair Haar nt 30, 111
hairbrush Haarbürste f 111
haircut Haarschnitt m 30
hairdresser's Friseur m 27, 30, 99
hair dryer Haartrockner m 119
hair dye Haarfärbemittel nt 111
hairgrip Haarklemme f 111
hair lotion Haarwasser nt 111
half Hälfte f 148
half a dozen halbes Dutzend nt 120
half an hour halbe Stunde f 153
half board Halbpension f 24
half price (ticket) zum halben Preis 69
halibut Heilbutt m 44
hall (large room) Halle f 81, 88
ham Schinken m 38, 41, 46, 64
hammer Hammer m 106
hand Hand f 138
handbag Handtasche f 116
hand cream Handcreme f 110
handicrafts Kunsthandwerk nt 83
handkerchief Taschentuch nt 116
handmade Handarbeit f 113
hanger Kleiderbügel m 27
hangover Kater m 108
happy glücklich, froh 151, 152
harbour Hafen m 74, 81
hard hart 52, 123
hard-boiled (egg) hartgekocht 38
hardware shop Eisenwarenhandlung
  f 98
hare Hase m 48
hat Hut m 116, 127
have, to haben 162
hay fever Heufieber nt 108
hazelnut Haselnuß f 53
he er 162
head Kopf m 138, 139
headache Kopfschmerzen m/pl 141
headphones Kopfhörer m 119
head waiter Oberkellner m 62
health food shop Reformhaus nt 98
health insurance Krankenkasse f 144
health insurance form Kranken-
  kassenformular nt 144
heart Herz nt 138
heart attack Herzanfall m 141
heat, to heizen 90
heath Heide f 85
heating Heizung f 28
heavy schwer 13, 101

heel Absatz m 118
helicopter Hubschrauber m 74
hello! (phone) Hallo! 135
help Hilfe f 156
help, to helfen 12, 21, 71, 100,
  134; (oneself) sich bedienen 120
her ihr 161
herb Kraut nt 51
herb tea Kräutertee m 60
here hier 15
herring Hering m 41, 44
high hoch 85, 141
high season Hauptsaison f 149
high tide Flut f 90
hike, to wandern 74
hill Hügel m 85
hire Verleih m 20, 74
hire, to mieten 19, 20, 74, 89, 91;
  vermieten 155
his sein 161
history Geschichte f 83
hitchhike, to trampen 74
hole Loch nt 29
holiday Feiertag m 151
holidays Ferien pl, Urlaub m 151
home address Wohnort m 25; Wohn-
  adresse f 31
home-made hausgemacht 40
homeopathic homöopathisch 109
honey Honig m 38
horse racing Pferderennen nt 89
horseback riding Reiten nt 89
horseradish Meerrettich m 51
hospital Krankenhaus nt 142, 144
hot heiß 14, 24, 38, 61, 155
hotel Hotel nt 19, 21, 22, 80
hotel guide Hotelverzeichnis nt 19,
  22
hotel reservation Hotelreservierung f
  20
hot water warmes Wasser nt 23, 28
hot-water bottle Wärmflasche f 27
hour Stunde f 153
house Haus nt 83, 85
how wie 10
how far wie weit 10, 76, 85
how long wie lange 10, 24
how many wie viele 10
how much wieviel 10, 24
hundred (ein)hundert 147
Hungary Ungarn m 146
hungry hungrig 35; (to be) Hunger
  haben 12, 35
hurry (to be in a) es eilig haben 21, 31

hurt, to weh tun 139; schmerzen 145; *(oneself)* sich verletzen 139
husband Mann *m* 93
hydrofoil Tragflächenboot *nt* 74

I
I ich 162
ice Eis *nt* 94
ice-cream Eis *nt* 54, 64
ice cube Eiswürfel *m* 27
iced tea Eistee *m* 61
ice pack Kühlbeutel *m* 106
ill krank 140, 156
illness Krankheit *f* 140
important wichtig 12
imported importiert 113
impressive eindrucksvoll 84
in in 14
included inbegriffen 20, 24, 31, 32, 40, 63, 80
indigestion Magenverstimmung *f* 141
inexpensive preiswert 35; billig 124
infect, to infizieren 140
infection Infektion *f* 145
inflammation Entzündung *f* 142
inflation Inflation *f* 131
inflation rate Inflationsrate *f* 131
influenza Grippe *f* 142
information Auskunft *f* 67, 155
injection Spritze *f* 142, 144, 145
injure, to verletzen 139
injured verletzt 79, 139
injury Verletzung *f* 139
ink Tinte *f* 105
inn Gasthaus *nt*, Gasthof *m* 22, 33
inquiry Auskunft *f* 68
insect bite Insektenstich *m* 108, 139
insect repellent Insektenschutz *m* 109
insect spray Insektizid *nt* 109
inside drinnen 15
instead statt 37
insurance Versicherung *f* 20, 79
insurance company Versicherungs-gesellschaft *f* 79
interest *(on investment)* Zinsen *m/pl* 131
interested, to be sich interessieren 83, 96
interesting interessant 84
international international 133, 134
interpreter Dolmetscher *m* 131
intersection Kreuzung *f* 77
introduce, to vorstellen 92

introduction *(social)* Vorstellung *f* 92; *(letter)* Empfehlungsbrief *m* 130
investment Kapitalanlage *f* 131
invitation Einladung *f* 94
invite, to einladen 94
invoice Rechnung *f* 131
iodine Jod *nt* 109
Ireland Irland *(nt)* 146
Irish Ire (Irin) *m/f* 93
iron *(laundry)* Bügeleisen *nt* 119
iron, to bügeln 29
ironmonger's Eisenwarenhandlung *f* 99
Italy Italien *(nt)* 146
its sein 161
ivory Elfenbein *nt* 122

J
jacket Jackett *nt*, Jacke *f* 116
jade Jade *f* 122
jam Marmelade *f* 38, 120
jam, to klemmen 28, 125
January Januar *m* 150
Japan Japan *(nt)* 146
jar Glas *nt* 120
jaundice Gelbsucht *f* 142
jaw Kiefer *m* 138
jeans Jeans *pl* 116
jersey Strickjacke *f* 116
jeweller's Juwelier *m* 99, 121
joint Gelenk *nt* 138
journey Fahrt *f* 72
juice Saft *m* 38, 61
July Juli *m* 150
jumper *(sweater)* Pullover *m* 116
June Juni *m* 150
juniper Wacholder *m* 51
just *(only)* nur 16, 37, 100

K
kerosene Petroleum *nt* 106
ketchup Tomatenketchup *nt* 51
key Schlüssel *m* 26
kidney Niere *f* 138
kilogram Kilo(gramm) *nt* 120
kilometre Kilometer *m* 20
kind nett, freundlich 95
king-size extra lang 126
knee Knie *nt* 138
knife Messer *nt* 36, 61, 107
knock, to klopfen 155
know, to wissen 16, 26; kennen 96, 114

L

label Etikett nt 105
lace Spitze f 114
lady Dame f 155
lake See m 23, 81, 85, 90
lamb Lamm(fleisch) nt 45
lamp Lampe f 29, 106, 119
landmark Wahrzeichen nt 85
landscape Landschaft f 92
lane (in town) Gasse f 154
lantern Laterne f 106
large groß 20, 101, 118, 130
last letzte 13, 68, 72, 149, 150, 151
last name (Familien)name m 25
late spät 13
later später 135
laugh, to lachen 95
launderette Waschsalon m 99
laundry (place) Wäscherei f 29, 99; (clothes) Wäsche f 29
laundry service Wäschedienst m 23
laxative Abführmittel nt 109
lead (theatre) Hauptrolle f 86
lead-free bleifrei 75
leap year Schaltjahr nt 149
leather Leder nt 114, 118
leather goods Lederwaren f/pl 127
leather trousers Lederhose f 116
leave, to lassen 26, 96, 156; (go away) abreisen 31; abfahren 68, 74
leek Lauch m 50
left linke 13; links 21, 30, 63, 69, 77, 79
left-luggage office Gepäckaufbewahrung f 67, 71
leg Bein nt 138
lemon Zitrone f 37, 38, 53, 54, 60
lemonade Limonade f 61
lens (glasses) Glas nt 123; (camera) Objektiv nt 125
lentil Linse f 43
less weniger 14
let, to (hire out) vermieten 155
letter Brief m 132
letter box Briefkasten m 132
letter of credit Kreditbrief m 130
lettuce Lattich m 50
library Bibliothek f 81, 99
licence (for driving) Führerschein m 20, 79
lie down, to sich hinlegen 142
life belt Rettungsring m 74
life boat Rettungsboot nt 74
lifeguard Rettungsdienst m 90

lift Fahrstuhl m 27, 100; Aufzug m 155
light leicht 13, 54, 59, 101; (colour) hell 101, 112, 113, 126
light Licht nt 28, 124; (cigarette) Feuer nt 95
lighter Feuerzeug nt 126
lighter fluid Benzin fürs Feuerzeug nt 126
lighter gas Gas fürs Feuerzeug nt 126
light meter Belichtungsmesser m 125
light music Unterhaltungsmusik f 128
lightning Blitz m 94
like, to (want) gerne haben 12, 23; mögen 20, 38; (take pleasure) gefallen 24, 92, 102, 112
line Linie f 73
linen (cloth) Leinen nt 114
lip Lippe f 138
lipsalve Lippenpomade f 110
lipstick Lippenstift m 110
liqueur Likör m 59, 60
liquid Flüssigkeit f 123
listen, to hören 127
litre Liter m 75, 120
little (a) ein wenig 14
live, to leben 83; (reside) wohnen 83
liver Leber f 46, 138
lobster Hummer m 41, 44
local hiesig 36, 60
local train Nahverkehrszug m 66, 69
long lang 26, 62, 76, 77, 78, 116
long-sighted weitsichtig 123
look, to sehen 123; sich umsehen 100
look for, to suchen 12
look out! Vorsicht! 156
loose (clothes) weit 116
lose, to verlieren 123, 156; (one's way) sich verirren 12, 156
loss Verlust m 131
lost and found office Fundbüro nt 67, 156
lost property office Fundbüro nt 67, 156
lot (a) eine Menge 14; viel 162
lotion Lotion f 110
loud (voice) laut 135
love, to lieben 163
lovely (wunder)schön 84; herrlich 94
low niedrig 141
lower untere 69, 70

low season Vorsaison f, Nachsaison f 149
low tide Ebbe f 90
luck Glück nt 152
luggage Gepäck nt 18, 26, 31, 71
luggage locker Schließfach nt 18, 67, 71
luggage trolley Kofferkuli m 18, 71
lump (bump) Beule f 139
lunch Mittagessen nt 34, 80, 94
lung Lunge f 138
Luxembourg Luxemburg (nt) 146

M

machine Maschine f 114
mackerel Makrele f 41, 44
magazine Illustrierte f 105
magnificent großartig 84
maid Zimmermädchen nt 26
mail, to aufgeben 28
mail Post f 28, 133
mailbox Briefkasten m 132
main Haupt- 40, 67, 80
make, to machen 131
make a mistake, to (bill) sich verrechnen 31, 63, 102
make up, to machen 28, 71, 108
man Herr m 115, 155; Mann m 159
manager Direktor m 26
manicure Maniküre f 30
many viele 14
map Karte f 76, 105; Plan m 105
March März m 150
marinated mariniert 44
marjoram Majoran m 51
market Markt m 81, 99
marmalade Apfelsinenmarmelade f 38
married verheiratet 93
mass (church) Messe f 84
match Streichholz nt 106, 126; (sport) Wettkampf m 89
match, to (colour) passen 112
material (fabric) Stoff m 113
matinée Nachmittagsvorstellung f 87
mattress Matratze f 106
May Mai m 150
may (can) können 11, 12, 163
meadow Wiese f 85
meal Mahlzeit f 24, 143; Essen nt 34, 63
mean, to bedeuten 10, 25
means Mittel nt 74
measles Masern f/pl 142

measure, to Maß nehmen 114
meat Fleisch nt 40, 45, 46, 62
mechanic Mechaniker m 78
medical ärztlich 144
medical certificate ärztliches Zeugnis nt 144
medicine Medizin f 83; (drug) Medikament nt 143
medium (meat) mittel 47
medium-sized mittlere 20
meet, to treffen 96
melon Melone f 53
memorial Denkmal nt 81
mend, to flicken 75; (clothes) ausbessern 29
menu Gedeck nt 36, 39; Menü nt 39; (printed) Speisekarte f 36, 39, 40
merry fröhlich 151
message Nachricht f 28, 136
metre Meter m 112
middle Mitte f 69, 87, 150
midnight Mitternacht f 153
mild mild 52, 126
mileage Kilometergeld nt 20
milk Milch f 38, 61, 64
milkshake Milchmixgetränk nt 61
million Million f 148
mineral water Mineralwasser nt 61
minister (religion) Pfarrer m 84
mint Pfefferminz(e) f 51
minute Minute f 21, 153
mirror Spiegel m 115, 123
miscellaneous verschieden 127
Miss Fräulein nt 9
miss, to fehlen 18, 29, 62
mistake Irrtum m 62
mixed gemischt 50
modified American plan Halbpension f 24
moment Augenblick m 11, 136
monastery Kloster nt 81
Monday Montag m 150
money Geld 129, 130
money order Postanweisung f 133
month Monat m 16, 150
monument Denkmal nt 81
moon Mond m 94
moped Moped nt 74
more mehr 14
morning Morgen m 151, 153
mortgage Hypothek f 131
mosque Moschee f 84
mother Mutter f 93
motorbike Motorrad nt 74

motorboat Motorboot nt 91
motorway Autobahn f 76
mountain Berg m 23, 85
mountaineering Bergsteigen nt 89
moustache Schnurrbart m 31
mouth Mund m 138
mouthwash Mundwasser nt 109
move, to bewegen 139
movie Film m 86
movie camera Filmkamera f 124
movies Kino nt 86, 96
Mr. Herr m 9, 131
Mrs. Frau f 9, 131
much viel 14
mug Becher m 107; (beer) Maß f 56
muscle Muskel m 138
museum Museum nt 81
mushroom Pilz m 41, 50
music Musik f 83, 128
musical Musical nt 86
music box Spieldose f 121, 127
mussel Muschel f 41, 44
must, to müssen 23, 31, 95, 101
mustard Senf m 37, 51, 64
mutton Hammelfleisch nt 45
my mein 161
myself selbst 120

N

nail (human) Nagel m 110
nail brush Nagelbürste f 110
nail clippers Nagelzange f 110
nail file Nagelfeile f 110
nail polish Nagellack m 110
nail polish remover Nagellack-
    entferner m 110
nail scissors Nagelschere f 110
name Name m 23, 25, 79, 136
napkin Serviette f 36, 105, 106
nappy Windel f 111
narrow eng 118
nationality Nationalität f 25
natural history Naturkunde f 83
near nah 13
nearby in der Nähe 77, 84
nearest nächste 78, 98
neat (drink) pur 59
necessary nötig 88
neck Hals m 138; (nape) Nacken m
    30
necklace Halskette f 121
need, to brauchen 29, 118, 137
needle Nadel f 27
negative Negativ nt 125

nephew Neffe m 93
nerve Nerv m 138
nervous system Nervensystem nt
    138
Netherlands Niederlande pl 146
never nie 15
new neu 13
newsagent's Zeitungshändler m 99
newspaper Zeitung f 104, 105
newsstand Zeitungsstand m 19, 67,
    99, 104
New Year Neujahr nt 151
New Zealand Neuseeland (nt) 146
next nächste 13, 65, 68, 73, 76,
    149, 150
next time nächstes Mal 95
next to neben 14
nice (beautiful) schön 94, 152
niece Nichte f 93
night Nacht f 9, 24, 151
nightclub Nachtlokal nt 88
night cream Nachtcreme f 110
nightdress Nachthemd nt 116
nine neun 147
nineteen neunzehn 147
ninety neunzig 147
ninth neunte 148
no nein 9
noisy laut 24
nonalcoholic alkoholfrei 61
none kein 15
nonsmoker Nichtraucher m 70
non-smoking Nichtraucher- 36
noodle Nudel f 49
noon Mittag m 153
normal normal 30, 110
north Nord(en) m 77
North America Nordamerika (nt) 146
Norway Norwegen (nt) 146
nose Nase f 138
nosebleed Nasenbluten nt 141
nose drops Nasentropfen m/pl 109
not nicht 15, 163
note (banknote) Schein m 130
notebook Notizheft nt 105
note paper Briefpapier nt 105
nothing nichts 15, 17
notice (sign) Tafel f, Hinweis m 155
notify, to benachrichtigen 144
November November m 150
now jetzt 15
number Nummer f 25, 65, 134,
    136; Zahl f 124, 147
nurse Krankenschwester f 144

DICTIONARY

O

occupation *(job)* Beruf m 93
occupied besetzt 13, 70, 155
October Oktober m 150
office Büro nt 22, 80
oil Öl nt 51, 75, 111
oily *(greasy)* fettig 30, 111
old alt 13
old town Altstadt f 82
omelet Omelett nt 64
on an, auf 14
once einmal 148
one eins 147
one-way *(ticket)* einfach 69
on foot zu Fuß 76
onion Zwiebel f 50
only nur 15
on time pünktlich 68
onyx Onyx m 122
open offen 13, 82
open, to öffnen 10, 17, 82, 108, 132; *(account)* eröffnen 130
opening hours Öffnungszeiten f/pl 82
opera Oper f 88
opera house Opernhaus nt 82, 88
operation Operation f 144
operator Vermittlung f 134
operetta Operette f 88
opposite gegenüber 77
optician Optiker m 99, 123
or oder 15
orange orange 113
orange Orange f 53, 64; Apfelsine f 53
orange juice Orangensaft m 38, 61
orangeade Orangeade f 61
orchestra Orchester nt 88; *(seats)* Parkett nt 87
orchestral music Orchestermusik f 128
order *(goods, meal)* Bestellung f 40, 102
order, to *(goods, meal)* bestellen 36, 62, 102, 103
ornithology Vogelkunde f 83
other andere 59
our unser 161
out of order außer Betrieb 155
out of stock nicht vorrätig 103
outlet *(electric)* Steckdose f 27
outside draußen 15, 36
oval oval 101
over über 14

over there dort drüben 69
overalls Overall m 116
overdone zu stark gebraten 62
overheat, to *(engine)* heißlaufen 78
overnight *(stay)* eine Nacht 26
overwhelming überwältigend 84
owe, to schulden 144
oyster Auster f 41, 43

P

pacifier Schnuller m 111
packet Packung f 120; Schachtel f 126
page *(hotel)* Page m 26
pail Eimer m 106, 128
pain Schmerz m 140, 141, 144
painkiller Schmerzmittel nt 109
paint Farbe f 155
paint, to malen 83
paintbox Malkasten m 105
painter Maler m 83
painting Malerei f 83
pair Paar nt 116, 118, 149
pajamas Schlafanzug m 117
palace Palast m, Schloß nt 81
palpitation Herzklopfen nt 141
panties Schlüpfer m 116
pants *(trousers)* Hose f 116
panty girdle Strumpfhalterhöschen nt 116
panty hose Strumpfhose f 116
paper Papier nt 105
paperback Taschenbuch nt 105
paperclip Büroklammer f 105
paper napkin Papierserviette f 105
paraffin *(fuel)* Petroleum nt 106
parcel Paket nt 133
pardon? Wie bitte? 10
parents Eltern pl 93
park Park m 82
park, to parken 26, 77
parking Parken nt 77, 79
parking disc Parkscheibe f 77
parking meter Parkuhr f 77
parliament Parlament nt 82
parsley Petersilie f 51
part Teil m 138
parting *(part)* Scheitel m 30
partridge Rebhuhn nt 48
party *(social gathering)* Party f 95
pass *(rail, bus)* Mehrfahrkarte f 72
pass *(mountain)* Paß m 85
passport Paß m 16, 17, 25, 26
passport photo Paßbild nt 124

Wörterverzeichnis

pass through, to auf der Durchreise sein 16
pasta Teigwaren f/pl 49
paste *(glue)* Klebstoff m 105
pastry Gebäck nt 54
pastry shop Konditorei f 99
patch, to *(clothes)* flicken 29
path Weg m 85
patient Patient(in) m/f 144
pay, to (be)zahlen 31, 63, 68, 102, 136
payment Zahlung f 131
pea Erbse f 50
peach Pfirsich m 53
peak Bergspitze f 85
peanut Erdnuß f 53
pear Birne f 53
pearl Perle f 122
pedestrian Fußgänger m 79
peg *(tent)* Hering m 107
pen Feder f 105
pencil Bleistift m 105
pencil sharpener Bleistiftspitzer m 105
pendant Anhänger m 121
penicillin Penizillin nt 143
penknife Taschenmesser nt 106
pensioner Rentner(in) m/f 82
people Leute pl 93
pepper Pfeffer m 37, 51, 64
per cent Prozent nt 148
percentage Prozentsatz m 131
perch Barsch m 43
per day pro Tag 20, 32, 89
performance *(session)* Vorstellung f 87
perfume Parfüm m 110
perhaps vielleicht 15
per hour pro Stunde 77, 89
period *(monthly)* Periode f 141
period pains Menstruationsbeschwerden f/pl 141
permanent wave Dauerwelle f 30
per night pro Nacht 24
per person pro Person 32
person Person f 32, 36
personal persönlich 17
personal call Gespräch mit Voranmeldung nt 134
per week pro Woche 20, 24
petrol Benzin m 75, 78
pewter Zinn nt 122
pheasant Fasan m 48
phone Telefon m 28, 78, 79, 134

phone, to telefonieren 134
phone booth Telefonzelle f 134
phone call (Telefon)gespräch nt 135, 136; Anruf m 136
phone number Telefonnummer f 96, 134, 135
photo Foto nt 124, 125
photocopy Fotokopie f 131
photograph, to fotografieren 82
photographer Fotograf m 99
photography Fotografie f 124
phrase Ausdruck m 11
pick up, to *(person)* abholen 80, 96
picnic Picknick nt 63
picture Bild nt 82; *(photo)* Foto nt 82
piece Stück nt 29, 52, 64, 120
pigeon Taube f 48
pill Pille f 141
pillow Kopfkissen nt 27
pin Nadel f 110; *(brooch)* Anstecknadel f 121
pineapple Ananas f 53
pink rosa 113
pipe Pfeife f 126, 127
pipe cleaner Pfeifenreiniger m 126
pipe tobacco Pfeifentabak m 126
place Ort m 25, 76
place of birth Geburtsort m 25
plaice Scholle f 44
plane Flugzeug nt 65, 159
plaster *(cast)* Gipsverband m 140
plastic Plastik nt 107
plastic bag Plastikbeutel m 106
plate Teller m 36, 62, 107
platform *(station)* Bahnsteig m 67, 68, 69, 70
platinum Platin m 122
play *(theatre)* Stück nt 86
play, to spielen 86, 88, 89, 93
playground Spielplatz m 32
playing card Spielkarte f 105
please bitte 9
plimsolls Turnschuhe m/pl 118
plug *(electric)* Stecker m 29, 119
plum Pflaume f 53
pneumonia Lungenentzündung f 142
pocket Tasche f 117
pocket calculator Taschenrechner m 105
pocket dictionary Taschenwörterbuch nt 104
pocket watch Taschenuhr f 121
point, to *(show)* zeigen 11
poison Gift nt 109

poisoning Vergiftung f 142
Poland Polen (nt) 146
police Polizei f 78, 156
police station Polizeiwache f 99, 156
pond Teich m 85
pop music Popmusik f 128
poplin Popeline m 114
porcelain Porzellan nt 127
pork Schweinefleisch nt 45
port Hafen m 74; (wine) Portwein m 59
portable tragbar, Koffer- 119
porter Gepäckträger m 18, 71; (hotel) Hausdiener m 26
portion Portion f 37, 54, 62
possible möglich 137
post (letters) Post f 28, 133
post, to aufgeben 28
postage Porto nt 132
postage stamp Briefmarke f 28, 126, 132
postcard Postkarte f 105, 126, 132
poste restante postlagernd 133
post office Postamt nt 99, 132
potato Kartoffel f 48, 49
pottery Töpferei f 83
poultry Geflügel nt 48
pound (money) Pfund nt 18, 102, 130; (weight) Pfund nt 120
powder Puder m 110
powder compact Puderdose f 122
prawn Garnele f 44
pregnant schwanger 141
premium (gasoline) Super nt 75
prescribe, to verschreiben 143
prescription Rezept m 108, 143
present (gift) Geschenk m 17, 121
press, to (iron) dampfbügeln 29
press stud Druckknopf m 117
pressure Druck m 75
pretty hübsch 84
price Preis m 40, 69
priest Priester m 84
print (photo) Abzug m 125
private privat 91, 155
private toilet eigene Toilette f 23
processing (photo) Entwickeln nt 124
profession Beruf m 25
profit Gewinn m 131
programme Programm nt 87
prohibit, to verbieten 155
pronunciation Aussprache f 6

Protestant protestantisch, evangelisch 84
provide, to besorgen 131
prune Backpflaume f 53
public holiday Feiertag m 152
pull, to ziehen 155
pullover Pullover m 117
pumpkin Kürbis m 50
puncture Reifenpanne f 75
purchase Kauf m 131
pure rein 114
purple violett 113
push, to (button) drücken 155
put, to stellen 26
put through, to verbinden 28
pyjamas Schlafanzug m 117

Q

quality Qualität f 103, 113
quantity Menge f 14, 103
quarter Viertel nt 148
quarter of an hour Viertelstunde f 153
quartz Quarz m 122
question Frage f 10
quick schnell 13, 156
quickly schnell 79, 137
quiet ruhig 23, 25

R

rabbi Rabbiner m 84
rabbit Kaninchen nt 48
race course/track (Pferde)rennbahn f 90
racket (sport) Schläger m 89
radiator (car) Kühler m 78
radio (set) Radio nt 23, 28, 119
radish Radieschen nt 50
railway station Bahnhof m 19, 21, 67
rain Regen m 94
rain, to regnen 94
rain boot Gummistiefel m 118
raincoat Regenmantel m 117
raisin Rosine f 53
rare (meat) blutig 47
rash Ausschlag m 139
raspberry Himbeere f 53
rate Tarif m 20; (exchange) Kurs m 18, 130; (inflation) Rate f 131
razor Rasierapparat m 110
razor blade Rasierklinge f 110
read, to lesen 40
ready fertig 29, 118, 123, 125, 145
real echt 121
rear hinten, Hinter- 75

receipt Quittung f 103, 144
reception Empfang m 23
receptionist Empfangschef m 26
recommend, to empfehlen 22, 35, 80, 86, 88, 145
record (disc) Schallplatte f 127, 128
record player Plattenspieler m 119
rectangular rechteckig 101
red rot 59, 113
redcurrant rote Johannisbeere f 53
reduction Ermäßigung f 24, 82
refill (pen) Ersatzpatrone f 105
refund Rückerstattung f 103
regards Grüße m/pl 152
register, to (luggage) aufgeben 71
registered mail per Einschreiben 132
registration Anmeldung f 25
registration form Anmeldeschein m 25, 26
regular (petrol) Normal nt 75
religion Religion f 83
religious service Gottesdienst m 84
rent, to mieten 19, 20, 74, 89, 91; vermieten 155
rental Verleih m 20, 74
repair Reparatur f 125
repair, to reparieren 29, 118, 119, 121, 123, 125, 145
repeat, to wiederholen 11
report, to (a theft) anzeigen 156
require, to verlangen 88
reservation Reservierung f 19, 65, 69
reservations office Reservierungs-schalter m 19; Platzreservierung f 67
reserve, to reservieren (lassen) 19, 23, 36
restaurant Restaurant nt 19, 32, 33, 35, 67
return (ticket) hin und zurück 69
return, to (give back) zurückgeben 103
reverse the charges, to ein R-Ge-spräch anmelden 134
rheumatism Rheumatismus m 141
rhubarb Rhabarber m 53
rib Rippe f 46, 138
ribbon Band nt 105
rice Reis m 49
right rechte 13; rechts 21, 30, 63, 69, 77, 79; (correct) richtig 13, 76
ring (on finger) Ring m 122
ring, to klingeln 155; telefonieren 134
ripe reif 52

river Fluß m 74, 85, 90; (major) Strom m 85
road Straße f 76, 77, 85
road assistance Pannendienst m 78
road map Straßenkarte f 105
road sign Verkehrszeichen nt 79
roast Braten m 45
roasted gebraten 47
rock Felsen m 85
roll (bread) Brötchen nt 38, 64
roller skate Rollschuh m 128
roll film Rollfilm m 124
roll-neck mit Rollkragen 117
romantic romantisch 84
room Zimmer nt 19, 23, 24, 25, 27, 28; (space) Platz m 32
room number Zimmernummer f 26
room service Zimmerbedienung f 23
rope Seil nt 107
rosary Rosenkranz m 122
rosé rosé 59
rosemary Rosmarin m 51
round rund 101, 117
roundtour Rundfahrt f 74
roundtrip (ticket) hin und zurück 69
rowing-boat Ruderboot nt 91
rubber (material) Gummi m 118; (eraser) Radiergummi m 105
rubber sole Gummisohle f 118
ruby Rubin m 122
rucksack Rucksack m 107
ruin Ruine f 81
ruler (for measuring) Lineal nt 105
rum Rum m 59
running water fließendes Wasser nt 23
rye Roggen m 38

s

safe (not dangerous) gefahrlos, ungefährlich 90
safe Safe m 26
safety pin Sicherheitsnadel f 111
saffron Safran m 51
sage Salbei m 51
sailing-boat Segelboot nt 91
salad Salat m 49, 50
sale Verkauf m 131; (bargains) Aus-verkauf m 101, 155
sales tax Mehrwertsteuer f 24, 40, 102
salmon Lachs m 41, 44; Salm m 44
salt Salz nt 37, 51, 64
salty salzig 62

same selbe 40; gleiche 118
sand Sand *m* 90
sandal Sandale *f* 118
sandwich Sandwich *nt* 64; *(open)* belegtes Brot *nt* 64
sanitary towel/napkin Damenbinde *f* 109
sapphire Saphir *m* 122
sardine Sardine *f* 41
satin Satin *m* 114
Saturday Samstag *m*, Sonnabend *m* 150
sauce Soße *f* 48
saucepan Kochtopf *m* 107
saucer Untertasse *f* 107
sauerkraut Sauerkraut *nt* 50
sausage Wurst *f* 47, 64
scallop Jakobsmuschel *f* 44
scarf Halstuch *nt* 117
scenic route landschaftlich schöne Straße *f* 85
school Schule *f* 79
scissors Schere *f* 107, 110
scooter Motorroller *m* 74
Scotland Schottland *(nt)* 146
scrambled egg Rührei *nt* 38
screwdriver Schraubenzieher *m* 107
sculptor Bildhauer *m* 83
sculpture Bildhauerei *f* 83
sea Meer *nt* 85, 90
sea bass Seebarsch *m* 44
seafood Meeresfrüchte *f/pl* 43
season Jahreszeit *f* 149; Saison *f* 149
seasoning Würze *f* 37, 51
seat Platz *m* 69, 70, 87
seat belt Sicherheitsgurt *m* 75
second zweite 148
second Sekunde *f* 153
second class zweite Klasse *f* 69
second hand Sekundenzeiger *m* 122
second-hand *(books)* antiquarisch 104
second-hand shop Gebrauchtwarenladen *m* 99
secretary Sekretär(in) *m/f* 27, 131
see, to sehen 163; *(check)* nachschauen 11
sell, to verkaufen 100
send, to schicken 78, 132; senden 102, 103. 132
send up, to hinaufschicken 26
sentence Satz *m* 11
separately getrennt 63
September September *m* 150

service Bedienung *f* 24, 40, 63, 100; *(religion)* Gottesdienst *m* 84
serviette Serviette *f* 36
set, to *(hair)* legen 30
set menu Tagesgedeck *nt* 36, 40
setting lotion Haarfestiger *m* 30, 111
seven sieben 147
seventeen siebzehn 147
seventh siebte 148
seventy siebzig 147
sew, to nähen 29
shampoo Haarwaschmittel *nt* 30, 111
shape Form *f* 103
shape, to *(hair)* legen 30
share *(finance)* Aktie *f* 131
sharp scharf 52; *(pain)* stechend 140
shave, to rasieren 31
shaver Rasierapparat *m* 27, 119
shaving brush Rasierpinsel *m* 111
shaving cream Rasiercreme *f* 111
she sie 162
shelf Regal *nt* 120
ship Schiff *nt* 74
shirt Hemd *nt* 117
shoe Schuh *m* 118
shoelace Schnürsenkel *m* 118
shoemaker's Schuhmacher *m* 99
shoe polish Schuhcreme *f* 118
shoe shop Schuhgeschäft *nt* 99
shop Geschäft *nt*, Laden *m* 98
shopping Einkaufen *nt* 97
shopping area Geschäftsviertel *nt* 81, 100
shopping centre Einkaufszentrum *nt* 99
shop window Schaufenster *nt* 100, 112, 124
short kurz 30, 116, 117
shorts Shorts *pl* 117
short-sighted kurzsichtig 123
shoulder Schulter *f* 138
shovel Schaufel *f* 128
show *(theatre)* Vorstellung *f* 86, 87
show, to zeigen 11, 12, 76, 100, 101, 103, 119, 124
shower Dusche *f* 23, 32
shrimp Garnele *f* 44
shrink, to einlaufen 114
shut geschlossen 12
snutter *(window)* Fensterladen *m* 29; *(camera)* Verschluß *m* 125
sick *(ill)* krank 140, 156
sickness *(illness)* Krankheit *f* 140
side Seite *f* 30

DICTIONARY

specimen *(medical)* Probe f 142
spectacle case Brillenetui nt 123
spell, to buchstabieren 11
spend, to ausgeben 101
spice Gewürz nt 51
spinach Spinat m 50
spine Wirbelsäule f 138
spiny lobster Languste f 41, 44
sponge Schwamm m 111
spoon Löffel m 36, 62, 107
sport Sport m 89
sporting goods shop Sportgeschäft nt 99
sprain, to verstauchen 140
spring *(season)* Frühling m 149; *(water)* Quelle f 85
square viereckig 101
square Platz m 82
stadium Stadion nt 82
staff Personal nt 26
stain Fleck m 29
stainless steel rostfreier Stahl m 107, 122
stalls *(theatre)* Parkett nt 87
stamp *(postage)* Briefmarke f 28, 126, 132, 133
staple Heftklammer f 105
star Stern m 94
start, to beginnen 80, 87, 88; *(car)* anspringen 78
starter *(appetizer)* Vorspeise f 41
station *(railway)* Bahnhof m 19, 21, 67; *(underground, subway)* Station f 73
stationer's Schreibwarengeschäft nt 99
statue Statue f 82
stay Aufenthalt m 31
stay, to bleiben 16, 26; *(reside)* wohnen 93
steak Steak nt 46
steal, to stehlen 156
steamed gedämpft 44
stew Eintopfgericht nt 42
stewed gedämpft 47, 51
stew pot Schmortopf m 107
stiff neck steifer Nacken m 141
sting Stich m 139
sting, to stechen 139
stitch, to nähen 29, 118
stock *(supply)* Vorrat m 103
stock exchange Börse f 82
stocking Strumpf m 117
stomach Magen m 138

stomach ache Magenschmerzen m/pl 141
stools Stuhl(gang) m 142
stop *(bus)* Haltestelle f 72, 73
stop! Halt! 156
stop, to halten 21, 68, 70, 72
stop thief! Haltet den Dieb! 156
store *(shop)* Laden m, Geschäft nt 98
straight *(drink)* pur 59
straight ahead geradeaus 21, 77
strange seltsam 84
strawberry Erdbeere f 53
street Straße f 25, 82
streetcar Straßenbahn f 72
street map Stadtplan m 19, 105
string Bindfaden m, Schnur f 105
strong stark 126, 143
stuck *(to be)* klemmen 28
student Student(in) m/f 82, 93
study, to studieren 93
stuffed gefüllt 47
sturdy robust 101
subway *(railway)* U-Bahn f 73
suede Wildleder nt 114, 118
sugar Zucker m 37, 51, 64
suit *(man)* Anzug m 117; *(woman)* Kostüm nt 117
suitcase Koffer m 18
summer Sommer m 149
sun Sonne f 94
sunburn Sonnenbrand m 108
Sunday Sonntag m 150
sunglasses Sonnenbrille f 123
sunshade *(beach)* Sonnenschirm m 91
sun-tan cream Sonnencreme f 111
super *(petrol)* Super m 75
superb prächtig 84
supermarket Supermarkt m 99
suppository Zäpfchen nt 109
surcharge Zuschlag m 68
surfboard Surfbrett nt 91
surgery *(consulting room)* Arztpraxis f 137
surname (Familien)name m 25
suspenders *(Am.)* Hosenträger m/pl 117
swallow, to schlucken 143
sweater Pullover m 117
sweatshirt Sweatshirt nt 117
Sweden Schweden *(nt)* 146
sweet süß 59, 62
sweet *(candy)* Bonbon nt 126
sweet corn Mais m 50**

Wörterverzeichnis

through train durchgehender Zug m 68, 69
thumb Daumen m 138
thumbtack Reißzwecke f 105
thunder Donner m 94
thunderstorm Gewitter nt 94
Thursday Donnerstag m 150
thyme Thymian m 51
ticket Karte f 87, 89; (plane) Flugticket nt 65; (train) Fahrkarte f 69; (bus) Fahrschein m 72
ticket office Fahrkartenschalter m 67
tide (high) Flut f 90; (low) Ebbe f 90
tie Krawatte f 117
tie pin Krawattennadel f 122
tight (clothes) eng 116
tights Strumpfhose f 117
time Zeit f 80, 153; (occasion) -mal 148
timetable Fahrplan m 68
tin (can) Büchse f 120
tinfoil Aluminiumfolie f 107
tin opener Büchsenöffner m 107
tint Tönungsmittel nt 111
tinted getönt 123
tire Reifen m 75, 76
tired müde 12
tissue (handkerchief) Papiertuch nt 111
tissue paper Seidenpapier nt 105
to zu 14
toast Toast m 38
tobacco Tabak m 126
tobacconist's Tabakladen m 99, 126
today heute 29, 150, 151
toe Zehe f 138
toilet paper Toilettenpapier nt 111
toiletry Toilettenartikel m/pl 110
toilets Toilette f 27, 32, 37, 67
toilet water Toilettenwasser nt 111
tomato Tomate f 50
tomato juice Tomatensaft m 61
tomb Grab nt 82
tomorrow morgen 29, 151
tongs Zange f 107
tongue Zunge f 46, 138
tonic water Tonic nt 61
tonight heute abend 29, 86, 87, 88, 96
tonsil Mandel f 138
too zu 14; (also) auch 15
tooth Zahn m 145
toothache Zahnschmerzen m/pl 145
toothbrush Zahnbürste f 111, 119

toothpaste Zahnpasta f 111
torch (flashlight) Taschenlampe f 107
touch, to berühren 155
tough (meat) zäh 62
tour Rundfahrt f 80
tourist office Fremdenverkehrsbüro nt 22, 80
tourist tax Kurtaxe f 32
towards gegen 14
towel Handtuch nt 111
tower Turm m 82
town Stadt f 19, 76, 105
town hall Rathaus nt 82
tow truck Abschleppwagen m 78
toy Spielzeug nt 128
toy shop Spielwarengeschäft nt 99
track (station) Gleis nt 67, 68, 69
tracksuit Trainingsanzug m 117
traffic (cars) Verkehr m 79
traffic jam Stau m 79
traffic light Ampel f 77
trailer Wohnwagen m 32
train Zug m 66, 68, 69, 70, 73, 159
tram Straßenbahn f 72
tranquillizer Beruhigungsmittel nt 109
transfer (bank) Überweisung f 131
transformer Transformator m 119
translate, to übersetzen 11
transport Transport m 74
travel, to reisen 93
travel agency Reisebüro nt 99
traveller's cheque Reisescheck m 18, 63, 102, 130
travelling bag Reisetasche f 18
travel sickness Reisekrankheit f 108
treatment Behandlung f 143
tree Baum m 85
tremendous außerordentlich 84
trim, to (beard) stutzen 31
trip Reise f 93, 152, 159; Fahrt f 72
trousers Hose f 117
trout Forelle f 44
try, to versuchen 135; (sample) probieren 60; (clothes) anprobieren 115
T-shirt T-Shirt nt 117
tube Tube f 120
Tuesday Dienstag m 150
tumbler Wasserglas nt 107
tunny (tuna) Thunfisch m 41
turbot Steinbutt m 44
turkey Truthahn m 48
turn, to (change direction) abbiegen 21, 77

turnip Kohlrabi m 50
turquoise türkisfarben 113
turquoise Türkis m 122
turtleneck mit Rollkragen 117
tweezers Pinzette f 111
twelve zwölf 147
twenty zwanzig 147
twice zweimal 148
twin beds zwei Einzelbetten nt/pl 23
two zwei 147
typewriter Schreibmaschine f 27, 105
typewriter ribbon Farbband nt 105
typing paper Schreibmaschinenpapier nt 105
tyre Reifen m 75, 76

U

ugly häßlich 13, 84
umbrella Regenschirm m 117; (beach) Sonnenschirm m 91
uncle Onkel m 93
unconscious bewußtlos 139
under unter 14
underdone (meat) blutig 47; zu roh 62
underground (railway) U-Bahn f 73
underpants Unterhose f 117
undershirt Unterhemd nt 117
understand, to verstehen 11, 16
United States Vereinigte Staaten m/pl 146
university Universität f 82
until bis 14
up hinauf 15
upper obere 69
upset stomach Magenverstimmung f 108
urgent dringend 12, 145
urine Urin m 142
use Gebrauch m 17
use, to benutzen 78, 134
useful nützlich 14
usual gewöhnlich 143

V

vacancy freies Zimmer nt 23, 155
vacant frei 13, 22, 155
vacation Ferien pl, Urlaub m 151
vaccinate, to impfen 140
vacuum flask Thermosflasche f 107
vaginal infection Scheidenentzündung f 141
valley Tal nt 85
value Wert m 131

value-added tax (VAT) Mehrwertsteuer f 24, 40, 102, 154
vanilla Vanille f 54
veal Kalbfleisch nt 45
vegetable Gemüse nt 40, 49, 50
vegetable store Gemüsehandlung f 99
vegetarian vegetarisch 37
vein Vene f 138
velvet Samt m 114
velveteen Manchester m 114
venereal disease Geschlechtskrankheit f 142
venison Reh nt, Hirsch m 48
vermouth Wermut m 60
very sehr 15
vest Unterhemd nt 117; (Am.) Weste f 117
veterinarian Tierarzt m 99
video cassette Videokassette f 119, 128
video-recorder Videorecorder m 119
view Aussicht f 23, 25
village Dorf nt 76, 85
vinegar Essig m 51
vineyard Weinberg m 85
visit Besuch m 92
visit, to besuchen 94, 144; (look around) besichtigen 84
visiting hours Besuchszeit f 144
vitamin pills Vitamintabletten f/pl 109
V-neck mit V-Ausschnitt 117
volleyball Volleyball m 89
voltage (Strom)spannung f 27, 119
vomit, to sich übergeben 140

W

waistcoat Weste f 117
wait, to warten 21, 95, 108
waiter Kellner m 26; Herr Ober m 36, 56
waiting-room Wartesaal m 67
waitress Kellnerin f 26; Fräulein nt 36
wake, to wecken 27, 71
Wales Wales (nt) 146
walk, to (zu Fuß) gehen 74, 85
wall Mauer f 82
wallet Brieftasche f 117
walnut Walnuß f 53
want, to (wish) wünschen 12
warm warm 94
wash, to waschen 29, 114

DICTIONARY

wash and wear bügelfrei 114
wash-basin Waschbecken nt 28
washing powder Waschpulver nt 107
washing-up liquid Spülmittel nt 107
watch Uhr f 121, 122, 127
watchmaker's Uhrmacher m 99, 121
watchstrap Uhrarmband nt 122
water Wasser nt 23, 28, 32, 38, 75, 90
water carrier Wasserkanister m 107
waterfall Wasserfall m 85
water flask Feldflasche f 107
watermelon Wassermelone f 53
waterproof wasserdicht 122
water-ski Wasserski m 91
wave Welle f 90
way Weg m 76
we wir 162
weather Wetter nt 94
weather forecast Wetterbericht m 94
wedding ring Ehering m 122
Wednesday Mittwoch m 150
week Woche f 20, 26, 80, 151
weekend Wochenende nt 20, 151
well gut 9, 115; (healthy) wohl 140
well Brunnen m 85
well-done (meat) gut durchgebraten 47
west West(en) m 77
what was 10
wheel Rad nt 78
when wann 10
where wo 10
which welche(r/s) 10
whipped cream Schlagsahne f 54
whisky Whisky m 59
white weiß 49, 59, 113
Whit Monday Pfingstmontag m 152
who wer 10
why warum 10
wide weit 118
wide-angle lens Weitwinkelobjektiv nt 125
wife Frau f 93
wig Perücke f 111
wild boar Wildschwein nt 48
wind Wind m 94
window Fenster nt 28, 36, 69; (shop) Schaufenster nt 100, 112, 124
windscreen/shield Windschutzscheibe f 76
wine Wein m 57, 58, 59, 62
wine list Weinkarte f 59

wine merchant's Weinhandlung f 99
winter Winter m 149
winter sports Wintersport m 91
wiper Scheibenwischer m 76
wish Wunsch m 151
with mit 14
withdraw, to (bank) abheben 130
without ohne 14
woman Dame f 115; Frau f 159
wonderful wunderbar 96
wood (material) Holz nt 127; (forest) Wald m 85
wood alcohol Brennspiritus m 107
wood carving Holzschnitzarbeit f 127
woodcock Schnepfe f 48
wool Wolle f 114
word Wort nt 10, 14, 133
work, to (function) funktionieren 28, 119
working day Werktag m 151
worse schlechter 13
wound Wunde f 139
wrinkle resistant knitterfrei 114
wristwatch Armbanduhr f 122
write, to schreiben 11, 101
writing pad Schreibblock m 105
writing-paper Schreibpapier nt 27
wrong falsch 13, 77, 135

X

X-ray, to röntgen 140

Y

year Jahr nt 149
yellow gelb 113
yes ja 9
yesterday gestern 151
yet noch 15
yield, to (traffic) Vorfahrt gewähren 79
yoghurt Joghurt m 64
you du, Sie 162
young jung 13
your dein; Ihr 161
youth hostel Jugendherberge f 22, 32

Z

zero null 147
zip(per) Reißverschluß m 117
zoo Zoo m 82
zoology Zoologie f 83

Inhaltsverzeichnis